Resettling Homeless People
Theory and Practice

Mike Seal

learning network
west

Russell House Publishing

First published in 2005 by:
Russell House Publishing Ltd.
4 St. George's House
Uplyme Road
Lyme Regis
Dorset DT7 3LS

Tel: 01297-443948
Fax: 01297-442722
e-mail: help@russellhouse.co.uk
www.russellhouse.co.uk

© Mike Seal

British Library Cataloguing-in-publication Data:

A catalogue record for this book is available from the British Library.

ISBN: 1-903855-65-9

Typeset by TW Typesetting, Plymouth, Devon
Printed by Antony Rowe, Chippenham

About Russell House Publishing

RHP is a group of social work, probation, education and youth and community work practitioners and academics working in collaboration with a professional publishing team.
Our aim is to work closely with the field to produce innovative and valuable materials to help managers, trainers, practitioners and students.
We are keen to receive feedback on publications and new ideas for future projects.
For details of our other publications please visit our website or ask us for a catalogue. Contact details are on this page.

Contents

For Eddie, Paul, Les,
and all the others who got lost on their way.

Preface

There is a growing awareness amongst practitioners and policy makers of the importance of a comprehensive resettlement strategy in the housing of homeless people. Despite this there has been little comprehensive examination of good practice or the theoretical concepts that support effective resettlement. This book sets out to explore in greater detail the theory and skills that underpin effective resettlement interventions with service users. As a starting point it sees resettlement as working with those homeless people for whom the solution to their homelessness goes beyond the securing of move-on accommodation. As such, resettlement should be seen as an ongoing process designed to empower homeless people to gain and remain in appropriate permanent accommodation.

It has three main, interconnected themes. Firstly, that there is a need to define and delineate the work to prevent the task of resettlement being over-simplified on the one hand, and having false expectation put on it on the other. As such the book will develop a generic model for working across the spectrum of homeless people, while emphasising the varying manifestations this may take. Secondly, workers and services must adopt a holistic approach, taking into account the cognitive, emotional and practical aspects of the individual's functioning. Finally, given the second theme, that the role of a resettlement worker is a complex and professional one. As such it needs some of the structures, values and attitudes that are associated with being a professional. Sections are dedicated to developing an overview of resettlement work and its historical background; to developing appropriate relationships with clients and other stakeholders; to structuring our work and to intervening on the aforementioned cognitive, emotional and practical levels.

Who this book is for

The book has multiple intended audiences. Primarily it is intended for practitioners involved in the resettlement and support of homeless people, and people in supported housing. It should be relevant whatever the working context: day centres, hostels, street work, tenancy support and floating support. It will also be of relevance to allied professions such as social workers, probation workers, Connexions teams, youth workers and other care professionals whose work involves problems with housing. It is intended as a text book for students undertaking the Advanced Professional Certificate in Working with Homeless People offered by the YMCA George Williams

College in London. In addition it explicitly covers elements of the underpinning knowledge requirements of both the NVQs in Housing and in Promoting Independence. It will also be of use to those undertaking options in Diplomas in Social Work and Youth and Community work. Finally, it should be of relevance to policy makers and those responsible for the development of homeless services, particularly given the recent expansion of such services under *Supporting People*.

Introduction: Resettlement, a Cinderella Service?

Resettlement has been described as the 'Cinderella service'. This statement could be interpreted in different ways. Some may hope that a worker can wave a magic wand and resettle the homeless person. Other agencies may have unrealistic expectations of what resettlement workers can do. Even colleagues in the same agency may lack understanding, and see resettlement workers as solely responsible for accommodation issues. Resettlement workers themselves may feel guilty when they cannot live up to expectations and solve every accommodation-related problem. Clients may well detect these dynamics and buy into them. It is only human that if a quick fix solution appears to present itself, a person will want to believe in it.

This background gives a context for several themes that run through this book. The first theme is the continuing project of resettlement workers, and homelessness services in general, to define and delineate their area of work. This means defining what the work entails and where its boundaries lie. This book takes a standpoint of not differentiating between our various work contexts such as day centre work, direct access hostels, supported housing, advice work etc. It also rarely distinguishes between our various client groups such as families, drug users, rough sleepers, women etc. (This is a subject that warrants attention, and will be the subject of subsequent works.) Instead it tries to examine the common areas in resettlement. It takes as a starting point that resettlement work consists of working with homeless people who need support beyond the securing of decent affordable housing. The question is what does this support looks like and how can we effectively deliver it.

A second related theme is that working with homeless people should be seen as a distinct field of work, with resettlement services as a distinct profession within it. In the UK there are over 2,000 practitioners of dedicated resettlement services for homeless people and a further 20,000 involved in supported housing for homeless people. This is likely to increase as the new *Supporting People* initiative develops. However, numbers alone are not enough to establish the need for a new profession. It is the distinctiveness of a role that establishes a profession. This book will attempt to set out what is distinctive about working with homeless people that warrants dedicated attention.

The third theme of this book concerns a particular aspect of how our work has been shaped and should be shaped in the future. It propounds that resettlement work in the UK has tended to over-concentrate on the practical aspects of the work, to its detriment. This is a legacy of a campaign that equated all homelessness with a lack of affordable housing. While this is still true for many homeless people, it does not serve those who currently undergo resettlement. While seeing homelessness as a housing problem represented a positive development in how people viewed homeless people, more subtle responses need to be developed. We have already given a baseline definition of resettlement as being work with clients where the solution to their homelessness goes beyond housing need. This book says that we need to examine and develop the more cognitive and emotional aspects of the work, and aims to move resettlement on if only by establishing an agenda that needs to be furthered.

The many comments and thoughts I have included from practitioners are largely drawn from training sessions I have facilitated over the years. I have also included any patterns I have seen and noted in these comments and thoughts. Some of these training sessions have been deliberately structured with an eye to research, using research questions, in an attempt to make my methodology more systematic. This has particularly been the case in the development of the set of ethical principles outlined in Chapter 3, people's thoughts on the client-worker relationship in Chapter 4 and people's reflections on the resettlement process in Chapter 12. I have conducted this training over a period of 12 years, involving contact with over 1,000 practitioners.

The book is divided into four sections. While not necessarily intended to be read sequentially, there is logic to the structure of the book and it would benefit readers to begin with the first section. This consists of three chapters on key debates in homelessness and attempts to define the boundaries and contexts of resettlement work. Chapter 1 examines the historical development of resettlement services, tracing changes in how homelessness and hence the services intended for homeless people have been socially constructed. It argues that views of homelessness have moved through three identifiable stages: as an individual problem on the outskirts of society; as purely a housing problem and lastly as a more complex problem needing more complex solutions. In tandem it will explore the changes in service provision for homeless people, tracing how the idea of resettlement emerged and developed and is likely to develop in the future.

Chapter 2 begins by examining the need for a definition of resettlement by different stakeholders including workers, managers and funders. It examines early models of resettlement arguing that they often concentrated on the differences between working environments such as operating from a hostel or outreach or a day centre, instead of looking at what was common between them. A definition of resettlement is suggested and there is an examination of three themes that stem from it. The chapter finally asks whether resettlement work is a distinct area of work or should be an adjunct of, say, social work.

Chapter 3 develops a notion of a code of ethics for resettlement workers and explores what possible principles it could contain. A contrast will be drawn between resettlement and the ethics of other care professions such as advice work, social work, and youth work.

Section Two focuses on our working relationships with a variety of stakeholders and again has three chapters. Chapter 4 examines the nature of a worker's relationship with the client. It will examine some of the policy definitions of this relationship, arguing that these policies are often set by worse case scenarios underpinned by a particular view of professional boundaries. It will build on work done by Brandon, Biestek (1961) and Illich on what makes for an effective working relationship, leading to the development of a set of principles upon which resettlement workers should base our relationships with clients.

Chapter 5 examines the importance of the effective management and support of workers. It will examine whether resettlement workers accept support, arguing that there is a culture of rejection that needs to be countered. It then argues that the support offered to workers needs to be sensitive to the demands of different clienteles and working contexts. It will examine the nature of support through recent work on the development of the Connexions service done by Christ Church Canterbury University College.

Chapter 6 looks at the wider issue of working with other agencies. It will develop a thesis that effective working with other agencies involves a subtle mastery of the relative arts of knowledge, flattery and threat. It will then examine differing notions of networking, building principally on the ideas of Gilchrist and Argyris on organisational defensiveness.

Section Three examines how workers should structure their work. Chapter 7 explores the nature of confidentiality and its moral and legal limitations. It then discusses the extent to which the records we keep should be reviewed and jointly owned with the client. This leads into an examination of the implications of the Data Protection Act (1998), highlighting its impact on different settings. Lastly, the chapter asks whether restrictions mean that the notion of confidentiality has become meaningless. It will argue that it is more relevant for workers to focus on building up trust in the client that the information they give will not be abused.

Chapters 8 and 9 explore different dimensions of assessment. Chapter 8 examines the assessment of need and the appropriateness of a service. In doing this it questions whether resettlement is for everyone, arguing that it is a discrete service. It examines alternative criteria for assessing the eligibility of clients under the broad headings of need, motivation and ability. Chapter 9 examines current models of needs assessment within resettlement, proposing an alternative model as developed by Brandon. This is followed by an examination of different styles of assessment and their relative advantages and disadvantages.

Chapter 10 outlines the rationale for having a support plan and examines the relevancy of Egan's model to resettlement work. It will expand on the idea of leverage, examining factors that need to be considered in identifying the issue that will move the client forward. It then evaluates the relevance of task-centred casework and seeks to develop a model integrating these ideas with those of Egan.

Chapter 11 explores different models of how to hold caseloads. It critiques the RSI index of need as a method of weighting cases. It seeks to develop an alternative based on the impact of the client on the worker, rather than basing weighting on the needs of the client. Finally it tries to place caseloads within the context of other aspects of our working practice.

Chapter 12 deconstructs the 14 stage model of resettlement as outlined in *The Resettlement Handbook* (Bevan, 1998). It examines several implications of the model based on a discussion of the aims, standards and good practice of three of the stages. The model is reviewed using the following framework: what is realistic from a practitioners point of view; what relative importance do practitioner's place on the various stages and what are the implications arisingfrom this.

Chapter 13 evaluates the relevancy of Prochaska and Diclemente's theory of change to resettlement work. It traces the origins of the model and then evaluates the relevance of the model to resettlement workers. It explores in detail two stages of particular significance to the resettlement worker, that of maintenance and pre-contemplation, examining typical reactions and danger signs within these stages.

Chapter 14 focuses on people's emotional reactions to change and tries to identify if there are any commonly discernible patterns. It will outline 'stage models' of people's reactions to critical life events and evaluate their transferability to resettlement.

Chapter 15 begins by considering the importance of working with people's cognitive and decision making abilities. It seeks to contextualise a number of approaches to cognitive working within a framework of the three main schools of thought; psychodynamic approaches, cognitive-behavioural ap-proaches and person centred approaches. The chapter then examines the ideas and principles behind four cognitive interventions of relevance to resettlement work: motivational interviewing, transactional analysis, brief therapy and neuro-linguistic programming.

Section One
Definitions and Key Debates

Historical Legacies: The Construction of Homelessness from Spikes to Supporting People

Since its inception, housing policy in the United Kingdom has been determined by the dominant political philosophy of the time.

(Balchin, 1998)

The struggle by different vested interests to impose a particular definition of homelessness on the policy agenda is critical to the way in which homelessness is treated as a social problem.

(Jacobs, Kemeny and Manzi, 1999: 15)

It is not my intention to examine the history of homelessness or the development of homelessness legislation and policy as this has been comprehensively covered in other works (Burrows et al., 1997; Daly, 1998; Banister et al., 1993; Bines, 1994). However, as the two quotes above indicate, the way homelessness has been thought about and conceptualised has influenced the development of the services created to deal with it. Homelessness and homeless services can be thus seen as social constructions (Hutson, 1984). In this chapter I therefore intend to examine how the concept of homelessness and conceptions of homeless people have changed and over time how services have developed in response to this. Secondly, it will specifically explore how resettlement services emerged, their position now and the challenges that face the sector in the future.

Historically, homelessness has been explained as arising for either structural or individual reasons (Johnson, 1991; Pleace, 1998; Main, 2003). Structural explanations see societal factors as the main cause of homelessness. Individual explanations put the blame on issues within the individual. More recently post-modern and feminist influences have started to come to the fore in our thinking about homelessness (Neale, 1997). The relative dominance of these different explanations has changed as different ideologies of social care have changed (Balchin, 1998; Hutson, 1994; Cranes et al., 2000). This evolution followed three distinct phases: individualistic explanations prevailed from the Poor Law until the Second World War; structuralist notions dominated from the end of the war until the early nineteen-eighties; and more post-modern ideas have come to the fore since then. There is fluidity between these competing ideologies, as all three continue to underpin different aspects of practical service provision, an issue I will come back to in the conclusion.

Individual explanations

Historically, individual explanations for homelessness have tended to dominate the discourse (Main, 2003). There are three inter-related assumptions that often underpin these explanations: that homeless people are bad, demanding minimal provision; they are mad, needing paternalistic intervention; or they are sad, needing pity and charity. Consequently provision that stems from this philosophy has tended to be minimal and punitive, excluding those who are seen as undeserving, and was paternalistic in nature (Daly, 1998).

These individual explanations for homelessness also place homeless people on the peripheries of society both culturally and physically (Daly, 1998). Culturally, homelessness is seen largely as an individual failure, a personal weakness or, at best, an emergency. Without this view of homelessness as an individual problem it would reflect on us as a part of society, which as Pratt says would be more disconcerting.

> When the third world is no longer maintained at a distance out there but begins to appear in here . . . (when it) emerges at the centre of our daily lives, in the cities and cultures of the so called advanced or 1st world, then we can perhaps begin to talk of a significant interruption in the preceding sense of our own lives, culture, languages and futures.

> (Pratt, 1992: 164)

Another historical individualist view, as embodied in the Poor Law, saw homeless people as making a choice not to embrace the work ethic. This, in turn, made them immoral. This law, outlining the earliest state provision for homeless people, enshrined this political view with notions of deserving and undeserving poor, linking it to this economic ethic:

> In the giving of relief, the public should impose such conditions as will help the individual and the country at large. Every penny given that helps to make the position of the pauper more eligible than that of the other workmen will encourage laziness.

> (Poor Law, 1834: 65)

While social housing provision changed radically after the First World War and even more so after the Second (Balchin, 1991) attitudes towards homelessness and homeless people did not change much, and individual explanations still predominated. Orwell's 1934 book Down and Out in Paris and London describes the services offered to homeless people that stemmed from this individualistic ideology, the successors of the Poor Law. The main provision was the 'Spike', a sort of hostel. It offered minimal provision and often systematically dehumanised people (Orwell, 1932). I personally worked with one elderly man who had experienced such provision. He told me how he had been de-loused upon entry, searched for money in case he could pay for lodgings, on the assumption he was lying about that and given a chore to do to combat idleness. Those regimes also encouraged homeless people to be a migratory population. The maximum length of stay varied from one to three days and, as Spikes were 20 miles apart, a migratory trail of homeless people developed from Canterbury to Glasgow. Ironically, Spikes were called 'resettlement units' but forced people to be unsettled and mobile. (Goodhall, 1999) Homeless people were not only located on the periphery of humanity in a philosophical sense, they were forced to the edges physically. The Spikes were on the outskirts of towns, to keep homeless people away from tourists, shoppers and businesses.

The first revision of this provision was enshrined in the National Assistance Act 1948, which changed the regimes of the Spikes, although they were still called resettlement units. The Act is often cited as a move forwards in how social policy makers viewed homelessness, yet in many ways it consolidated the earlier attitudes and constructions, rather than challenging them (Donnison and Ugerson, 1982) Responsibility for dealing with homeless people was changed from a 'parish concern' to state provision. However, it still had weaknesses and underlying assumptions about homeless individuals.

The 1948 Act provided the wrong powers (imposing a weak obligation to provide temporary shelter for small numbers when the problem of homelessness called for stronger obligations to provide permanent housing for large numbers) and these powers were in the wrong hands (resting ineffectually with the DHSS and the county social services departments instead of the DOE and the local authority housing departments.

(Donnison and Ugerson, 1982: 271)

This legislation was predicated upon notions of homelessness as a consequence of vagrancy, alcoholism, destitution, pauperism and unwillingness to work.

(Jacobs, Kemeny and Manzi, 1999: 15)

Structural explanations: the nineteen-sixties onwards

A structuralist explanation locates the reasons for homelessness in social and economic factors, rather than in the individual. It perceives homelessness as being primarily a housing issue due to the shortfall in affordable suitable accommodation and says basically that, if people were given houses, there would be no more homelessness. This structuralist explanation grew out of a more general structural attitude towards housing in the aftermath of the Second World War. The solution to the post-war housing crisis, as opposed to the lack of response after the First World War, was seen as a state responsibility and resulted in an extended council house building programme (Balchin, 1998). The formation of organisations such as Shelter, CHAR and Crisis galvanised the argument, culminating in the passing of the Housing Act 1977, acknowledging the link between homelessness and housing. Many campaign groups saw this as being a positive move away from moralistic judgements about homeless people that had been enshrined in the National Assistance Act 1948 and towards a more structural explanation. This is illustrated by the words of Wilson, the first Director of Shelter:

> The aim . . . was to relate homelessness to housing scarcity, and not to welfare (in its administrative sense) and to get full recognition of the scale of the problem.

(Wilson, 1970: 19)

Interestingly the 1977 Act and all subsequent homeless legislation (the Housing Act 1985, the Housing Act 1996 and the Homeless Persons Act 2002) preserve some of the ideas of deserving and undeserving poor from the individualistic perspective (Foord et al., 1998). Firstly, they talk about 'priority need' i.e. that some homeless people are not a priority, and deserve only limited help, and also of 'intentionality', enshrining the idea that some homeless people choose to become homeless and therefore deserve virtually no help.

Whilst the shift towards a structuralist explanation was undoubtedly a positive move, it did not explain or take account of the full range of homeless people's experiences. While it is clear that homelessness is precipitated by a lack of suitable accommodation, for some, the nature of the problem is more complex. Randall (1999) estimates that up to 80 per cent of hostel dwellers are in need of support in addition to accommodation. This need for support can also continue beyond the acquisition of accommodation. Randall (2002) recently recommended that support should continue for up to a year after permanent accommodation has been secured. On a similar vein, from a survey conducted in Liverpool examining the use of street homelessness services, over 40 per cent of people who used street services such as soup runs had a place to stay (Seal et al., 1993). However, people were not there primarily for food but for company, and for many of them, using the provision was actually uneconomic.

Nevertheless, structural explanations prevailed for some time. Campaign groups such as Shelter did not acknowledge until the late 1990s the importance of looking at support needs (Jones et al., 2002). Prior to this such attempts were labelled as a distraction from the main issue of fighting for enough affordable housing and attempts to address support needs were labelled as services trying to be quasi social workers and were asking the wrong questions. It was not until the advent of Supporting People that there was a development of supported provision within local authorities to any significant degree (Randall, 2002).

The nineteen-eighties: the changing face of homelessness and the need for new explanations

The structural approach to homelessness assumed that the homeless person was capable of sustaining accommodation once that was attained. In doing so it did not answer some of the basic questions: Who is homeless? Why are they homeless? What role is homelessness playing for them? What effect is the experience of homelessness having on them? What effect have homelessness services had on them?

Neal (1996) traces theoretical developments in the late 70s and 80s in which feminist authors challenged binary assumptions that homelessness was either for individual and structural reasons: homeless people's identities, their issues, and the structures they are subject to are not homogenous but contested and shifting. In turn we need to think about homeless services more flexibly and creatively. As an example, she traces how concepts such as 'home' are social constructions and have different meanings for men, women and children (Watson and Austerbery, 1986; Munro and Madigan, 1993).

Neal (1996) also traces how postmodernism and post structuralism sought to challenge the idea that there was any single oppressive force or single solution to any predefined social problem. This was then applied by different authors to homelessness (Hewitt, 1992) challenging notions that homeless people's needs could be neatly quantified and suitable accommodation could be provided by the state as an adequate response. Importantly such analysis allows us to challenge the simplicity of structural solutions without falling back into individualist assumptions. As Neal says:

The lives of homeless people are structured by numerous public factors but they are not determined by them and change is possible. Issues of individuality, subjectivity and personal experience should therefore be recognised, but without neglecting shared experiences and common oppressive forces.

(Neale, 1996: 48)

Partly because they did not account for the complexities of homelessness, structural approaches failed to respond to the changing nature of homelessness that occurred in the eighties and nineties. It was during these decades that a raft of new legislation was passed that had consequences for the demographics of homelessness. It is not my intention to cover all of these issues or changes, only to give an overview of them.

Community Care Act 1990

Much has been written about the Community Care Act 1990 (Franklin, 1999; Leigh, 1993: 1994; Means and Smith, 1996). Over the past three decades the UK government decided to close asylums and psychiatric institutions or to severely reduce their size. However, that did not necessarily mean that those who were discharged from hospital received appropriate services, as Daly notes:

The concept of deinstitutionalisation was predicated on an optimistic belief in the compassionate capacity of the community, on the discovery of psychotropic drugs and on the belief that large medical and psychiatric hospitals failed to provide tangible benefits to patients.

(Daly, 1998: 121)

Many people with mental health issues did not have their housing needs met (CHAR, 1990). Furthermore, the savings realised by these closures were not redirected to special needs housing or to community care: the National Association of Housing Associations (1998) estimated that only nine per cent of special needs housing schemes in England are allocated to people with mental illness. Daly (1996) views that many people who were supposedly deinstitutionalised ended up in bed and breakfast accommodation, often un-medicated, noting that in Portsmouth alone, the number of such institutions springing up to meet this demand increased five fold in the 1980s.

While some of the causes and effects of this dynamic are still debated, the level of mental health issues is now very high amongst the homeless population. Daly (1996) reports that the level of diagnosed mental health issues amongst homeless people has risen to 28 per cent in bed and breakfasts, 36 per cent amongst day centre users and 40 per cent amongst soup run users compared to 10 per cent in the1970s. Other authors, such as Gillet et al., (1996) put the figure for the incidence of mental health in hostel dwellers as high as 60 per cent.

Children Act 1989

Before examining the Children Act 1989 we should acknowledge the fact that social services budgets have been under great pressure for years. Many authors (McCluskey, 1994; Banister, 1993; Brody, 1994) identify a lack of resources as being one of the major factors in the failure of this Act to meet the needs of young homeless people. The 'advise and befriend' aspect of this Act, which should have enabled services for young homeless people, became more or less meaningless. This is compounded by other factors: the needs of homeless people are not well understood by social workers; there is a lack of clear guidelines and policy; there is a lack of multi-agency working; and a fear of being overwhelmed by demand (McCluskey, 1994).

Erosion of benefits

This has been of particular effect on young people under 25, who as well as receiving £10 less a week in income support on job seekers allowance are also disadvantaged by the single room rent restriction on their housing benefit entitlement (CHAR, 1994). That restriction means that young people normally only receive housing benefit to the average cost of a single room, to prevent them renting self-contained accommodation of their own.

A significant general change affecting homeless people in particular was the introduction of the discretionary social fund. (CHAR, 1994), replacing the previous system of one-off benefit payments. Previously when a person got a new flat they could claim an allowance for furniture, clothing etc. Social fund legislation introduced a budget-limited (and so competitive) system of grants and loans that again brought in criteria that discriminated between deserving and undeserving homeless people. The deserving were defined as families, people coming out of institutions or in danger of returning to them. This has been extended to those engaged in 'recognised' resettlement programmes, again tying people to another form of institution. People's needs are also subject to the judgements of individual social fund officers, their area and national budget priorities and the competing needs of other applicants.

Whatever the impact of the reduction of benefits and the ineffectiveness of the Children Act 1989, the proportion of homeless men under 25 grew from 11 per cent to 39 per cent between 1972 and 1991 and from 24 per cent to 60 per cent for homeless women, of whom over 50 per cent, in both cases, had been in local authority care (Kemp, 1997).

Drug use

Drug use is not a new phenomenon, drugs having been used by civilisations for centuries (Shapiro, 1996; McKennsa, 1998) but drug use has always been an integral part of the lifestyle of the homeless population, particularly alcohol (Orwell, 1943; London, 1913). What has perhaps changed has been the drug of choice, the style of use (i.e. poly-drug use) and the prevalence. Some authors argue that homeless people have a pre-disposition for substance use. This need not be seen as an individualist explanation about choice: if it is a functional part of the homeless lifestyle, then it may be acquired as a part of that lifestyle (Klee and Reid, 1998). Daly illustrates this functionality in relation to alcohol but this is increasingly becoming equally true of drug use.

People on the street drink to cope with the cold weather, depression, isolation, and physical or emotional pain. Because it dulls pain, induces euphoria, and fills idle time, alcohol is accepted as the drug of choice and as a means of fostering sociability amongst homeless men and some homeless women.

(Daly, 1996: 117)

Evidence of the acceptability, or at least normality, of drug use is evident from many sources. Klee and Reid (1998) document how 69 per cent of homeless people do not know anyone who does not take drugs. The Big Issue (1998) estimates that 70 per cent of their vendors use drugs not prescribed to them. These figures need to be contextualised, a survey in the same year said that recreational drug use amongst young people aged between 16-25 is as high as 30 per cent (ONS, 1998). What seems to be markedly different is the drug of choice. The Big Issue said that, of its users, 53 per cent were using heroin, 28 per cent were using crack cocaine, 23 per cent were using diazepam and 21 per cent were using temazapam. Comparative figures for young people were only 1 per cent for cocaine, 1 per cent for heroin, 1 per cent for crack cocaine and abuse of prescription drugs was minimal.

Development of services and the search for new explanations

During this time services, particularly in the voluntary sector, recognised the changes in the demographic nature of homelessness, with the resulting gap in service provision, and attempted to respond to this need (Bevan, 1998). Provision developed organically and locally, according to perceived local need (Randall and Brown, 1994). Funding was obtained from a variety of sources, but predominantly agencies funds from trusts supplemented by some local authority monies (Seal and Stretch, 1992). Positively, this made for a bottom up approach, one that was sensitive to workers experiences of their clients. Negatively, no statutory funding base was established for resettlement work and there were no established models of good practice.

People were looking for new explanations of homelessness and new models of services that should be provided to them. Existing models either emphasised agency factors, such as the difference between the contexts in which people worked, (day centres, hostel drop-ins, etc) or they perpetuated some of the patriarchal assumptions of the individual model of homelessness (Seal and Stretch, 1992) For example, a prevalent model at the time was one of "good housekeeping' that reduced resettlement to 'teaching' homeless people skills such as how to cook and keep a household budget (Randall, 1994).

A common version of this model was to run a course for clients, often lasting several weeks or months, on developing these skills. As an example of the paternalistic nature of some of these approaches, one agency I worked with had a ten-week course with incentives, (or disincentives). The participants had an allocated stock of furniture, but for every session that was missed an item of furniture was removed. They had a high rate of successful resettlement for anyone who completed the course: little wonder given that by default they had weeded out those who were potentially problematic.

Not withstanding this confusion the term resettlement came into common usage for projects working with people who needed more intervention than simply the securing of accommodation. However, the term remained ill-defined and contested. The nineties was a decade of change in terms of homeless provision and particularly for resettlement services and rough sleepers. In 1991 the government launched the Rough Sleepers Initiative in central London. Resettlement services were a central plank of this initiative. In addition, this funding was provided outside of London (DETR, 1990). The first published piece of research on resettlement was produced (Randall and Brown, 1994; The Moving-in Experience, Crisis).

The aforementioned locally developed services started coming together, often in dedicated resettlement forums. Initially they were often for networking or training but they began to develop models of good practice. In 1992 forum members came together with CHAR to form the National Resettlement Forum. A series of good practice conferences followed in 1994, 1995 and 1996. Funding for workers was achieved in 1996 and the forum drew together good practice in the Resettlement Handbook (Bevan, 1998). This provided practical tools but also sought to facilitate the development of a common framework of understanding by setting out good practice in resettlement.

Rather than attempting to present one 'correct' model of resettlement, the handbook saw resettlement as more post-modern and provided information on all elements of resettlement work, to be interpreted and implemented according to local circumstances. It also included an attempt to develop a framework for homelessness interventions going beyond structural or individual explanations, recognising the need for more than housing with some people, but avoids falling into the blaming trap of individual explanations. These themes will be explored in the next chapter on definitions of resettlement. Before we do this I think it is useful to bring us up to date with how resettlement has developed as a field.

2000 and beyond

While statistics do not tell us everything, it is useful at this juncture to establish a baseline of the demographics of homeless people, their needs, and the range of services that are provided for them. In 2000 in England, there were 172,760 households accepted as homeless. Of these:

- 110,790 were classified as unintentionally homeless and in priority need.
- 8,140 intentionally homeless and in priority need.
- 52,830 homeless and not in priority need.
- In 1999 30 per cent lost their home because friends or relatives could no longer accommodate them, 23 per cent because of relationship breakdown, and 3 per cent because of mortgage arrears.
- It is estimated that the 172,760 households represents over 415,000 people.

The numbers of households in temporary accommodation arranged by their local authority in 2000: 72,440 in total, of which:

- 9,860 were in bed and breakfast hotels.
- 10,320 were in hostels or women's refuges.
- 25,390 were in private sector accommodation.
- 26,870 in other accommodation (housing association or local authority stock).

Source: The Department of the Environment, Transport and the Regions.

There are no comprehensive or reliable figures for single homelessness nationally due to the complexities of the situation and any figure would have to include single people in hostels and bed and breakfasts, rough sleepers, squatters, etc. However:

- 28,353 households accepted by local authorities as homeless in 1996/97 had a single occupant (see above).
- A report by the London Research Centre in 1996 estimated there to be over 100,000 single homeless people in London.
- 9,600 people were estimated as squatting in England in 1995.
- 80 per cent of squatting is thought to happen in London.

The government produced the first official national estimate of the extent of rough sleeping in England in 2001. This was based on local authority counts and estimates, but many authorities did not provide any statistics. There are no definitive and robust figures to rely on, due to the transient nature of the population.

- In October 2000, the DETR estimated there to be 1,180 people sleeping rough on any given night in England.
- A report by Shelter in 1997 gave an estimate that in England outside London 2,000 sleep rough each night and 10,000 people drift in and out of rough sleeping over the course of a year.
- An estimate by the Housing Services Agency in 1998 gave a figure of 400 on any given night in London and 2,400 throughout the year.
- In Scotland it is estimated that 11,000 people sleep rough on at least one occasion in any one year.

It is also useful to discuss the number and extent of services provided to homeless people. We will explore the nature of the services more in the next chapter. There are over 500 hostels (emergency and non-emergency) in London.

- Of these, there are around 50 emergency (direct access) hostels. These provide 2,574 bed spaces.
- There are nearly 1,900 hostels, containing around 27,000 beds, being provided or used by local authority housing departments in England.

Day centres provide a wide range of essential services for homeless people, from food and shelter to advice and health care.

- Around 300 day centres for homeless people operate in the UK.
- Day centres provide essential support for around 14,000 people every day.
- Former rough sleepers make up 45 per cent of the client base.

Youth homelessness includes young people living on the streets and those sleeping in hostels or on a 'friends' or 'relatives' floor. Between a fifth and a half of all young homeless people have been in care.

- 32,100 people between the ages of 16 and 21 were estimated to be homeless in 1995 by the London Research Centre.
- A report by CHAR (now NHA) in 1995 gave an estimate of 246,000 homeless people between the ages of 16 and 25.
- 20 per cent of homeless young people in London in 1999 had attempted suicide at least once in the past year.
- Homeless young people are twice as likely to have been physically or mentally abused.

Ethnic minority groups are over-represented in applications to housing departments and in general homelessness figures.

- 20 per cent of the young homeless population in urban areas in 1996 were from ethnic minorities. Other national surveys have showed 31 per cent.
- 25 per cent of applicants for housing to local authorities in England in 1994 were from ethnic minority groups.

- 52 per cent of applicants for housing in London in 1994 were from ethnic minority groups.
- 10 per cent of rough sleepers in London were from black or ethnic minorities in 1998.

In terms of resettlement, Randall and Brown (2003) recently estimated that 70-80 per cent of homeless families had needs beyond housing. The research identified a wide range of needs among homeless families including: vulnerable lone parents, many of them young and with little or no social support; women made homeless by domestic violence; people with mental health and emotional problems, and often experiencing repeated homelessness; people with neighbour disputes and victims and perpetrators of anti-social behaviour; people with drug and alcohol problems; people with mental health problems; people with physical health problems, poverty and debt, unemployment; literacy and educational difficulties; children's behavioural and educational problems; childhood histories of abuse and local authority care among parents in homeless families; histories of unsettled accommodation and repeated homelessness and multiple needs combining two or more of the above. For single people Randall and Brown estimate that over 50 per cent had multiple needs, by these definitions.

In terms of developments and thinking about homelessness, this decade can perhaps be seen as a period of consolidation and contradictions. Positively, funders, practitioners and government are recognising and embracing the idea of resettlement. Currently there are over two thousand practitioners of resettlement-specific services for homeless people in the UK and this is likely to increase. Legislatively it has finally been acknowledged as part of the jigsaw of solutions to homelessness. The new Homelessness Act 2002 puts a specific duty on local authorities to conduct, and act upon, a strategic review on homelessness services including those services that:

Provide support for people who are or may become homeless, and those who have been homeless and need support to prevent them becoming homeless again.

(Homeless Act, 2002: DTLR)

The act restored some of the erosion of duties to homeless people that had happened since the 1986 Housing Act. This included changing the duty to people from being effectively temporary accommodation, a short-hold tenancy in the private sector, to permanent accommodation. People also have strengthened rights of appeal and choice. However, while the priority categories have been extended, the notion of 'deserving' and 'undeserving' homeless people has been preserved. While local authorities now have the power to give housing to non-priority people, this is a power not a duty.

Resettlement has been bolstered by the formation of the new government Homeless Directorate. This builds on the continuing recognition that the government has given to resettlement services via the Rough Sleepers Unit's work on tenancy sustainment and 'meaningful occupation' initiatives.

> *Resettlement services can help former homeless families and single people make an effective transition to a new home . . . Schemes that provide practical, emotional and financial help . . . have proved successful in ensuring that tenancies do not break down. These schemes should be as much a part of supporting people as a homeless strategy.*
>
> (More Than a Roof, 2002: DTLR)

There is also international recognition of the need to develop expertise in resettlement. In its latest statement of purpose FEANTSAH (European Federation of National Organisations Working with Homeless People) and that:

> *In general terms, the role of resettlement agencies (NGOs) as social mediators, must be developed and encouraged, particularly in relation to public and private landlords.*
>
> (FEANTSAH, 2001)

In fact some of the earliest research into homeless services was done by the Council of Europe (Social Co-operation in Europe: Homelessness, 1992) which came out with the specific recommendations on resettlement for member states:

> *That personalised rehabilitation schemes be designed and implemented at local level . . . and to seek for this purpose . . . the best ways of achieving social integration.*

This culminated in the introduction of the Supporting People Programme in 2003. This programme funds the support costs of housing for vulnerable groups including homeless people. All supported housing services in operation in April 2003 had the support element of their funding switched to Supporting People. Prior to this most support services for homeless people were funded through housing benefit. This was a legacy of homelessness being seen in terms of housing and it had several consequences. Firstly, it meant that clients were effectively barred from working. If they worked they were no longer entitled to benefits, and would have to pay rents of several hundred pounds. Secondly, support was defined in terms of housing and practical support, explaining the emphasis of the work that we shall explore in subsequent chapters. Supporting People still funds what it calls 'housing costs', but these are defined as:

- *Support in establishing a suitable home.*
- *Support with daily living skills.*

- *Support in accessing benefits, health and community care services.*
- *Help in establishing and maintaining social support.*

As such, the potential of supporting people as a means of funding resettlement services for homeless people is great. However, in the first two years there was an over spend on the programme of almost 200 per cent (Homeless Link, 2004). As such services are facing a cut of 7 per cent in the coming financial year. The programme is funded through the local authority with a dedicated supporting people team that is responsible for drawing up a local strategy. This structure has its dangers, as Jenny Edwards, director of Homeless Link pointed out recently:

> *Inevitably, local authorities will be under pressure to preserve their in-house services and to focus on vulnerable groups who may be perceived as more popular with their electorates. This would place in jeopardy the high cost, but high value services that successfully transform the lives and chances of homeless people with complex and multiple needs.*
>
> (Edwards, 2004)

In terms of the development of practice, it seems to be a period of consolidation. Homeless Link is developing NVQs in Housing for resettlement workers and the National Learning Skills Council is consulting on developing a wider accreditation framework for all homelessness workers. The first higher education courses dedicated to working with homeless people have been developed. Work has also been undertaken on developing quality assessment frameworks for the sector. However, quite what the shape of the service will be is still undecided.

Old legacies and new challenges

Despite this progress the continuing influence of structural and individual explanations for homelessness in the services we provide for people needs to be acknowledged. The Rough Sleepers Initiative (RSI) has been accused of being a displacement activity, an aesthetic problem (Pleace, 2001). RSI originated after a Tory MP famously said that he was 'fed up of stepping over homeless people to get to the opera, RSI was as much about social exclusion as it was about inclusion (Pleace, 1998). In its first phase new units of accommodation were built, significantly these did not tend to be in central London but in outer London boroughs, reminiscent of Spikes. Practitioners have told me how in Edinburgh, homeless people are still cleared away using the 1834 Vagrancy Act, just before the festival, and allowed back afterwards. I have had similar reports in Nottingham and experienced them during Zero Tolerance measures at the end of the nineties in Kings Cross.

Another dimension of the continuing influence of individual explanations is paternalistic practice such as the destruction of spaces that homeless people had made their own. A recent example is the closing of the 'Bull Ring' at Waterloo in London. This has been a recognised cardboard city for over 20 years and has had a population in the hundreds, yet it was torn down to make way for a new cinema. As agencies provided services for the displaced, it being a planned eviction, it was cited as good practice (Thames Reach, 1998). The principle of it being homeless people's space was not countenanced. Even squatters, another much maligned group, get rights to their properties after some years.

In the final phase of the RSI, a target was set to reduce street homelessness by two thirds. Behind this policy decision is an interesting assumption that if the existing street homeless population are resettled they will not be replaced. This is a denial of social closure (Weber, 1976) regarding homeless people. That street homelessness may be because of more fundamental structural issues seems to have been lost.

Finally in the subtext of the policy document for the final phase of the RSI there was a distinct implication that for those street homeless people who do not accept the resettlement that is offered them, the police will be involved in dealing with them. This represented a return to the individualist model, characterising homeless people as having chosen their lifestyle and that those who do not take what they are charitably offered are 'bad' and must be dealt with accordingly. Interestingly in the 'street service teams' that have replaced street workers, there is an obligation to work with the police and there has been an active increase in police using their old powers of enacting the 1836 Vagrancy Act.

In conclusion, it seems that despite recent recognition of resettlement there is a task of work to be done. There has been little exploration of good practice in supporting people through resettlement, particularly at a more theoretical academic level. I intend this book to contribute to the building and development of this project. We also need not to let structural or individual discourses over-dominate the debate on how homelessness is thought about and legislated for. We need to create a more flexible and responsive arena for debate. Positively, Neal (1996) gives us a starting point for this agenda, setting a tone for what the rest of this book would like to achieve.

Individuals do not cause their own homelessness and it is therefore unacceptable and indeed impractical to leave them to their own devices when housing and support networks fail. Through increased communication, greater co-operation and more participation, enhanced understanding and subsequent improvements to policy and provision for homeless people seem likely to result.

(Neal, 1996: 49)

Chapter 2

Common Themes in Resettling Homeless People

Introduction

Front-line workers have many different job titles: resettlement workers, project workers, support or key workers. In many projects the resettlement role is separate from the day-to-day support or housing management function, but in others different stages of the resettlement process are undertaken by staff with wider responsibility than resettlement. They work in housing associations, local authority housing departments, hostels, day centres, outreach services, probation services, youth services and many others (Bevan, 1998: iii).

As Bevan (1998) illustrates, resettlement is a broad church. In fact it could be considered so broad that some workers do not even recognise they are part of it. In this way it is more of a role, but a role that needs some definition. In addition to the contexts of working given above a variety of different services are offered to homeless people within these settings. Recently Randall and Brown (1996) identified the variety of support services given to homeless people that are beyond purely housing services:

- **Tenancy support** focuses on preventing tenancy failure. They either work with people who are moving into a tenancy and have a history of tenancy breakdown or with people where the tenancy has been identified as breaking down:
- **Domestic violence** services provide specialist support to people who have experienced domestic violence. They have recently started to concentrate more on the moving out stage.
- **Money and debt** advice is a key area of support work with tenants at risk of homelessness. Help with access to settled housing. However, there is a new concentration of finding the most suitable housing in an area where the tenant will not be socially isolated, so it is an important part of preventing repeat homelessness (Randall and Brown, 2003).
- **Housing advice.** In the past advice has tended to focus on the housing options and rights of clients rather than their personal support needs

(Randall and Brown, 2003). Increasingly there are some tenancy support services linked to advice agencies.

- **Family mediation services** are designed to reconcile young people to their parents and prevent homelessness resulting from the breakdown of family relationships (Randall and Brown, 2003).
- **Rough sleeping services**. While many hostels are dedicated to working with this client group, there is also dedicated outreach work working with people on the streets. These can be called outreach workers, street workers, contact and assessment teams and more recently street services.
- **Drug and alcohol services**. Interestingly, Randall identifies that there are currently very few services that specifically target homeless families.
- **Mental health services**. Mental health problems affect both homeless adults and children. Specialist services have helped clients to sustain tenancies which might otherwise have failed. Many agencies will have specialist mental health workers, whether it is in day centres or hostels.
- **Health services**. There is a wide range of specialist health services for homeless people, including GPs, health visitors, Community Psychiatric Nurses (CPN), nurses and surgeries in day centres. Housing advice services in hospitals can help to ensure patients do not become homeless on discharge (Randall and Brown, 2003).
- **Social support**. These range from organising social events, volunteer befriending and linking people into local social networks.
- **Children's services**, including child care and ensuring attendance at school when they move areas.
- **Adult education** includes vocational training and English language classes for refugees.
- **Support for families with very high needs**. Many homeless families with very high and difficult to meet needs, such as chaotic life styles, a history of anti-social behaviour and rent arrears have in the past been excluded from social housing. But some authorities have developed schemes which offer both high support and a regime of compliance to rules governing acceptable behaviour. These schemes have proved effective in destabilising such families (Randall and Brown, 2003).
- **Former offenders' services**. Some local authorities have services such as housing advice sessions in prisons and specialist tenancy support for former offenders, including some for high risk offenders who would not previously have been housed or supported.
- **Services for current and former asylum seekers** include specialist tenancy support and day centre services offering mutual support and language classes. Multi-agency work is developing in some areas including,

for example, multi-disciplinary teams for the assessment of support needs and the co-ordination of services.

(Adapted from Randall and Brown, 2003)

Many other authors (Williamson, 2000; Bradley et al., 2004) have written good practice guides dedicated to looking at these services and their specific contexts. As such it is not my intention to revisit these ideas here. Similarly it is not the focus of this book to explore the specific needs and dimensions of different client groups. (While a worthy and needed piece of work this will be covered in a subsequent work.)

I mentioned in the previous chapter how early work on definitions focused almost exclusively on the differences between contexts of resettlement and the client groups they serve. Whilst this is invaluable to agencies seeking to understand their own role and focus, it inevitably stresses difference at the expense of what services hold in common. In doing so it misses a broader set of linkages which show resettlement to be a wide ranging yet discrete area of work.

As covered in the previous chapter, the emerging discipline of resettlement has faced a second difficulty, that of establishing itself in a context of ideology and legislation that perceives homelessness as primarily a housing issue. It is important that the boundaries of the work are broad enough to cover the different kinds of work carried out under the name resettlement. It is my intention now to outline a framework designed to help us think through what is within and what falls outside the concept.

A framework for discussion

We've got no definition of resettlement, nothing to measure it by. We're just working on a gut reaction most of the time to what somebody wants and in the light of what they are telling us, which is not always the truth

(Worker quoted in Smith and Wright, 1992: 29)

As illustrated above, the term resettlement has an ambiguous ring to many in the housing and caring fields. It may conjure up images of the old spikes, or, even the United Nations controversial involuntarily mass resettlements (MRGI, 2004). 'Re-settle-ment' can all too easily be seen as something workers 'do' to clients. These negative associations are further compounded by conceptual confusion; few seem to be clear about what resettlement involves.

Despite these difficulties, as we saw in the previous chapter, funding bodies such as the Department of the Environment and a number of charitable trusts were prepared to back a wide ranging, if unco-ordinated experiment in resettlement work. Across the country, a considerable variety of projects have developed with different funding bases, agency contexts, methods of intervention, involvement in the stages of resettlement process, etc. The fact that resettlement is still an undefined area of work has implications for those who use the service, those who provide the service and those who fund it. There are a number of reasons why each group would clearly benefit from the content and the boundaries of resettlement work being mapped out more clearly.

- **Service users**: require resettlement projects to meet their needs and to be accountable. Lack of clarity about what resettlement is makes it difficult for prospective referees to assess its relevance to their situations. They need to know what is on offer and what standard of services to expect. A common definition of resettlement increases accessibility, relevance and accountability.
- **Workers**: lack of clarity as to who they should work with and exactly what their jobs entails, leaves many resettlement workers demoralised, and with a disquieting sense of failure at being unable to meet increasingly fluid demands. In addition to answering the organisational questions raised above, a common frame of reference helps workers begin to clarify practical questions, such as, how to make relevant assessments, how to structure work, and where and when to make appropriate referrals.
- **Funders and policy makers**: need to be educated about both the need for, and the possibilities of, resettlement work. With the development of *Supporting People* it could be said that this battle has been largely won, funders need to know and be convinced of what they are buying. Clarity of definition, role and tasks is inextricably linked to the accountability that purchasers of services require.

More generally, it is vital to identify how resettlement differs from and complements other services, for example the rehousing work done by housing associations and local authorities, care in the community and other social service provision, probation, youth work etc. Without recognition of resettlement as a unique and discrete area of work within housing and caring services, there is a danger that funding sources could dry up. It is only by drawing together what is effectively a language of need and response that a credible agenda for the development of resettlement work can be set out.

Early research work by Crisis identified a widespread lack of clear of goals and objectives within agencies delivering resettlement services (Randall and Brown, 1996). Organisations had to grapple with fundamental questions with very few benchmarks. In 1994 the resettlement forum thought that a common definition of resettlement would provide a starting point for addressing these issues, by beginning to clarify the tasks and boundaries of resettlement work (Oldman, 1995). As a working definition, it described resettlement as involving 'a planned supported process of change in an accommodation context'. Within this definition I will seek to outline three themes:

- Support and the need for change.
- Process and the nature of change.
- The accommodation context.

I will also begin to consider differences and points of contact with related provision e.g. social services and rehousing work.

Support and the need for change

The central tenet of resettlement work is that it is possible to intervene usefully in situations where homelessness is the result of something more than difficulties in accessing accommodation. 'Support' is the general term used for interventions. Perhaps more important is the implication of the need for change. This is implied because resettlement is commonly understood to be a discrete piece of work (Bevan, 1998). If support is withdrawn, without change having occurred, then the situations that led to the initial homelessness will recur. Something needs to change if that person is to avoid becoming homeless again and that some kind of 'support' is needed to enable them to make that change. Change can occur on one of the following levels. (The nature of interventions that can be made on these levels will be covered in subsequent chapters.)

- **Cognitive** (thinking about it): making the right decisions about how and where to live is fundamental to an individual's chance of succeeding in their aims (Dane, 1998). A repeated cycle of accommodation breakdown can often be the result of a poor evaluation of options and unrealistic choices. The development of decision making skills can lead to lasting solutions, which are arrived at by the individuals themselves (Miller and Rollnick, 1991).
- **Emotional** (feelings about it): the way we feel about ourselves, other people and the place that we live, plays a large part in our ability to sustain any given lifestyle (Rowe, 1999). Negative emotions – whether the result of a bad experience in our past, or of coping with the present can lead to people repeatedly giving up their attempts to change accommodation at a similar point, even if they made an appropriate decision. Moving home is considered to be in the top 20 stressful events (Holmes and Rahe, 1967). Enabling people to be aware of, and to cope with, their feelings can take away the blockage and help them to proceed.
- **Practical** (doing it): changing accommodation often requires the adaptation of old skills and the need to learn new ones. Competence or adequate support in these things is essential for someone coping in their new

environment. There are also practical changes that need to occur, often external to the individual such as the acquisition of accommodation, furniture, the connection of amenities etc.

Historically, resettlement services in Britain have tended to concentrate on the practical aspects of the work (Randall and Brown, 1994; 1995). This is perhaps explained by its roots in housing, rather than social work and the legacies of structural approaches to homelessness. This approach ignores the more emotional and cognitive aspects of the work such as the need for social support (Randall and Brown, 1996; Rog and Holupka, 1999; Crane, 1999) and help on decision making (Birch, 1999). Interestingly other countries take a different stance. The Dutch model of resettlement allows support to be withdrawn only when the client has two positive relationships apart from the worker (Tavecchio, 1999). Some American authors such as Rowe (1999) also take this view, 'A positive relationship with another human being is a prerequisite for a successful exit from homelessness' (Rowe, 1999: 86).

Practical considerations are seen to be secondary to this and will probably come in time. While it would be premature to say that this is a better model or more accurate, it is interesting in its difference to the practice of many British resettlement projects. The British projects tend to have criteria such as whether people seem to be coping in practical terms, with amenities connected etc. An example illustrates the dynamics of these potential levels of intervention, and the dangers of neglecting any of the levels.

Case Study: Jimmy

Jimmy is a client known to the worker for several months. He had lived with his mother until her death in his 30s. It was her death that led to Jimmy's drinking, a deterioration in the flat, and ultimately Jimmy's homelessness. Jimmy then had a pattern of street homelessness followed by stays in hostel accommodation and then tenancies that subsequently broke down, for 10 years. He also had slight learning difficulties. Jimmy's initial perspective was that if you 'just got him a flat it would all be sorted.' After some work on his decision making Jimmy accepted that perhaps he initially needed some kind of supported accommodation. He was moved to a cluster house where he had his own flat but there was a communal lounge and a support worker who visited him. After a month the support worker contacted the resettlement worker to say that the arrangement did not seem to be working. Jimmy was sleeping in the communal lounge. Discussion with Jimmy initially centred around whether this was the right decision for him, he still felt it was the right choice. Discussion then moved onto whether he was coping with practical matters such as budgeting, but this again was not the issue. It was only when discussion centred on the emotional level that the real issue came to light.

> Whether it was a subconscious thing or simply what he associated with home; he had decorated his front room to resemble his mother's front room. Every time he walked into the flat he was faced with feelings that he could not cope with as he had not really dealt with his mother's death.

This case study is important for two reasons. Firstly it illustrates the importance of considering all three levels of change that a person may go through. Secondly, it does raise the question of boundaries, as we are not bereavement councillors. However, we can see that to get Jimmy to access these services will be no simple matter, an issue we will return to in considering the accommodation context.

The recognition that change occurs on these three levels provides resettlement workers with a clear focus for the support they offer, three aspects to be considered in assessments, and three areas in which they can develop skills and methods of intervention. The three levels also provide a dynamic model which recognises that change at one level is likely to have an effect on another; the way we think about something often changes the way we feel about it; a positive feeling about something is unlikely to be maintained if our lack of practical skills will ultimately let us down: and so on. This simple recognition points to the need for a high level of skill and competence on the part of resettlement workers.

The need for support and change then defines the starting point of resettlement intervention. It makes a broad distinction between needs that can be met by one-off pieces of work and those which require a more sustained form of intervention. This distinction may be useful for clarifying the practical application of rehousing and resettlement services. The two models are not mutually exclusive: rehousing work often extends into advocacy and practical help, but by its very nature offers a strictly limited form of intervention. Resettlement workers, on the other hand, may take on a case only to find out that all that was needed was a brief form of intervention covering practical issues. Their intention and rationale, however, is to provide an appropriate level of support in order to enable the individual to achieve and sustain their chosen lifestyle. In essence, resettlement work involves a process – something we will explore in the next section.

Process and the nature of change

If resettlement is about supporting someone through change, it will involve some kind of process; there is an assumption of movement, which relates to the individual and their environment. Perhaps more significantly, change is not an instant thing, it takes time and this is not always an easy thing for people.

This may be very uncomfortable for people to accept, and counsellors (sic. workers) need to recognise that people may give out mixed messages. 'The traveller may be tempted to stop completely – perhaps with mixed feelings about the need to go on with the guide, or with the belief that the destination has in fact been reached' (Kent, 1991: 314).

The question then arises of what is the nature of this process. A definition of it helps us explore that:

An actual or intended move in accommodation, and the individual process of adjustment and change which accompanies it.

(Seal and Stretch, 1992)

Once resettlement is seen as a process in which support enables people to alter the situation in which they find themselves, a number of things fall into place. The resettlement process cannot be reduced to something solely relating to a change in accommodation. This approach misses the human dynamics involved in any transition. It makes for poor quality resettlement work and a high percentage of placement breakdowns (Dane, 1998; Randall and Brown, 2003). If we resist the temptation to reduce resettlement merely to moving house, we soon become aware of an implicit ethos which views as a learning experience what could have been seen as a failure: where accommodation breaks down we have a broader set of questions to ask. Is this the end of the process or a stage in raising someone's awareness? Were the decisions the move was based up on the right ones? How did the person feel and how did this influence things?

Process, then, needs to be understood in a holistic way, which takes full account of the individual's, interaction with their accommodation context. The pace at which the resettlement process moves is crucial and needs to be managed in terms of the three levels outlined above (thinking, feeling and doing). A balance also has to be found between the expectations of service users, the input of workers and the often overriding influence of external factors e.g. the unavailability of accommodation and the timing of an offer. A way of viewing that process can be illustrated thus:

Internal process

Thinking about → Making → Making → Getting used → Becoming
decisions   decisions   changes   to changes   that change

External process

Unsatisfactory → Temporary → New accommodation
accommodation   accommodation

It is important, therefore, as workers, we attend to the internal processes as well as the external ones. We then have to find a way to articulate such a model to our clients, as their focus and belief, as already explored, may well be that the process of change is over at the point where they gain their accommodation.

We should not underestimate how difficult a change in perception this may be. Snow and Anderson (1993) note how at a certain point being a homeless person becomes an identity in itself. In these cases we are not simply asking people to make changes in their thinking, behaviour and circumstances: we are threatening their very identity:

> *The thought of giving up one's homeless identity, of giving up homeless acquaintances for the isolation of apartment living, raising doubts about self-worth that can be pushed down more easily in the day-to-day foraging for subsistence*

(Rowe, 1999: 106)

In addition, and perhaps as a consequence, the resettlement process is not necessarily a linear one from dependence to independence to interdependence. There are a number of difficulties with this idea:

- It initially labels people dependant, some of whom have been surviving 'on the road' for 50 years or more!
- It prescribes the nature and direction of change – our 70 year old traveller may now want nursing care at home: definitely resettlement work, but hardly a move towards independence.
- As a result, this approach is in danger of seeing necessary and appropriate events, such as leaving a flat, as failure.

Placing the emphasis on 'change in an accommodation context' bases our work on the recognition that we are all, to some degree, interdependent. Resettlement is about enabling service users to re-negotiate the balance of relationships and circumstances in their lives at any given time.

The resettlement process inevitably brings an awareness of limits, of a beginning and an ending, which places legitimate boundaries around resettlement work. In practical terms the resettlement process begins with a referral and ends at a point where support can – or must – be withdrawn. Beyond this, service users will either be able to sustain on their own or will need some form of longer-term support. One of the major tasks facing resettlement workers is to identify ways of assessing when support can be effectively withdrawn. i.e. when the process of adjustment and change associated with the move is completed.

The accommodation context

Having a home involves expressive as well as instrumental needs, a sense of control over one's life and the ability to create one's own environment. It involves creating or reclaiming one's personal identity as a housed person with social and community status and respect.

(Ridgeway et al., 1994: 410)

The term 'accommodation context' refers to individuals' housing situation in the very broadest sense and provides the backdrop against which resettlement work takes place. In addition to the basic need for shelter, as indicated by Ridgeway et al.'s quote above, 'accommodation context' recognises that the place where a person lives affects their health and well being, their ability to socialise and participate in society, their safety and their identity.

As a point of departure the accommodation context initially locates the problem with the accommodation rather than the individual (De Shazer, 1985). This allows the service user and the worker to meet with the neutral and common aim of solving accommodation difficulties that the individual has identified for themselves. This allows other issues to arise naturally in the process of the work and at the individual's pace.

As a central focus the accommodation context also provides workers with 'leverage', a source of motivation and commitment that has been identified by the service user themselves (Egan, 1998). This is particularly important when working with people leading chaotic lifestyles or having to face a number of issues such as mental health or a dependency. It enables workers to address such issues as they relate to an accommodation context. A dependency issue for example may come to light during a session of budgeting and could be addressed via a harm reduction approach, which enables the person to come to terms with paying bills. Resettlement intervention involves facilitating decision making inside this situation and enabling individuals to act upon their choices effectively.

Addressing issues as they relate to obtaining or maintaining accommodation delineates the boundaries of resettlement, but the concept of an accommodation context acknowledges that this is a blurred boundary. Work is carried out as it relates to the accommodation context, but at the same time we need to recognise that referring on to other agencies for other issues is no simple matter.

The case study of Jimmy illustrated this with the example of counselling: the resettlement process often elicits disclosures about significant issues which may require more in-depth work. Sometimes, however, the worker may not have the skill or it may not be appropriate to engage in in-depth counselling. In this instance the role of the resettlement worker is not to provide such counselling but to act as a bridge to other services.

This bridging role in itself requires a high level of expertise and understanding on the part of the worker, and can often take a considerable length of time. They do not simply refer on, which distinguishes them from an advice worker; they hold clients until they are in a position realistically to access that service. In the case of Jimmy this meant working with him until he recognised he needed the service, made an appointment, turned up, at the right time, on the right day, sober, sat down in front of a stranger and talked about the issues as he saw them. Without such work it is possible that a contributing factor to the person's accommodation difficulties, such as Jimmy's grief, will not be addressed and they may soon move on again and repeat previous patterns.

The accommodation context shows why resettlement is unique in its tasks and approaches. Although many agencies work with people on housing issues, few see this fundamentally shaping the nature of their interactions. This is reflected in the fact that there are currently no professional qualifications, include teaching, on the process of homelessness and its effects on the service user. In addition to this the new role of social workers as care package managers and the high number of cases they are expected to deal with suggests that it would be difficult for them to fully engage with the tasks we have outlined.

Conclusion

The three themes are intended to begin the process of defining resettlement for the situation we face at present. They allow it to be seen as an inclusive area of work, which has room for many different styles, approaches, and levels of intervention. They also illustrate how resettlement is responding to needs that cannot me met through traditional models of rehousing work, youth and community work or by the current nature of social work intervention.

One writer has suggested that 'needs which lack a language adequate to their expression do not simply pass out of speech: they may cease to be felt'. However, the recent development of resettlement services around the country has been a response to an increasingly well defined area of unmet need, that of homeless people who, with the right support, are able to improve their accommodation situation and the way they manage it. In practice this often involves bridging the crucial gap between a cycle of homelessness and being able to sustain a tenancy. In struggling with these issues resettlement workers are, in effect, making the silent and private dilemmas of many homeless people into a clearly identified public issue.

Within this context we need to recognise a fundamental standpoint we are adhering to. This is that the care system for homeless people we are operating within has fundamental flaws. Many needs are not, and indeed may never, be met (Park, 2002). The on-going development of resettlement services, and the maintenance of this political stance is one of the best ways to ensure that these needs do not cease to be felt by funders and policy makers. It is implied through the continued development of a 'language of need and response'.

Chapter 3

The Ethos of Resettlement: Managing Values and Tensions

In any circumstances where as individual or group of individuals takes responsibility for aspects of the lives of others on the grounds of special knowledge or expertise . . . ethical issues arise and some form of guidance for action is required.

(Tomlinson, 1997: 1)

Professionalism and ethics

Tomlinson (1997) goes on to explain that this is particularly important where the worker is working alone, often on a one-to-one basis, has managerial support that may be remote and has relative autonomy. These seem to be typical circumstances for a resettlement worker. At present, there is no professional body and no statement of ethics for our sector. Statements on values are occasionally reflected in the mission statement or literature of individual agencies but there are none that are both specific and common to resettlement workers in general.

At the 1996 resettlement conference, practitioners voted to professionalise the service (Oldman, 1996). While this could have different meanings and motivations, it represented a claim that resettlement is, or could be, a distinct profession (Oldman, 1996). There are many aspects we could consider as to what constitutes a professional: undertaking professional training, having autonomy over one's work, an apprenticeship or a statement of public duty (Dingwall and Lewis, 1983; Torstendahl and Burrage, 1996). Unfortunately there is little agreement over which of these traits constitutes a professional (Banks, 1995). Koehn (1994) believes that the public pledge is the most defensible trait of professionalism, and is the one from which all the others stem. The most common form of this pledge is the code of ethics or statement of values (Dawson, 1994; Lash and Urry, 1987). If then for reasons of our working context and in developing our professional status, we see the need for a stated set of common ethics, we need to identify what these should be. This is no easy feat; Timms (1983) found 180 different definitions of statements of values within the context of professional ethics.

It is worth here making a distinction between a code of ethics, a code of practice and rules. The first is a statement of general principles and the second gives more detailed guidance on how to interpret these in particular circumstances or situations (Banks, 1995). However, what neither of these provide is the third, which is a set of precise rules for our conduct 'telling practitioners how to act in every possible type of situation they may encounter in their everyday work' (Banks, 1995: 6). Social workers are explicit that their code of conduct does not represent such a thing:

> In itself, this code does not represent a set of rules that will prescribe all the behaviours of social workers in all the complexities of professional life. Rather, it offers general principles to guide conduct, in situations that have ethical implications.
>
> (NASW, 1998)

In my experience trainees often have a desire for a body of precise instructions that tells them what they should explicitly do in any given situation. Rice (1975) warns that to create such a thing would be a 'substitute for ethical reflection'. In other words this would be a denial of the need for a public declaration of our ethics, the need for which recognises that we are autonomous, and, in the end only have our own consciousnesses to answer to. Perhaps to be professional is to recognise this; that we will always have ethical dilemmas and decisions to make with only ourselves and perhaps a set of guiding values as a reference point. This chapter will attempt to start developing this reference point.

Without wishing to open up a large philosophical debate, ethics or values are normally seen as ontological in derivation (coming from the nature of existence, i.e. they are intrinsic) or teleological (coming from the purpose in existence or from what our activities intend to achieve). Putting this into context, we have two ethical dimensions, or sources, to consider. As resettlement workers we are professionals that are concerned with people, our ontological ethics should then come from what is generally accepted about how humans should treat each other (Hayes, 1998). To be specific we will look to other care professions and our own practice to see if there are common denominators in how we should treat clients.

To understand our teleological ethics, we should look to any principles that derive from our specific role i.e. to support people through a process of change in an accommodation context. In reality, as Tomlinson (1997) says, our ethics often derive from a combination of the two and they will interact. As a methodology I therefore intend to examine our ontological ethics (accepted ways to treat clients), to then interpret them in the context of our role and then to see if any other (teleological) ethics arise. I will be using in addition my reflections on the courses I have run with practitioners about the subject of ethics (Seal, 2002). I have generated nine ethical statements that can perhaps give us a basis for a code of practice:

1. **Non-labelling:** Clients are not inherently homeless, drug users, alcoholics, un-housable etc. We should use labels carefully for the benefit of people and have regard to how clients label themselves.
2. **Individual responsibility:** The client is responsible for assessing their situation and what they need to do about it. Decisions that people 'own' are the ones that they stick to.
3. **Internal attribution:** Realising that the power to change, within the limits of outside constraints, lies with the client themselves. Everyone has a right and a potential to make decisions about their lives.
4. **Conscientisation:** Recognising that clients may need to be educated to believe in themselves, developing consciousness of their situation, to see what has happened to them and why. You cannot just ask people what they want, people have to learn how to ask, analyse and question.
5. **Non-directiveness:** Clients have a right and the potential to make decisions about their lives. The worker should not seek to impose their values but facilitate the client in developing their own without pressure or coercion.
6. **Intervention:** Can be a necessity for workers but at a point that fosters development not dependency. The goal of the intervention is that the person can see and accept the reality of their situations so that they can change accordingly.
7. **Utility:** Workers should work for the good of the client, balancing this with taking into account the needs of other users of the project and the wider community. Policies that affect clients should be designed with this in mind rather than organisational convenience in mind.
8. **Responsibility:** The right and duty to bring to the attention of those in power the ways in which activities of government, society or agencies create or contribute to hardship and suffering.
9. **Competence:** We have a duty to train, become qualified, network and keep up to date with developments in practice. We should see these activities as opportunities that enhance our practice and are an important part of it.

In examining the codes of ethics of social work, nursing, counselling and youth work Banks (1995) identifies five core themes that run through them all concerning how we should treat our clients (ontological ethics).

Non-labelling/Banks' first theme

The first of these, Banks (1995: 89) calls 'the recognition of the value and dignity of every human being'. Specifically in our context, one value that many practitioners (Seal, 2004) have cited under this category is that of non-labelling, expressed here as values statement one. While laudable we should consider three complicating factors. Firstly many services are targeted at people on the basis of their label, being young, having issues of mental health, drugs etc. While this can acknowledge the commonalities in a particular experience it can become a crude reason for exclusion or labelling people as a problem. Carter (1999) notes how the presence of drugs, mental health and alcohol accounted for a high percentage of exclusions in hostels in Birmingham, regardless of circumstances. Legislation such as the various Homelessness Acts and the discretionary social fund distinguishes between people by what it calls priorities, but this also divides and labels people as the deserving and undeserving poor (Frost et al., 1998).

A second dimension of labelling is that of self-labelling; this can take both negative and positive forms. A mental health label can be a relief as it gives an explanation and a hope of treatment, for distressing experiences a person may have gone through (Craig et al., 1995). On the other hand labelling can be an evasion of responsibility; for example some drinkers use their 'alcoholism' as an evasion of responsibility – everything that happened was as a result of their 'disease', and not something they have a responsibility for (Miller and Rollnick, 1991). (Some ways of working with these dimensions of labelling will be explored further in Chapter 4 on the client-worker relationship.) These factors influence the phrasing of the second half of the value statement.

Individual responsibility/Banks' second theme

Bank's (1995) second common feature of codes of practice she phrases as 'the facilitation of the realisation of each individual with due regard to the interests of others'. This statement seems to have many conceptions within it, some of which may conflict in the context of working with homeless people. The words 'facilitation' and 'realisation of an individual' would seem to relate to the next five value statements (Seal, 2002), the first three of which concern what part clients should play in the process and the next two which consider the worker's resulting role and responsibility.

The first complicating factor of these values is that often the power to effect what needs to be done about an issue does not lie with the person, it lies with other agencies or in wider societal structures. This effect is further compounded when, as Smith (2002) notes, a casework approach is one where 'the focus is on the individual, ignoring the social factors that impact on specific groups'. We will return to this issue, exploring how we can preserve our integrity and politics and not blame the client for their situation, in the next chapter on the client-worker relationship, and in subsequent chapters on how we operationalise this relationship with issues like assessment and support planning.

Another complicating factor seems to stem from the very project of resettlement itself. Many individuals we encounter have had profound problems 'assessing their situation and what to do about it', and this is why they are in front of the worker. This presents a dilemma in that we do not want to label them as useless or patronise them as being incapable, yet they do not seem able to make informed choices, a concept that is often taken for granted and oversimplified in our work.

Conscientisation

We are partly helped here by Freire's (1968) concept of conscientisation, as expressed in the fourth value statement. He believes that people need to be educated to develop consciousness of their situation, to understand what has happened to them and why. You cannot just ask people what they want, people have to learn how to ask, analyse and question. It is a dialectical process rather than an information giving one. Friere (1968) believes that people may deliberately not have been allowed to develop this conscious ability. In another context, that of education, the reasons for this deliberateness are spelled out worryingly clearly by an early non-advocate of education for the working classes:

> However specious in theory the project might be of giving education to the labouring classes of the poor, it would, in effect, be found prejudicial to their morals and happiness, it would teach them to despise their lot in life, instead of making them good servants in agriculture, and other laborious employments to which their rank in society had destined them; instead of teaching them subordination, it would render them fictitious and refractory . . . It would enable them to read seditious pamphlets, vicious books and publications against Christianity; it would render them insolent to their superiors; and in a few years . . . legislators would find it necessary to direct the strong arm of power against them.
>
> (Giddy quoted in Donald, 1992: 20)

However, the concept of conscientisation has its limitations. It shares, with both the values of internal attribution and internal responsibility, Rogerian (1995) assumptions that all clients have the powers and ability to self actualise. What these values ignore is that some clients, with issues such as mental health, some forms of learning disability and personality disorder will never be able to do this, as they cannot gain insight into their situations. Given the levels of these issues around homelessness mentioned in Chapter 2 this may have a substantial impact on this field. That said, we should not underestimate the levels of insights these client groups may have.

Non-directiveness and intervention

There are then two values (statements 5 and 6) that inform the role of a resettlement worker. The first is from counselling in its Rogerian form, that of non-directiveness. This value is central to being client centred (Rogers, 1955) with the belief that we should hold certain ideas about a client:

Non-directivity is part and parcel of client-centered theory and practice and, as well, a behavioral result of adhering to the central conditions of client-centered therapy. For those who believe the critical foundation of client-centered theory, i.e., that the client is his or her own best expert about his or her life, non-directivity is a natural stance that emerges from the theory.

(Bozarth and Evans, 2000)

This client centred approach has become almost axiomatic in the care professions (Park, 2002). However, this approach needs to be counter balanced with the realities of our interventions as resettlement workers given our context of change. Broadly the difficulty seems to be the fallacy of informed choice. Many workers talk about informed choice as though it is simply a matter of giving people options and then supporting them through the choice they make. Many clients come to us with ambivalence towards change and the difficulties that this might entail. Miller (1993) helps us identify four common reactions in clients that can demand interventions that go beyond such a rigid definition of what it is to be non-directive:

- *Clients who seem stuck in certain patterns of choices and behaviour that does not work or are on a downwards spiral.*
- *Clients who want to change but do not know what to change or keep changing their mind.*
- *Clients who know where they want to be but do not think they can do it or that they are not worth it.*
- *Clients who are not realistic about what they want, sometimes setting their goals deliberately too high.*

Certain interpretations of non-directiveness (Kahn, 1999) would hold a worker should never interpret, give advice and definitely not argue with a client. In training, workers have reflected this notion, saying that we do not have the right as workers to interfere with a client's decision. Conversely, do we have the right not to intervene when a client may be leaning towards a decision that we may feel could be damaging to themselves or others? The challenge seems to be able to intervene without abandoning the tenets of a person centred approach. Bozarth and Evans (2000) argue that we should concentrate less on the primacy of non-directiveness, but on empathy and how this is expressed, 'The issue is not the behaviour of the therapist but whether or not the therapist's actions emerge from the therapist's dedication to the client's frame of reference'. Miller takes reinterpretation as far as redefining this as confrontation; for our purposes we should be content to redefine it as intervention (value statement 6).

There are dangers in intervention but, done carefully, it can nevertheless be powerful, as Miller acknowledges, 'coming face to face with a disquieting image of oneself may be the precipitating force in many changes that occur'. In Chapter 15 on cognitive interventions, we will explore how Miller develops these ideas further into motivational interviewing.

Utility/Banks' third theme

Banks (1995) third common theme in codes of practice is the 'Relief and prevention of hardship and suffering'. In its widest sense Banks (1995) interprets this as being our commitment to equality and to the very enterprise of working in the care professions – that of caring for people. Within the context of homelessness it has two major implications. Firstly, as Brandon (1998) mentions, we have to recognise that homelessness is an equal opportunities issue. Homeless people are discriminated against in a number of ways both structurally and within our institutions. Examples of structural discrimination are well documented in terms of benefits (Kemp and Rugg, 1998; Wyler, 1999) access to health (Pearce, 1996; North et al., 1996; Crisis, 1998) voting (CHAR, 1997) media representation (Hutson and Clapham, 1999; Hutson and Liddiard, 1996) as victims of crime (Jones, 1999; Hawes, 1997) as well as within homelessness legislation itself. We will return to what duty this places upon the worker when considering the next value statement.

Perhaps most important for us, is that this value is utilitarian in that we work for the 'good' (Banks, 1995). A question that stems from this in our working context is what balance we strike between meeting individual needs and those of the wider community. While it would be unwise to reach a precise answer or formula for this, it would seem to be important to establish a framework for considering it. Within homelessness and resettlement we need to consider the needs of an individual client and the needs of the other people within the project. As an example I will examine admissions policies and evictions policies within such a framework.

Case study

A common reason given for not allowing the use of alcohol on the premises is that it would be unfair on those giving up within the hostel. Analysing this in terms of whose need this serves, we see that the rationale is a utilitarian one, taking the greater good of the hostel into account rather than the individual's need for a service whilst still drinking. However, an assumption behind this decision is that people drinking in the hostel would lead those not drinking into temptation. It also either ignores the world of drink the client exists in once they step outside of the hostel or at best makes the assumption that they need their hostel space to be drink free to cope with the outside world.

Sometimes other residents within the hostel have been consulted to establish the truth of these assumptions, but often they have not. Assuming we do consult the residents, there are questions of time and precedent as to whether that should set a consultation precedent for other residents and for how long. One dispersed project in Southampton adopted an interesting approach: every week the house met and decided what the drinking policy for that week should be, including the sanctions for breaking it. This would seem to call for greater involvement of users in the dynamic of decision making and implies that the policy should be an evolving one according to the individual and group needs within the project. As it was a house for people with personality disorders, excuses that clients would not be interested or in a fit state to participate are hard to maintain. Such opportunities for participation are seen by authors such as Neale (1998) and Hutson (1996) as utilitarian in itself, being as important for people's well being as the design of the building.

Responsibility/Banks' fourth theme

Bank's (1995) fourth theme in codes of practice is 'the responsibility to report and act on evidence of suffering being caused' I have expressed this as value statement 8. This value has interesting implications for workers as it places a duty on them both politically and in their workplace. Given the structural discrimination we mentioned earlier, it seems to give rise to a campaigning role. This is important in terms of the emphasis we place on the different aspects of our role. As we shall discuss in Chapter 6 on networking, many workers have a reluctance to engage in this wider role, even in the form of networking or joining local inter-agency forums. A common reason given is that workers see this as less important and as detracting from face-to-face work with their clients. This value implies, however, that we are being derelict in our duty if we do not engage in these wider issues at least to some extent.

This value also means that we have a duty to speak up about discriminatory practices within our own and other agencies. During my training (Seal, 2004) a common complaint from workers is that they are not in a position to implement some of the good practice they are learning and do not feel empowered to challenge some of the bad practice they are experiencing. People expressed fears about the personal consequences of doing or saying something. The implications of this value (Banks, 1995) are that we nevertheless have a duty to do so, the question shifting to how we make ourselves feel safe when we fulfil our duty.

Competence/Banks' fifth theme

Bank's (1995) final common theme of codes of practice is the 'commitment to serve those purposes with integrity and skill.' I have paraphrased this as value statement 9. There are many barriers to developing these 'skills and integrity' and within our field the way to do this is still contested. There is no recognised qualification in working with homeless people (Seal, 2000) and the debate about the merits of a qualification and what it should be like, have gone on for some years. The 'pro' lobby seems to feel it will give acknowledgement for the work that workers do; it will set standards, avoiding resettlement being reduced to its lowest common denominator and will delineate resettlement as a discrete area of work. The counter argu-ments are that we will become restricted both in the scope of the work, who becomes a worker and which agencies practice it (Seal, 2000). Workers have traditionally come from a variety of backgrounds and there was a desire not to establish accreditation that would become a barrier. Similarly, resettle-ment work has developed organically within small agencies responding to need.

However, there has been some work in recent years to develop such accreditation and avoid the pitfalls mentioned. Homeless Link has developed a route through the Housing NVQ that is designed for resettlement workers at levels two and three. Other agencies have gone through the Care Route or Open College Network. (It is not the scope of this chapter to debate the relative merits of these attempts, suffice to say that there is an imperative at the moment.) The National Learning Skills Council has launched a pilot into the area and *Supporting People* see workforce development as a key factor in its Quality Assessment Framework. Similarly, work needs to happen on developing practitioner journals. Many second tier organisations such as Homeless Link, Shelter, Crisis etc produce newsletters, but there is no journal dedicated towards practice. There is not a culture of valuing training, qualifications and disseminating good practice among workers. As with the attitude mentioned above towards networking, it is seen as distracting from front-line work at best and avoidance of work at worst. It is for this reason that I have phrased the value as it stands.

Conclusion

Codes of practice do not guarantee good practice. At best they are a reference point for discussion, which is the intent of the nine statements above. Resettlement work as a profession does not have some of the traits of a professional: a recognised qualification, a professional association that monitors and censors individual behaviour, a professional journal or established standards. Given this and the largely autonomous working context, resettlement workers often truly have only themselves to answer to, making the need for some guiding principles even more imperative.

Section Two
The Environment and Working Relationships

Chapter 4

The Client–Worker Relationship

We place great importance on the formation of a trusting relationship and see it as the single most important factor in ensuring a formerly homeless person makes a successful transition to permanent housing.

(Director of Wintringham, a service for older homeless people in Melbourne)

All those who make their living in the helping professions are in the paradoxical position of working to eliminate their own jobs, at least insofar as they actually try to help people help themselves. Regardless of the proclaimed goals, the brute economic fact is that the helping professions need neediness, disability, incapacity, and helplessness, and this fact is not lost on the burgeoning bureaucracies of the aid industry.

(McKnight, 1996: 74)

If we examine the implications of these quotes we see that it is a necessary task, if one that is occasionally overlooked, to examine the nature of our relationship with the client so as to temper these 'brute economic facts'. John McKnight (1996) in his insightful piece called *Professionalising Service and Disabling Help* discusses how workers, when they design and deliver services often underpin them with a particular construct of the concept of 'need'. Need, he says, is often defined as 'deficiency' and this deficiency is located in the client. Needs are understood to reside in the individual rather than in the system and judgements are made about people who do not comply with services that meet these needs. Parson (1952) identifies four aspects of the role of a sick person: one is an obligation on the sick person to get well, and another is an obligation for the sick person to seek technically competent help and to co-operate with that help in trying to get well. Those who do not seek help are seen as amoral, and where someone does seek help, but cannot cope with the system, this is seen as non-co-operation and incurs blame (Parson, 1952). My experience of workers' attitudes, including my own, of people who do not engage with services, or 'make trouble' in a hostel would echo this.

Furthermore, deficiencies are translated into a set of disconnected 'issues' and treated with specialised services. With every increase in professional social services given to people (in our case homeless people), it pulls them into a network of services which diagnose the individual as defective and in need of further services. The development of care management models in social services (Park, 2002) is a reflection of this. Workers then keep focusing on these services until the client becomes compromised and disabled by them. As Illich (1977) notes, while people initially become dependent on professionals for specialist skills, gradually they become dependent on them for services which, in the past, people provided for themselves or for each other. The result is a state of social service dependency, social control, a loss of personal autonomy and the creation of needs in the client. This phenomenon is explored within the context of homelessness in more detail in Chapter 12 on models of resettlement, where we examine how agencies find difficult the stage of letting go, the temptation being to create or find unmet needs in the client.

A similar concern arises commonly in day centres (Bradley et al., 2003) and to a certain extent hostels, where clients may use the services (even on a casual basis) for years. Agencies are torn between wanting to provide a safety net, but *not* wanting people to become dependant on the service. On the positive side, there is a live debate amongst workers, and in some agencies the issue has been addressed operationally. One day centre in Liverpool I know, employed workers specifically to engage with clients who seem stuck in the service, in an attempt to move them on.

In this chapter we shall consider the implications of the above for our relationships with clients. The destructive dynamic described is not purely structural; it can be a part of our relationships with clients. This is supported by Hutson and Clapham (1999) who, in investigating relationships in hostels, takes the view that more informal approaches and building on the support clients give each other is a way forward and that traditional approaches can be dependency creating. As Neale (1998) says, in investigating factors determining successful resettlement, 'whether or not hostels increased or decreased independence depended on the particular hostel concerned and on the individual worker'. With this in mind the question we need to ask ourselves is what the relationship with clients should be. To do this I will firstly develop some principles about the relationship and secondly I will examine issues that arise from them.

The principles outlined below are developed from three sources. As a starting point, Illich (1977: 45) identifies characteristics for workers who are becoming 'disabling professionals', 'they hoard knowledge, consolidate power, exercise privilege in ways that disempower clients and make clients more dependent upon professionals'. This gives us a model to avoid. Secondly, I have sought to take account of a series of challenges Brandon sets for workers in their relationships with clients as outlined in the *Resettlement Handbook* (1998). As a third source I have used Biestek, (1961) *The Casework Relationship*, particularly the opening chapter on the essence of the relationship one needs to develop with clients.

Principles of an effective client-worker relationship

1. Be holistic rather than partial or pathological. People are always much more important than just a list of syndromes, however complex. The nature of people is more important than the nature of their problems.
2. Help people to understand the vast labyrinth of professionals and services, and their sometimes competing ego battles. Oppose a professional colonialism that thinks it knows best.
3. Seek out and provide information; both concretely and clearly, avoiding jargon which hinders fuller involvement while not underestimating a person's understanding or undermining a person's knowledge.
4. Believe in and act on the rights of homeless people, putting them first and where possible, acting under their direction.
5. Acknowledge the power you and the client have in the relationship and seek ways to make this productive.
6. Seek to break down the barriers between workers and clients, humanising themselves and you. Confess your ignorance and human feelings at a point that helps their development rather than just your own.
7. Take as your starting point that people are coping and can cope, but that your client may not realise this. Seek ways to build upon this.
8. Reflect on your own practice and learn to differentiate from when you insufficiently support people, setting them up to fail and when you create dependency or perpetuate client's 'needs'.

There are many issues that could be drawn from these principles and I will consider only three in this chapter in detail: issues of professional colonialism (Principle 2), issues of power (Principles 5 and 6) and language and information (Principle 3). Principles 1 and 4 stem from our earlier debate on values and from issues outlined in the opening paragraph of this chapter. Principle 7 is covered in more detail in the chapter on assessment, but it is worth noting here that it should become integral to the whole of the relationship we maintain with clients as well as during the assessment period. Principle 8 derives from the aforementioned tendency of services to perpetuate or create needs; a phenomenon to be explored more in subsequent chapters. We will examine how the principle can be put into practice in the chapter on worker's support mechanisms.

Professional colonialism

Principle 2 implies, firstly that the care system is flawed (Park, 2002) and secondly that many agencies are self-serving and self-perpetuating; the latter is generally accepted by practitioners (Seal, 2002), the former less so. Many workers in training express a model of brokering or matching people to 'appropriate services'. This is a very 'New Labour' model and can be seen in allied fields in the new case management approach to social work (Park, 2002) and initiatives such as Connexions (Smith, 2001). We will return to the implications of such a model and how this affects our practice in the chapter on assessment.

Practitioners often felt uncomfortable at the idea of sharing their concerns about other agencies and the failures of the care system in general. Some felt that to do so would be imposing their opinions on a client and we should instead allow clients to form their own opinions. However, workers agreed that the concerns they had with other agencies effected their own judge-ments and working practices, from the extreme of not referring to an agency to the milder form of not fostering working relationships with them. Worker's opinions therefore impact upon clients anyway. To say that we would not want to impose our opinion on a client also has an underlying assumption that we are capable of discerning between opinion and fact but our clients are not.

Some practitioners were concerned at sharing their opinions of their own agency and its inconsistencies with clients, fearing that they would take advantage of that. A different view practitioners expressed (Seal, 2002) is that clients would take advantage this. A particular working model lies behind this assumption and it is worth spending some time un-packing it:

> We (workers) create a 'them' and 'us' model of working with clients, a siege mentality. The client group were seen as exploitative and would manipulate any perceived weaknesses in the staff team. I have seen many examples of these attitudes when working in the field of homelessness and they determined working practices. Policies were based on worse case scenarios which were then taught as best practice.

(Seal, 2002: 99)

One example is that of socialising with clients, or meeting a client in a social situation. Many agencies have strict policies about this, to the extent that if a worker enters a pub with clients, or clients are in a pub which the worker enters, the worker must leave, and certainly not socialise with them, even briefly. The common rationale for this is that it would create an 'inappropriate relationship' or that the client would take advantage of the situation. While there is no denying that it would not be appropriate to have a drink with many clients, this does not explain the extremes of these policies or the blanket nature of them. It emphasises a 'them and us' mentality. It also shows a lack of trust in our clients, although we expect them to have trust in us.

An ex-resident may wish to come back to a project as a worker or a volunteer; often projects have outright bans or a policy of a period of years needing to lapse before they can volunteer. They may give reasons such as not wanting to foster dependency but those are again blanket policies, labelling people as not being able to move on beyond their experiences. Such policies are rarely drawn up in consultation with clients. Rarely is the experience of homelessness seen as a possible asset, but it is often seen as a potential problem to the extent where some workers have felt it necessary to lie about their histories to gain employment in the field (Groundswell, 2002). These processes are not neutral and serve to extenuate perceived differences between our clients and ourselves. As to why we do this, Satyamurti gives a worrying view that we should be careful to make sure does not apply to us:

> To the extent that 'our' clients are incompetent, then this reinforces 'our' competence – we are capable when they are not.
>
> (Satyamurti, 1981: 131)

Satyamurti sees this polarisation as quite natural and rooted in our working cultures. This creation of the other is also a thing that can be reinforced by the client themselves, as Rowe (1999) has explored:

> Such themes (clients as sinners, workers as missionaries) are rooted in our culture and to some degree in the ideology of professional workers. Homeless persons seek a sense of belonging; workers seek to be the experts, friends and even the heroes who provide it.
>
> (Rowe, 1999: 56)

Hugman (1991) explains this dynamic in terms of power. He gives an example regarding drugs workers that is transferable to homelessness, with hostel places and resources replacing scripts as the instrument of control:

> As well as having material power e.g. the control of someone's script, they (workers) have ideological power in the creation of boundaries; they dominate in the production of images and meanings concerning the status and roles of clients and patients.
>
> (Hugman, 1991: 22–3)

Issues of power

These possible abuses of power lead to the ideas expressed in the fifth and sixth principle as things to bear in mind in countering them. We will return to the ideas in the Principles again when considering working contracts.

Suffice to say that often workers do not acknowledge the power they have with clients (Seal, 2002).

Principle 6 relates to a common expression of boundary, how much we talk about ourselves and our own life histories with our clients. While views on this vary wildly, there is a general tendency to believe that we should not talk about ourselves at all. When we are allowed it is often in terms of innocuous details such as our age, if we have children, if we are married etc. I have even heard some agencies, and courses, advise people to make their experiences anonymous, or pretend it is the experience of a third party i.e. lie about them. Reasons given for these policies often retread the manipulation fantasies explored earlier, rather than a more legitimate claim, made by person-centred councelling, that to talk about the worker is an obstruction.

An alternative reason is that other details are a private matter that a client does not have a right to know, missing the irony that this is a right we have just systematically denied the client. Perhaps the most legitimate reason is about us not working out our own issues through the client. Most practitioners feel that it can be appropriate at times. Given this we need to ask why, when and how it is appropriate. Returning to Biesteck (1961), this is why we need to be 'controlled' and 'purposive' about when we do share our experiences with clients. Interestingly his two principles are fully expressed as 'purposeful expression of feelings and controlled emotional involvement'. Significant is the emphasis on feelings and emotions, very different from the 'facts' we often feel permitted to share. It also avoids a different tendency, perhaps more with those workers who are ex-clients of a service, which is to share the detail or 'facts' of our experiences in the belief that this will somehow make the clients feel better about theirs (Biesteck, 1961). While this may make them feel not alone, it can equally give the message that 'this is how to do it' or even 'I am here now, why aren't you?' The worker's experience is not the client's experience and the dynamics of each experience might be wholly different. To share the content of our experiences may also create an expectation that the worker would have to have had a particular experience in order to be able to talk to a client about it, which, apart from anything else, would be a hard thing to achieve.

Sharing emotions, on the other hand, does not require details, although it remains personal and most importantly fairly universal. As we noted in Chapter 1, moving home is one of the top three traumatic experiences anyone can go through. Might not clients sometimes benefit from knowing that workers also have felt scared or apprehensive about moving, or that at times we regretted it or questioned the decisions we have made. More generally, we can even say that we find change difficult or do not make decisions easily. In this way we humanise the experience and give people permission to feel the mixed emotions that change can bring. We will return to the emotional side of our work in the chapter on emotional interventions, sharing frailties gives common ground and a client may feel reassured that their feelings are normal. I have also given some attention to other emotional reactions in other chapters, particularly the chapters of the resettlement process and the process of change.

Finally, on the subject of personal boundaries, we should perhaps recognise that we often have less than we think to lose sharing information with clients. While giving out our address or telephone number is not necessarily useful, we should lose the fear that it will definitely be dangerous. If a client really wants to know where a worker lives then there are numerous ways to find this out. (Buchy, 2005) writes about the curiosity that clients develop about workers and the gossip that circulates about them. This can be what Giddens (1996) calls 'structuration': denied power in a system a client will gain it where they can. If a client is denied details about the worker then they may deliberately try and find them out, even if it is by testing people's boundaries. If information is not available, clients may make it up – rumours about staff are common in hostels (Neale, 1996).

Language and information

Principle 3 is about the extension of power into the realms of knowledge, information and language. It is a subject of much contention during training, with a common perception that 'professional language' is used to hide things, to complicate issues, and to exclude people (McKnight, 1996). This perspective has a fine legacy (Illich, 1976) and resonates with many workers. Practitioners readily agree with the first statement of the principle and endeavour to make their language accessible to the client group. The corollary, that we can underestimate people, was brought up less often. Sometimes workers called things 'jargonistic' and alienating to the client, when I suspect they really mean is that they themselves did not understand what was meant. How much we should have to learn professional language is a moot point, if we understand it can be used to disempower us as well, this puts the onus on us to learn these languages so as to be able to explain them to our clients and avoid people being able to manipulate us and ultimately deny our clients the services they need.

There is a need to examine our own potentially misleading language. An example of this is the use of the term 'independent'. It features in the mission statements of many organisations in forms such as 'working towards independence' or 'independent living skills'. However, a client could interpret this to mean that they should be independent of all support and self-sufficient, needing no-one. Perhaps we need to explain clearly what we mean by independence or perhaps change the phrase. We are often not expecting total self-reliance, rather that people will live in a community and may continue to use services, like anyone else. 'Interdependent', may be more accurate and although there is again a danger in becoming jargonistic the challenge is to find a precise word to convey this concept.

Another example of how we create images and boundaries is in the illusion of choice for clients in hostels. It can be all too easy when dealing with disciplinary issues to inadvertently disempower clients further by saying that they 'chose to come into the hostel', implying a tacit acceptance of a contract with the hostel's rules, when in fact they had little choice in the matter. I have heard workers tell clients that they have excluded themselves from a service, a great example of Hugman's (1991) notion of how workers control boundary and role. Clients do not have the power to exclude themselves; exclusion is something that we do to them. This is not to deny a responsibility on the part of the client, it is merely to acknowledge the reality of the balance of power in the situation.

The name we give to clients is similarly not neutral. Clients are often called service users, or members or even customers. All these terms have implications of the clients having chosen the service, at least in terms of consumer choice, when often the choice people have is minimal or none at all. I asked clients in a focus group what they thought was the most appropriate terms for themselves. The answer was 'used' and while there was considerable irony in this choice of term, it betrayed a feeling of powerless in their relationships with workers and services. In this book I have used the term clients – while it is a medicalised term, it expresses to me a more accurate portrayal of the power dynamic between worker and client, with a resulting implication of the professional responsibility of the worker for their actions.

It can be argued that our tendency to use words like independent rather than, say, community is not neutral. Margaret Thatcher famously said 'there is so such thing as society, only families and individuals' (1987). It was also in this period that the voluntary sector grew massively, doubling between 1979 and 1987, when at the same time public services were cut. Some authors saw this as ideological rather than democratic (Burns, Hambleton and Hoggett, 1994) in that a Conservative central government at this time sought to break the power of Labour controlled local authorities by diverting funds into unaccountable quangos; something voluntary sector agencies have been accused of being (Meekosha, 1993; Burns, Hambleton and Hoggett, 1994). Instead of engaging with the political structures, segregated agencies were channelled into 'organising the provision of specific, usually volunteered-operated services' (Meekosha, 1993: 87). Even when agencies engaged with wider issues, their separate interests made the communities vulnerable to being picked off or set against each other (Taylor, 1995). Running a forum for agencies in the late 1990s gave me experience of this as a very real concern for agencies, with workers bemoaning earlier times when homelessness agencies were far more explicitly political in their stances (Seal, 1999). Without demeaning their achievements both current and historically second tier organisations such as CHAR moved from being campaigning organisations (Campaign for the Homeless and Roofless) to being a group representing agencies, and other stakeholders. Voices (National Homeless Alliance) to being a link between agencies and policy makers (Homeless Link). This legacy translates into language used by workers. Stewart and Taylor (1995) explore how, in public services we have moved to saying that our clients are consumers rather than citizens (service-users rather than clients); services and solutions are individual and not collective (independence not community).

As a final consideration I would like to suggest the use of a working contract with some clients. In terms of process this will often come after an assessment, after the decision that a person is eligible for a service, but before you have discussions about specific work to be undertaken. This approach is recommended by Bevan (1998) in *The Resettlement Handbook*, but his approach is orientated more to rules of the service provider. I consider a working contract to be more concerned with the relationship between the worker and client.

To contextualise this, a few years ago I undertook a small research project with service users, asking them which professional, of all those they encountered, they had the *clearest* but not necessarily the *best* relationship with (Seal, 1998). Interestingly lawyers came top while resettlement workers languished down at second from bottom. Practitioners have come up with many legitimate differences between a resettlement worker's relationship with a client and that of a lawyer (Seal, 2004). Clients have specific expectations of lawyers, their job is more delineated, they can obtain specific resources etc. However, the fact remains that they knew what a lawyer's role was whereas they remained confused about resettlement workers who sometimes acted like mates, sometimes like social workers and sometimes like jailers (Seal, 1998).

With this is mind I looked at what lawyer's do differently from resettlement workers, in establishing a relationship with a client. The main difference was the establishment of a working contract, not about what the lawyer would achieve but more about the nature of their relationship. These contracts have four principles that I will explore: mutual consent, valid consideration, competency and lawful object.

Mutual consent

Interestingly the emphasis with lawyers was less about everybody consenting to the process but is more about establishing who agrees the terms of the contract, and the rights that a person has. It is in this space that things like confidentiality can be explored, which (as we shall see in Chapter 7 on recording information) is a complex process (Park, 2003). It is also here that we can explore things like appeals and complaints procedures, as well as reviews and their purposes.

Valid consideration

Interestingly this is an exploration of who gets what out of the relationship. With a lawyer it is very clear what the lawyer gets out of the relationship: money. Apart from needing to explain this in terms of filling out the appropriate forms this is also covered so that the client feels they have some power in the situation, even if it is at a distance through legal aid. It is also so that the client feels as though there is some worth to the intervention. In our case resettlement workers in training rarely articulate what they get out of the situation (Seal, 2004).

Under *Supporting People* agencies have to calculate a unit cost per hour so we could compare ourselves to lawyers. Yet when I ask practitioners in training whether they feel they ought to share this with the client, the response is normally a resounding 'no' (Seal, 2004). People's reasons normally fall into two camps, the first is that clients may feel that the knowledge gives them an advantage over the worker and secondly that they may feel the service is not worth the money. I see that as no reason to withhold the information. While it may cause a few debates, surely that is a more empowering position for the client than to believe that the worker's services are free or, even worse to believe that they are provided through charity, making the client an object of charity.

Another reason is a general discomfort about mentioning money, sometimes because the worker comes from a more political perspective and feels that the client's rights are more important than the worker's wage, and sometimes because the client might get the impression that the worker provides the service just for the money. However the worker does do it for money, by getting paid. Would we want the client to think the reason we do it is because we are good or nice people. What is more empowering to the client, that we do the work because we are good people, or because we are paid? We are paid to have integrity, to look after the client's interests, payment means that there is a system of accountability to make sure that we do so.

What the lawyer's client gets from the relationship is representation. A lawyer once told me that he found it important to reiterate this with a client and to explore people's expectations as they often expect justice. He is careful to clarify a number of things here. Firstly, that his job is about the administration of the law, which is a separate thing from justice. Sometimes the law and justice coincide and sometimes they work in the opposite direction. Secondly his job is representation but he cannot guarantee to win.

The first point was because the client would often try and convince him of their innocence. When they did this he would emphasise that this was not necessary and may actually get in the way, as his job was to represent the person's point of view, not to determine his innocence.

Similarly we have to establish our role and manage clients expectations, something that we may need to do for ourselves, if clients expect that we can get them many resources, even physical flats and make lots of things happen, we may feel compelled to try and do this, even where that is impractical. The worker may know of some services or resources that the client does not know about, and services may be prepared to listen to a worker slightly more than the client, but the worker's power, if workers have any at all, is in the conversations they have with clients. The main role is therefore to discuss their thoughts with them, to help them make decisions for themselves and to be available to talk through frustrations when accommodation is a long time coming, when it is then not quite what they wanted, and if moving is more difficult than they thought it would be. We need to realise our real roles, admit our limitations to ourselves and find ways of communicating this to our clients.

Competency

This stems from the above discussion and is where we outline our skills, experience and time constraints. It is also where we discuss what we expect a client's commitment to be, what they need to be responsible for and what ability you expect them to have or develop. It can be a way to explain many of the ideas in Chapter 2, about support, change and accommodation.

Lawful object

This is where we need to outline our rules and legal obligations. While it sounds easy, we need to do it explicitly, and perhaps separate it from our resettlement work. This is because we are often subject to laws that we may not agree with or rules of the agency we work in that while they may or may not be legitimate, nonetheless work against some of what we are trying to achieve in terms of resettlement. I will expand these ideas in Chapters 8 and 9 where we explore how we should separate our information gathering for the separate assessment tasks of needs assessment, risk assessment and assessment in terms of housing management. Even at the stage of a working contract we should make the client aware that we ride these tensions. To take an example, it can be as simple as saying:

> That there is a law that says that if you as the client smoke marijuana on the premises, I as a worker have to take action. I may not agree with this, and we can debate that if you wish. It's not fair that I could probably smoke

it at home and no one would do anything, and if I had the choice I might want a different law, but I will still take action if I catch you with the drug. What I really hope though is that this does not affect the relationship we have and your willingness to discuss the issue of drugs.

Sometimes we try and find a legitimate reason for a rule that we find difficult to implement. This is again a common reaction of workers to something that is difficult to live with about their organisation or role, particularly when they are keen to look consistent and 'fair' (Wilson, 1987). The temptation can be to justify it as a benefit to the client. At a hostel I worked in, the service charge was justified as a part of the clients' learning processes because they will need to do that when they have their own place. However, as a non-residential resettlement worker, I later came to view the service charge as one of the many competing demands on a client's resources that we were trying to juggle. In the hostel they were not paying the service charge to learn how to budget, they were paying it because they had to and probably lost respect for me for saying it was for budgeting.

Conclusion

A working contract will not be the whole story in establishing a working relationship with a client, it is merely one tool to help it along its way. Like any relationship, the one we have with our clients will need constant attention and review. We have only touched on some of the elements of a successful relationship with a client in this chapter. To foster a relationship with clients is a process of continual negotiation with many factors to look out for and tendencies to avoid.

Chapter 5

Management and the Culture of Support

Agencies often lacked continuity and were constantly being thrown back on a circle of problems met almost annually. They were always adjusting to intakes of new staff. They (workers) fought tendencies to not care, to vent exasperations on clients and colleagues, to be self indulgent and protective of their practices. Many recruits last only a few months or a year before exhaustion and disenchantment overcome them. Among the few who last longer, the strain can be a form of self flagellation. In the homeless field breakdowns tend to be an occupational hazard.

(Brandon et al., 1980: 40)

Many helpers, when they themselves are suffering, are incapable of accepting support, or at least receiving it easily ... yet they may be impatient with those they are working with for not accepting aid or counsel readily enough. Chances are, if you can't accept help, you can't really give it.

(Ram Dass, 1985)

Writing in the early 1980s, Brandon detected a culture of both workers and managers that had adverse effects on workers and the organisation alike. In my personal experience it was not uncommon for fellow workers to leave the profession or burn out, needing periods of long-term sick leave. It was interesting to see how workers, including myself, dealt with this phenomenon. For those who did leave, although colleagues expressed sympathy and even anger that it had got to that point, there were also expressions that perhaps the person 'could not hack it', or that they were somehow 'not cut out for the work'.

More generally managerial responses to workers were often suspicious. Smith and Wright (1992) detected a worker/manager culture in hostels that was, 'based on a divisive 'them and us' attitude involving minimal contact and consultation, non-existent team work and the adoption of a 'restrictive practices mentality'. In light of these comments this chapter will examine two main considerations: the support workers receive and how we think about support as workers and managers. The main model of support I will examine will be supervision, as it is the model that practitioners are most familiar with.

Whatever our culture, and Ram Dass indicates one aspect of it, it seems important to consider the way that support is operationalised, as this can often determine what we think about it (Andrews, 2003). The industry structure for supporting workers tends to be line managerial supervision, given every four to six weeks. However, in practice supervision may be conducted less frequently than this, if at all. It seems to me, from practitioners reports on courses I have given, that the percentage who receive any supervision has shifted from 40–50 per cent to 60–70 per cent in the past 10 years, an increase, but still a concern. Even given the industry standard, one wonders whether this standard is compatible with the many contexts and client groups that workers deal with, what model of supervision agencies are working to and whether supervision, alone, is the most appropriate model of worker support.

Models of supervision

Regarding the first question, the model of supervision frequently found seems to be based on a social work model relating to field work (Bucknell, 2003). To copy this model wholesale does not look at other factors like the client group and working context. For example on the issue of time, once every four to six weeks may be appropriate for field social work, but not for resettlement work. Looking at a different context, a colleague of mine, working in a residential home for chaotic drug users, received half an hour's supervision a day in recognition of the complexity and difficulty of his work.

In looking to develop an appropriate model of supervision there are several questions that we need to ask ourselves. The first question is what is the aim of support and supervision? The common bottom line is that supervision is there to provide a better service for the client (Reynolds, 2001; Edwards, 1997; Scaife, 2001). While readily agreed as an overall aim by practitioners and managers, what does this mean in terms of emphasis and how this is to be achieved. Reynolds (2001) identifies three common functions to supervision across the care sector: monitoring, education and support/development. He suggests that *monitoring* is the functional management of a worker. In our context this normally means the monitoring of worker's caseloads and their ability to perform their role. *Education* is alerting the worker to new working practices and helping them develop their skills, understanding and capacities. *Support and development* as themes, are more contested. One view, as espoused by Field and Philpott (2001), sees support as a similar function to education, giving workers skills on how to deal with particular situations. The development aspect then follows in looking at opportunities that will enable the individual to develop professionally. Another view (Reynolds, 2001; Inskipp and Proctor, 1993) sees support as far more personally focused, recognising the inherent stress of the job and the way it can touch on and bring up personal issues. These functions are acknowledged in the *Resettlement Handbook*, which sees the purpose of supervision as being:

> *To check progress and to prioritise individual tasks; to provide and seek guidance and support; and to tackle ad hoc issues that the pressure of daily activity tends to exclude.*
>
> (Bevan, 1998)

The emphasis here is interesting; it illustrates some of the clashes we have seen between these functions and interpretations of them, the philosophies that underpin them and conflicting models of how to achieve both those and the ultimate aim of supervision – to give a better service to the client. One way of exploring these models and the tensions between them is to examine a key debate. The one I have chosen is the role of the supervisor. This question broadly maps over the contested models of supervision and its functions. One model says that a supervisor should be a manager of a person and their work, a second says that the supervisor should be a mentor, guiding a person's development and the third sees the supervisor as a facilitator in the worker's permanent need to be a reflective practitioner. We will examine each in turn.

Management model

A management model sees the supervisor as someone with authority over another at work; essentially it is an authoritarian role of making sure a person does what they are paid for (Reynolds, 2001). Going back to the functions of supervision, tension arises with the emphasis placed on the educative and support functions. Lawton and Feltham (2000) examining supervision for counsellors in universities, noted a perceived hostile attitude towards the educative function of supervision, not understanding why 'qualified and experienced practitioners needed expensive external consultation'. This tension can be detected within resettlement. Despite the above definition of supervision given by Bevan, when describing the purpose of supervision in resettlement, he lists six managerial purposes and only one educational – specifically about training. There are none given on the realm of support. Reinterpreting Bevan's definition of supervision the emphasis seems to be less about dealing with the pressure of the situation and its impact on the worker and more about the dealing with the issues that could not be dealt with immediately because of this pressure. Bevan seems to be operating very much from a managerial perspective on supervision.

Mentor model

The second model is that of a mentor who aids the worker in their development (Shipton, 1997). In this model the supervisor is seen as an exceptionally clear sighted and omniscient 'expert' who has knowledge and insight into the role to impart to the supervisee (Reynolds, 2001). This model has a long pedigree in professional development with origins in the idea of an apprenticeship (Reynolds, 2001) and its modern manifestations in the ideas of Wenger (1997) who believes that we are to become a part of a 'community of practice' that has a distinct culture to be learnt. We therefore need a key person to educate and induct us into this community, who would be the supervisor. Difficulties arise with such models in saying how we identify these individuals, their skills and knowledge base and how they will impart their knowledge. If we adopt Wenger's notion of this knowledge base being a culture that we somehow become 'encultured' into, it becomes particularly hard to define how a mentor is going to achieve this, a criticism also levelled at Wenger (Anning, 2001; Engestrom and Mietten, 1997).

Even if these questions are answered, mentoring models minimise the role of support as short term until a person is 'encultured'. A longer-term role may exist in these models and this is often called Continuous Professional Development (CPD). It comes from a belief that a person has perpetual things to learn or more simply that we need to offer people development opportunities as an employer, either morally or in the hope of retaining them. The lack of adequate progression routes has been identified by the profession as a key reason for the current crisis in retention (Homeless Link, 2004). While the retention rate in the field may have improved since 1980, practitioners on my courses have still identified a time period of between two to three years for 'burn out' and while that does not necessarily result in people leaving the field, it is a commonly identified time period for front-line workers to stay within any particular job (Seal, 2004).

What mentoring does not take into account is that the job itself may be inherently stressful – a factor for which a worker needs support. Brandon identifies at the beginning of the chapter that many people leave the profession for reasons of stress and burn out and this may not be due to faulty practices by the worker. As the psychotherapist Michael Balint (1991) commented 'working with disturbance is disturbing'. The emphasis here is to give the worker an opportunity to offload their emotions and talk through issues as it personally affects them; and may therefore be affecting the client.

Reflective practitioner model

A third interpretation of the role of the supervisor bridges the educative and supportive role of a supervisor. It is underpinned by a different model of what it takes to become an effective worker. In that model the worker needs to become a 'reflective practitioner'. That was developed by Schön in the 1980s when he described the life of a professional as being characterised by, 'complexity, uncertainty, instability, uniqueness, and value conflict' (Schön, 1985: 39). To become effective as a practitioner is not as simple as gaining knowledge and learning procedures. The situations we face are complex, and as such we need to learn, develop and change constantly, and often on our feet, in order to react in any given situation. The model was also developed with a view to those professionals who work in relative isolation:

> The worker functions in relative isolation, often alone and in the evenings when other professionals are at home; within a framework where there are few restrictions on the kind of activity they engage in; and meets situations charged with emotions. All this means that the worker is more prone to confusion, and more subject to chaos, than those working in more structured ways.
>
> (Christian and Kitto, 1987: 1)

While this observation was made about youth workers, much of it seems pertinent to homelessness workers, whose case work is undertaken alone, who often work nights, and with the expansion of floating support under *Supporting People*, often alone in relatively alien environments. In these conditions, Schön holds that to become effective, a practitioner needs to learn how to systematically reflect both on their actions while they are in action and afterwards (Christian and Kitto, 1987). The role of the supervisor is to provide a space where the worker can do the former and develop the skills to be able to do the latter. As such the supervisor is being neither managerial nor an 'expert'. The supervisee chooses the piece of work to examine and it is the worker's perception of the incident under scrutiny that is that starting point of the process. Significance is seen in how they see the situation, what they felt during the incident and what motivations may underlie the actions they took.

A different supervision role would be to tell people what to do rather than enable them to develop their own powers of reflection (Woods, 2001). Nor is the supervisor merely a counsellor who purely reflects, they will ask questions and give perspectives, however the autonomy remains with the worker to identify the best solution and way forward for them. Perhaps the difficulty with this model in the homeless field is in what Woods (2001) calls the importance of 'good faith' – the supervisor having faith that the worker can and will bring appropriate cases with a will to learn and reflect and the supervisee believing in the supervisor's ability and confidentiality in these matters.

Practitioner and Management perceptions

It is worth reflecting at this point on the reciprocal nature of the relationship that Woods (2001) refers to. Workers have their part to play in the supervisory relationship and for it to be a success that needs as much commitment to the process from the worker as from the supervisor. From the evidence of my interactions with practitioners, attitudes towards supervision and supervisors are contested. Some of these attitudes can be put down to negative experiences of supervision. Reynolds (2001) also notes that supervision has unfortunate connotations, particularly for workers who originate from industries where supervision did indeed mean checking whether you could do your job or not. I have noticed a mixed attitude to the support and supervision people receive that extends beyond this simple fear.

What people want from a supervisor/manager often echoes the aforementioned functions of supervision, someone to make decisions when needed, someone who has a wealth of experience to impart and someone who will support them when it all gets a bit much. The complexity is that people often want different mixes of these at different times and might want their manager (the person giving supervision) to second guess what was appropriate at any one point, playing out the different tensions between the models of who should be a supervisor. When asking for practitioners perceptions about whether the manager could fulfil the three roles of monitoring, educating and supporting, they betrayed a certain attitude towards management in principle (Seal, 2004). People thought that managers could generally do the first role and it was seen as the managers' primary concern. However they did not always agree with the manager's perception of what constituted the job. This leads into their thoughts on the second educative role of a supervisor. A common perception of management was that they did not have knowledge to impart. They were seen as either not coming from the 'front line' or that if they had they were either promoted because they could not do it; had 'sold out' for making the move to management or had simply 'lost touch'. Within this context people often did not believe that the final support function would be genuine, and thought that managerial considerations would always take precedence.

Whether these perceptions are based on experience or defensive positioning is difficult to ascertain, but given our earlier Smith and Wright comment, we can see that the culture between workers and managers in the homeless field is rarely characterised by the 'good faith' that Woods (2001) sees as essential to the supervisory relationship. Yet in this field supervision and support is most commonly embodied in the line manager, indeed Bevan (1998) sees this arrangement as one of the crucial principles of supervision. Perhaps this is a further symptom of the mutual mistrust managers and workers have of each other, neither would entrust responsibility for supervision to another.

The breaking of this damaging culture would seem to be a priority with the need for both sides to approach support and supervision without a culture of fear and suspicion. Edwards (2001) identifies how a key component of the professional training of care professionals including social work, youth work, careers, teaching and counselling is on supervision and support including what it is, why it is important and the expectations we should have of our supervisors and supervisees. According to Bucknall (2001) supervision is a part of social work culture. Social workers appreciate and want good supervision, even if it does not always meet the ideal in practice. This seems to be a cultural lesson that we need to learn.

A broader question remains – whether all the functions of supervision can be (or need to be) embodied within the same person. Edwards sees three tensions in trying to embody all the roles of supervision in one person. Firstly there is a,

> . . . *confusion of interests and roles, especially where assessment and personal development are both a part of the supervisory role. Secondly there may be reluctance on the part of the supervisee to fully disclose issues, needs and concerns that could be construed as weaknesses by a line manager, or indeed concern with the line manager themselves. Finally there may be external agenda issues, such as the accountability pressures to meet external targets or the supervisor's inclination to follow their own personal agenda. These pressures can interfere with the personal development of the supervisee.*

> (Edwards, 2001: 54)

With these tensions in mind other care professions have support mechanisms beyond the line manager. Edwards (2001) identifies that the debate often concentrates on the use of non-managerial supervision to overcome the limitations of line managerial supervision. Non-line managerial supervision is supervision of a worker by someone external. Youth workers, for instance, have as part of their working conditions an entitlement to such supervision in addition to line managerial supervision (JNC, 2001). Broadly, the split in roles is that the line manager fulfils the monitoring role and the non-managerial fills the support role, with the educational role being the cross-over point (Woods, 2001).

The disadvantage of this approach is that the non-managerial supervisor is not in a position to address some fundamental issues as they may be left with a limited grasp of the worker's issues and concerns.

Ultimately, Andrews says this debate clouds a wider truth in that a multitude of supervisory/support mechanisms are used by other care professions in a variety of combinations: line managerial supervision, non-line managerial supervision, mentoring, group supervision and peer supervision. Definition is needed here of the last two as practitioners have reported that they can be adopted for the wrong reasons, such as lower cost (Seal, 2004). Group supervision is with a trained facilitator, experienced in group skills. Peer supervision is also not just a question of bringing practitioners together, as Woods (2001) says, 'the other members of the group work as supervisors to the presenter of the issue'; this presupposes an understanding of the supervisory process and skills in being a supervisor.

In his 2001 paper, Edwards evaluates the relative pros and cons of these various mechanisms but concludes that it is more relevant to seek to develop an integrated model of support and supervision that incorporates all these mechanisms. He outlines a model that also identifies the differing support and supervision needs of a worker at different points in their career and time with any particular organisation. The relative roles of different mechanisms and the emphasis on different elements of support change accordingly. I would recommend this paper to the reader.

Conclusion

It seems that three changes are needed with regard to workers need for support. The first, and perhaps paramount, is a change of culture in how workers and managers see each others work, roles and colleagues. Secondly we need a systematic programme of training in both how to give and receive supervision and support. Thirdly we need to be flexible and imaginative in designing structures for support, using the full range of mechanisms available and taking account of the changing need of workers in their personal and professional development.

Chapter 6

Networking Within Resettlement: Dumping and Referring on

There are sometimes problems of misunderstanding between statutory and voluntary agencies, with statutory agencies seeing the voluntary sector as unprofessional and unqualified, while the voluntary sector can see statutory agencies as rule bound, inflexible and bureaucratic.

(Randall and Brown, 2003)

Services for homeless people are not a coherent whole in the manner of, say, health or education services, where when most people access them they can be sure of the depth of training and the extent of responsibility of the people they are consulting, and that if they are referred onward this will have been done with proper understanding of the service offered. Some homelessness agencies offer something similar, while others claim to do so but do not. Telling them apart can be difficult.

(Parks, 2003: 10)

As identified in Chapter 2, an essential feature of a resettlement worker's role is to act as the bridge between the homeless person and significant others. This will at times include other agencies. Yet whilst an essential part of the work, many practitioners complain that trying to involve other agencies is the bane of their life. To illustrate this, and to raise some of the questions and surrounding issues, I will relay an anecdote. The easiest strategy to deal with any tension that arises during a training course of resettlement workers it is to create unity by shifting the group's focus to a common enemy. This normally takes the form of talking about other agencies, in particular social services. Significant questions stem from this illustration and the opening quotes that will form the focus of this chapter.

I will not be examining some of the wider issues that pertain to this subject such as structural approaches to multi-agency working, inter-agency proto-cols, voluntary sector compacts etc; these have been covered admirably elsewhere (Cameron et al., 2000; Secker and Hill, 2001; El Ansari et al.,

2001). Instead my focus will be on the issues facing a front-line worker. I will consider the dynamics of accessing services for clients. I will argue that there are three dimensions that we must consider in effectively advocating for our clients; knowledge, flattery and threat. Each of these has, in turn, three factors to bear in mind.

Knowledge

- Know how you are perceived by the other agency.
- Know what the other service actually provides.
- Know the internal politics of that service.

Considering the first factor, many agencies have their own perception of homelessness workers. As we discussed in the first chapter, such services and their development have not been neutral, influencing other services' views of them (Balchin, 1998). Brokering can be challenging in itself as it can imply that there is something wrong with the other agency, even if it is only that their referral systems are at fault (CSNU:2000). As an illustration of the perceptual barriers we may face, here are three opinions of statutory workers about homelessness workers in the voluntary sector (Seal, 2004):

Homeless workers are a bunch of unqualified, unskilled, untrained and inexperienced people doing my job on the cheap who do not realise the damage they are doing.

(Senior social worker, anon)

They criticise me for evicting people even though it's gone through the right procedure when they kick people out of their hostel daily for no reason and with no appeal . . . criticising me for being a rent collector, forgetting that I used to do their job, and was better at it.

(Housing officer, anon)

They ring me up when they want someone taking away, pretending it's because the user needs a service. They do not know what they are looking at, insulting me by saying they think that a client should get into detox immediately, just because the client says they are ready or they have judged that they are.

(Senior drugs worker, anon)

We can therefore see that resettlement workers are not viewed neutrally. A starting point would therefore seem to be to seek out and acknowledge the perspectives of other agencies. There may be truths in the accusations and that we need to acknowledge them. Social services have shrunk in the same period that resettlement services in the voluntary sector have grown (Rowntree, 1995). Under *Supporting People* this process has accelerated, and the question needs to be asked – whether this is because our worth has been recognised or because we are cheap. In truth, we are largely unqualified and untrained compared to social workers and because of our rapid expansion, many workers are not experienced. In the same period the role of housing officers has changed rapidly, their previous role was similar to what we now term floating support (Balchin, 1998). As to how and when we refer on, can any agency honestly say that it never dumps on another agency in the guise of referral?

On the other hand these reactions can be defensive on the part of individuals or organisations; this is something we need to discern, especially when we ourselves may be the ones being defensive. It is perhaps most important here to consider a second, more institutional, idea of defensiveness, where it goes beyond the individual and becomes part of the culture of the organisation or profession. As Schein (1985) says, this form of defence becomes unconscious as it employs 'assumptions, that eventually, are taken for granted and finally drop out of awareness'.

Hornstein's (1986) concept of 'organisational defensiveness' is useful here. This is the notion that every organisation protects its routines, its habits and its culture through defensive measures, even when those routines lead to errors, to dissatisfaction or incompetence. Individuals are still important as it is often through them that the defensiveness is put into operation and perpetuated. Argyris (1990) gives us examples of how this defensiveness manifests in worker's behaviour:

- **Actions intended to increase understanding and trust often produce misunderstanding and mistrust.** As an example, people take out of meetings and case conferences what they want to, rather than listening to others, even when it appears that a common understanding is reached. Many partnership meetings, forums or case conferences can take this form. There is an illusion of people co-operating when in fact they are seeking to try and get hold of any resources that may be available or persuade others of their view of the situation (Argyris, 1990). Another manifestation of this is when workers leave a meeting with a confirmed view of the other agencies ineptitude. While that may, at times, be a legitimate conclusion, a worker needs to ask themselves whether they were genuinely open to what the other person was saying or whether they were waiting for a comment or action allowing them to write the meeting off and have their negative view reinforced.
- **Workers blame others or the systems for poor decisions.** Instead of reflecting, evaluating and seeking to change a policy, workers will either seek someone else to blame, claim impunity or claim that the decision is out of their hands and that they are powerless. This is a phenomenon we

have considered in relation to ourselves and our resulting responsibilities in these situations in Chapter 3 on ethics.

- **Organisational inertia: the tried and proven ways of doing things dominate organisational life.** Can often take the form of an idea killer (Hornstein, 1986) in the form of comments like 'we have tried that before and it will not work'. It can also be that the report is in the post or that events cannot move forward without a particular individual's presence who is invariably on holiday.
- **Upward communication for difficult issues is often lacking.** This is the converse of the second example. Sometimes there is a lack of upwards communication; managers are not listening, understanding or appreciating the perspectives of their workers. Conversely workers need to reflect on when they ask management to make a decision and when they do not.
- **Budget games are played and become necessarily evils.** People defend their own corner in terms of finances, even if it is to the detriment of other agencies. Resources can become a reason or excuse for not doing a thing, or, occasionally a thing that will unite an otherwise disparate and fractious team.
- **People do not behave reasonably, even when it is in their best interests.** This can take many forms, mainly to do with avoidance, including procrastination, indecision, analysis without action, sabotage or ignoring.
- **Management as a myth.** This can take many forms, sometimes it is to blame the team, or a wider ethos, when in fact it is just a particular individual who is causing the issue. At other times it is the opposite, management is blamed when in fact it is the team's resistance that does not allow a change to happen.

Countering these defensive strategies is difficult and the rest of this chapter gives some indication of how this can be attempted. However, as stated previously understanding is the appropriate starting point.

The second two factors under the heading knowledge perhaps need less explanation but are nonetheless very important. It is easy from the point of view of the resettlement worker, to attack other agencies for not meeting expectations of what they should do, rather than for what they actually did. That may be due to a lack of appreciation of what the other agency does or a misunderstanding of legislation pertaining to that service. Another deeper reason is that we are working in a care system that has some fundamental flaws (Park, 2003). Within this context an attack on other agencies for not doing what we think they ought is born out of frustration. This frustration becomes all the more acute from the belief, often correct, that we are the client last or best chance and if we or the agencies we rely on mis-serve them, there may not be another opportunity to pick up the pieces. While this may or may not be true we need to recognise that it may be the source of our misdirected frustration.

The final factor to consider is the difference between what an agency says about itself and its reality. We talked in the previous chapter about how an organisation, and the workers in it, will develop its own culture of practice, irrespective of its policies and aims (Wenger, 1998). Wenger (1998) asks us to combine the first two factors and examine how the agency actually functions, the cultural assumptions that have arisen over time and the ways it has chosen to interpret and put its duties into practice. Examples of this would include: knowing what criteria a social services community care team has to trigger a full assessment for a client or whether Jobcentre Plus's budget for the discretionary social fund is calculated on a yearly or monthly basis. Under the Children Act 1989, it has been well documented (McCluskey, 1993; 1995; 1997) that the interpretation of this Act varied enormously due to political preferences and budgeting imperatives and could amount to as little as a list of bed and breakfast accommodation handed to a homeless young person.

The question then arises of how to understand this culture. Participants on my courses have said that the main way they attempt inter-agency working is to find an individual they can relate to and work with and build on that relationship. While practical, I have three concerns with this approach. Firstly it is time limited, only working for as long as the other party is in the organisation, and continues to be receptive. Secondly, it is only open to the two parties concerned and thirdly it relies on the strength of that individual relationship rather than of the organisation as a whole. However, as Kilman (1984) indicates, that person is a part of a wider organisational culture and the fostering of a relationship with them could be done most effectively with a mind to developing understanding of this culture:

> *Culture is to the organisation what personality is to the individual – a hidden yet unifying theme that provides meaning, direction and mobilisation.*

(Kilman: 1984: 54)

Schein (1985) identifies two aspects for us to consider about an organisation's culture, its norms and its assumptions. The result when responses to a series of both internal and external situations have worked (Geoffman, 1971). These responses are then taught to members as the correct way to think about, feel about and perceive certain situations. In addition to stated norms such as standards and procedures this includes unstated ones such as generally accepted ideas, unspoken codes of behaviour, expressed and unexpressed belief (Douglas, 1986). Assumptions can include the beliefs upon which norms and other aspects of culture are built upon, stories that endure within an organisation, what is accepted about the outside world and other agencies and what people generally accept is possible and not possible (Geertz, 1998). To learn how to relate to this culture is the key to multi-agency working and the focus of our knowledge seeking (Schein, 1985). While running forums of agencies in the homeless field there was often a perception that they were useful for sharing information, I would contend that the real learning came in beginning to appreciate, deal with and perhaps influence, each other's working cultures.

Flattery

- Acknowledge if you are the best person to do this role.
- Acknowledge what the other service knows and can do better than you.
- Explain what you can offer with the client.

A common refrain I hear from practitioners is that their main worry about passing a client over to another agency is that they feel they have a strong relationship with the client, who would not trust another person. While there are various questions that arise from such a statement, (Do you think that you can do everything for this person? Why did you make them so dependant upon you etc.) the first one that comes to my mind is, what makes a worker think this? There is a danger of falling into some of the assumptions outlined in Chapter 4 on the client-worker relationship, of our centricity and importance, and consequently the client's relative incompetence. Rowe (1996) examines how, while in the early stages trust is more of an all or nothing proposition, in the long term the homeless person's perspective on the relationship is far less dependant than this:

> *When the homeless person and worker have known each other for some time, trust is tied to an investment in the relationship and negotiations over long term needs . . . The homeless person wonders whether the worker will write him off as a failure or be willing to see him through to the next opportunity.*

(Rowe, 1996: 83)

When I have asked training participants why they think they are critical to the client's well being, a common response is that the client told them so. Given Rowe's perspective, we need to understand why a client would give a false impression of their dependency.

Smith (2002), in a different context, gives us some insight into why this may sometimes be the case. In critiquing Demos's perspective on multi-agency working he suggests that it is not always in the client's interest to have agencies working together. Given that the care system cannot structurally meet all needs, to compensate, some clients actively shop around with agencies, playing them off against each other in order to maximise the resources available to them. Ironically flattering workers achieves this end, emphasising how important we are and how much would fall apart if we ended our liaison. To give an example, I remember one client would always tell me how important I was, how down to earth I was, the one who cut through the rubbish etc. I believed him until I heard him telling another worker the same thing. When challenged, he said workers wanted to hear it and it made us do things for him. Brandon (1980) has a slightly different take on this, seeing these respective roles as a part of the culture, a way in which both parties had learned to behave:

> The appeal of homelessness lies in the themes of marginality, loneliness, vulnerability and deprivation. The central characters – the homeless and the agency workers – respectively play out the role of victims, outsiders or sinners, champions, befrienders or saviours.
>
> (Brandon, 1980: 56)

A compounding factor here is that while it is positive that many services have moved in recent years to embrace inter-agency working they have at the same time developed a model which puts them at the centre, bringing in agencies as and when appropriate (Cameron et al., 2000; Secker and Hill, 2001; El Ansari et al., 2001). This is the principle behind community care management (Coleman, 1997) the Connexions Programme (CSNU, 2002), new definitions of holistic health (NHS, 2002) and *Supporting People* (2002). Questions arise about who is at the centre and who is at the periphery.

While a general malaise, it seems from the perceptions of the senior drugs worker that we are susceptible to it. There is perhaps something about the proximity of our clients, especially true of hostel workers, that gives us an illusion that we therefore 'know' them better and consequently have a better insight into their needs. In order to break these patterns we need to look towards more objective criteria of whether we are the appropriate worker for a client. Taking the second and third point of this section together, we need to know where we fit in the jigsaw of this person's care and the place of others. As an example, I worked with a client who to me seemed to be coping well without his medication, he was lucid and appeared to be motivated and could remember and relate what had happened that week. A psychiatrist who assessed him found that he could not answer questions about his mother's birthday, where he was born and who was the prime minister. I was surprised when the client could not answer. It was part of his condition to function in the present but not in the past and to be unable to contextualise himself. It therefore seems important to ascertain what other services assess on and why.

I turn now to the remarks of the senior drugs worker. Assessment of the appropriateness of detoxification is commonly based on based on four factors (Baker and Seal, 2002); motivation and commitment, immediate factors (such as withdrawal, seizure), history (personal and of treatment) and recent behaviour. Mental health diagnosis (Baker and Seal, 2002) is commonly assessed on: history of behaviour and treatment, immediate response at interview and recent behaviour. Of those factors resettlement workers or hostel workers may have the most insight into recent behaviour. This knowledge can be crucial as it may cover how they have reacted to medication, how their behaviour patterns have changed, triggers for their actions etc, but it is not the whole picture.

We can cast light upon some of the other factors, particularly clients' perception of things like their history but we need to remember the relativity of our perceptions. Following our detoxification example, it could be argued that we also have insight into a client's motivation. How can we tell when the individual is now motivated enough to make a detoxification programme work? Miller (1993) says that, 'Motivation emerges from the interpersonal interactions between worker and users'. While positively meaning we can impact on the motivation of a person, it also means that when this person engages with a new worker or agency that motivation will shift, their motivation which seems high with us will change when they are in another context. While not trying to suggest that we should blindly accept other agencies tests of motivation and beliefs that a client cannot change, we should recognise that our perceptions are contextual.

It may be at an organisational level that we negotiate our place within another agency's assessment process but this will always be mitigated by an individual worker. It is perhaps enough to remember to have some humility and importantly to talk as much about what we can offer the other agency as well as what we want from them.

Conclusion: the use of threat

- Let them know if there are legal implications.
- Let them know how this may affect your individual relationship.
- Let them know how this may affect your organisational relationship.

Threat is an emotive word but I thought it appropriate as it is pertinent at the limits of the other two approaches. When knowledge, understanding, being humble and outlining the support we can offer fails, we then need to know where we then go next. Our knowledge should then extend to the complaints procedures and any legal aspects to the case. Use of threat is often implied. It may be enough to hint that this legal course could be invoked, acknowledging that, while it would not be in the interests of your relationship and that of your respective organisations, it is nevertheless the option of last resort that may benefit your client.

I mention this as a last resort because that is what I believe it to be; after that you have nowhere to go. Practitioners on my courses have unfortunately said that they may move to this course of action a lot quicker than that. Often it is their second port of call – if they do not get what they want initially then they start quoting law and procedure at the person in the other agency. It is not through these actions that cultures and perceptions change.

Section Three
Structuring Our Work

Chapter 7

Recording and Managing Information

While it is a mistake to depend on recording stationery as a shortcut to good assessment, well-designed forms are invaluable for minimising error, speeding up administration, monitoring service delivery and, potentially, encouraging interagency exchange.

(Park, 2003)

It is not possible to judge how far the differences in case records reflect variations in quality of service. However, where there were no structured needs assessments or support programmes on file, it seems less likely that the work was being carried out as effectively, or at least that it was not possible to monitor effectiveness.

(Randall and Brown, 2003)

This chapter will ask how we hold information and keep records. It will discuss the extent to which the documents we keep should be reviewed and jointly owned with the client. This will lead into an examination of the implications for workers of the Data Protection Act 1998, highlighting its impact on different settings. It will also examine the nature of confidentiality towards the client, its moral and legal limitations and recent challenges to it. However, before we address these issues, I think it is important to explore both the reasons for record keeping, the culture of resettlement workers and the context that surrounds it.

Both quotes above illustrate that, while information recording may be a contested area, it is one where funders and policy makers, including *Supporting People*, have their own imperatives, and this is something that resettlement work needs to be able to respond to effectively.

When I introduce my courses, often a collective groan goes up when I mention the session on the recording work. When mention is made of *Supporting People* there is a similar reaction, despite the fact that *Supporting People* has been instrumental in the mass expansion of resettlement services (Chapter 1). In exploring this reaction practitioners respond that, while *Supporting People* represents an expansion in funding, there has been a parallel expansion of bureaucracy and paperwork. Many workers also saw paperwork as the bane of their lives (Seal, 2004).

Historically, resettlement workers have not had to write down much about clients, many homeless projects having been funded through housing benefit where the demand for recording was only enough to be able to process the claim (Bradley et al., 2004). Bradley et al., in their good practice guide for day centres, list eight different forms they see as useful to the work and there are parallel demands from *Supporting People*. It seems then that, irrespective of this history, the question of record keeping becomes, 'when is it useful and beneficial to our clients and when is it not?' A second question will be 'what should we record and how we should do that?'

I have asked many practitioners why they did not like paperwork. I found that one of the main reasons workers did not like paperwork was exactly that, it was not an enjoyable task. However, various other reasons were given for not liking paperwork as well as, or in avoidance of this simple truth. Common reasons were that it took away from 'face-to-face work', or that clients 'did not like having things written down about them'. As far as the former is concerned it seems to betray a view that anything that does not involve being in front of the client is somehow secondary or invalid in our work. Interestingly, when I have asked clients the same question, often as not they felt that we should and would be working behind the scenes, making things work, making phone calls, etc. It seems that face-to-face work is our priority rather than theirs. The second statement is quite a sweeping one and again when I asked clients their opinion, while many did agree with this sentiment, just as many thought that the existence of records about them at least meant they were worth having something written down about them. We will explore other reasons and concerns of workers around paperwork in the context of justifications for comprehensive record keeping as outlined by the CSNU (2002). While this was written in another context, the Connexions service for young people, their reasons are a good starting point for our own discussion. They list reasons for record keeping as:

1. To ensure young people's needs are met.
2. To provide a clear history of the work done with a young person.
3. To protect the young person.
4. To help to ensure that she or he receives a consistent level of service and support.
5. To provide continuity of service to the young person in the event of the Personal Advisor being unavailable, ill, or changing role.
6. To support practitioners in providing evidence of their work with young people and the basis upon which key decisions have been made, particularly in the event of a challenge or an inquiry.

7. To offer information that Personal Advisors can use to monitor and review their own work.
8. To provide key information to managers so that quality and performance of the service can be monitored and evaluated.
9. To furnish an audit trail for inspection.
10. To contribute to the ongoing improvement of the Connexions Service.

(CSNU, 2003)

The opening reason needs qualification, as it is not immediately obvious why recording will 'ensure a young persons needs are met'. Unfortunately, the authors do not go on to justify this statement, instead taking it as a given. Park (2003), in the context of assessment forms, detects a similar kind of assumption in the culture of some homelessness workers. While seemingly contradicting the anti-form culture expressed earlier, it illustrates how people have a mixed attitude towards, and perhaps a fear about, record keeping and form filling:

> *First, there is some concern that there may be a widely, though fortunately not universally, held belief that assessment means filling in a form. There has been much recent talk of assessment 'tools' – often seemingly with the tacit assumption either that such devices reduce the need to learn about assessment or that these abilities are already present – and managers often quickly turn to a discussion of form use and form design when the issue of assessment is raised.*

(Park, 2003: 16)

We need to ask why such a culture may exist. In my own discussions with workers, two phenomena shed some light on it. Some workers used forms as a crutch when they were unsure about themselves and what they were meant to be doing. Others were taking on the managerial concerns and lack of confidence that Park (2003) alludes to. Practitioners reported that this was mainly an organisational concern that if they did not get the paperwork 'that *Supporting People* want' then they would lose their funding. Worryingly they reported many organisations complaining that *Supporting People* would not 'tell' them what paperwork they should use, rather than doing as the standards indicate and looking at their practice to see how they could develop paperwork that accurately reflected it.

Going back to the reasons for systematically recording information, 6, 8, 9 and 10 are mainly about auditing and evaluation. Taylor (1989) identified some common concerns of practitioners about evaluation and how it is used:

- It is 'done' to a project by an 'objective outsider' (usually an 'academic').
- It is concerned with measurable facts, figures and statistics (leaving out the most important parts).

- It concentrates on 'flavour of the month' parts of the project ignoring other more important parts.
- It involves the views of 'outsiders', 'experts' who don't really understand what is going on or what it is like to be part of the organisations activities.
- Its conclusions are one way, i.e. used to cut funding or it is ignored and not acted upon by projects and funders alike, particularly if the results are challenging.

The problem here is trying to discern what is about fear and what is a genuine concern. Park (2003) follows his earlier quote by critiquing some of my own work on developing an NVQ in resettlement. He sees a danger in reducing assessment to being able to fill in a form, when it is a far more subtle process than this, a criticism that he is right to make. The problem is that NVQ demands this kind of 'evidence', something tangible that can be kept to show that a person can do a thing. As Randall and Brown (2003) illustrate in the opening quote, this certainly seems to be a prime motivation behind keeping paperwork with *Supporting People*. It is also enshrined in practice, the need to record for auditing purposes is mentioned in 20 of the standards in the Quality Assessment Framework (OPDM:2002). Some authors (Challis, et al., 1990; Jeffs and Smith, 2001) see this as a wider push in governmental policy towards keeping ever more records on our clients and people in general for reasons of claimed accountability and the ability to be audited (CSNU, 2002).

Positively, auditing can also be about standards and accountability, for without the ability to monitor and evaluate, both internally and externally, how do we know we are doing our job (CSNU, 2002).When projects were funded under housing benefit, some good work but also some poor work was done (Brandon et al., 1980). the problem being that people did not know how to show the difference between the two. This is not the space to have a wider discussion about monitoring and evaluation, suffice to say that we should try and make the *Supporting People* standards work for us. Our record keeping should be able to demonstrate the good standard of our work, rather than something we should fear.

At the same time we should heed Park's (2003) warning that forms should not become ends in themselves. Either by letting them take precedence over our work with clients, or by falling into the trap of thinking they do our work for us. With this last point in mind, we should take note of the fourth and seventh justifications for recording information. It should help us develop consistency in our work and enable us to look back and evaluate it. I do not think any worker could truly say that they can remember everything that they have done with a client, making a claim for total consistency, without keeping some kind of records. We will go on in the following chapters on assessment and then support planning to examine how recording our work can help us develop our practice. For now we will consider more general issues of how we hold information.

Confidentiality and managing information with clients

Once we write down things about our clients, one of the first questions that arises is who else will we share this information with, and how we will share it with our clients. Confidentiality is seen as a mainstay of our work; Parker (2003) sees it as one of the only identifiable ethical principles we have. However, what we mean by confidentiality is open to debate. Many policies seem to start from a point of view of confidentiality as secrecy (Park, 2002) in that what is said between the worker and the client stays 'their' secret. Beyond this there are exceptions that need to be explained to the client. The exceptions are varied but I will use them as a basis for examining the idea of information sharing. I will classify them broadly as legal, moral and finally instrumental reasons – the latter of which has taken an interesting turn recently that we will explore. I will also consider the Data Protection Act 1998, under legal reasons. While it is more of a framework than a restriction, it is nevertheless relevant to confidentiality.

Legal factors

These primarily concern children, (Children Act 1989) if a worker feels that a minor is being put at risk they are duty bound to inform social services of the matter. Other exceptions are around terrorism, something that could have increasing relevance with the passing of the Terrorism Act 2002. Another theoretical concern is treason. A common misconception is that beyond these confines, workers are not legally obliged to tell the police or others if someone commits, or intends to commit a crime. More recently there have been implications for confidentiality in homelessness under Section 8 of the Misuse of Drugs Act 1971, concerning the use and supply of certain drugs on premises that workers 'are involved on the management of' (Release, 2001). Under this law, steps need to be taken by an agency to prevent drug use on premises they 'manage'. Judge Howarth, (2000) ruling in the Winter Comfort Case, said a valid step in preventing drug offences on a premises might be to contact the police and inform them that there is a person who has been banned for supplying drugs on or near the premises. While this may be against many confidentiality policies, the Judge directed that such a policy could not prevent the disclosure of information to the police if such disclosure was a step that would prevent a prohibited act under Section 8. The situation here is continually changing, and the reader will need to keep abreast of recent developments.

The Data Protection Act 1998 sets out rules for processing personal information about living, identifiable individuals. It applies to paper records as well as those held on computers and can cover information as sparse as the client's name and address. Data subjects (clients) have new rights of access to personal data. A data subject is now entitled to know the source of personal data and may demand cessation of certain kinds of processing, such as when it is 'likely to cause damage or distress', or in relation to automated decision making. The person also has the right to rectify, block, erase or destroy inaccurate data. A distinction is made between aggregated data (i.e. used for statistics and monitoring), personal data such as birth date, gender, education etc and sensitive data relating to racial or ethnic origin, political opinions, religious or other beliefs, health, sex life and criminal convictions. Consent must be 'explicit' with sensitive personal data covering the detail and purpose of the processing and the type of data to be processed. Workers will have to give individuals certain kinds of access to all manual information covered by the Act, including:

- A description of the data being processed.
- The purposes for which it is being processed.
- Potential recipients of the data.
- The source of the data.

These principles have several implications for resettlement workers. Firstly, it begs the question of what information we do not allow them to see. The difficult aspect here is that, while clients do not have a right to see the information, they have a right to know the information is accurate and not likely to cause them 'damage or distress'. It is difficult to see how they could be assured of this without actually seeing the information. In this context, not giving clients access to their files, or parts of them, becomes a difficult position to maintain. Many agencies have long since abandoned closed access, often for reasons of good practice rather than the law, something we will return to.

Many agencies have policies whereby a client has access to their own files with certain exceptions, one being third party information. Justifications for this exception are often linked to 'risk', either that it is information about their potential risk or that them knowing the information would be a risk in itself. We will cover the degree to which we share our own risk assessments with clients in the relevant chapter, but assuming we do, it is unclear about why would we apply different rules to a third parties information. Under the Act it seems that while clients may not have the right to know what a third party, such as probation, mental health services etc, are saying about them but as, discussed before, they will still need to know that it is safe reliable etc. In this light, some organisations such as Mind have made third party information equally accessible to clients, as they have their own risk assessments. They are clear about this policy with other agencies, as one should not give out information from third parties without their permission. Their policy puts the onus on the third party to make sure they would not write down something that they would not want the client to find out about.

To complicate matters the Data Protection (subject access exemption) Health Order 2000 allows information not to be disclosed to the client if it is likely to 'harm their mental or physical heath'. Even if the agency decides to declare its information anyway, a third party may object to their information being released on these grounds. Finally, I mention the automated decisions part of the act because it could imply that agencies should not reject a client on the basis of information such as a risk assessment, without first discussing it with that client. The act implies that the client would have a right to question the use of the data in this way.

Other implications arise from the principles of the Act. They state that data must be:

- Processed fairly and lawfully.
- Obtained and processed for specified purposes.
- Adequate, relevant and not excessive.
- Accurate and up to date.
- Held for no longer than necessary.
- Processed in accordance with subjects rights.
- Kept secure.
- Transferred outside the European Economic Area (EEA – i.e. the 15 EU Member states plus Iceland, Liechtenstein and Norway) only if adequate safeguards exist.

Again these principles have several implications for us in practice. *Fairly and lawfully* means that the client must 'signify' their consent to the processing. This is not tacit or implied consent as in you cannot infer consent from non-response to a communication, such as failure to return or respond to a form. A further distinction is made between 'agreement' which can be token, forced, linked with other power relationships and mask resistance and 'informed consent' which should be knowledgeable, voluntary, based on accessing skilled support and withdrawn at any point.

In practice there could be problems if agencies tie the giving of a service to the signing of a consent form, particularly if it has accommodation tied to it. It could be argued that they knew they agreed to this when they signed up but to be informed consent it needs to be able to be withdrawn. The agency could counter by arguing that withdrawal of consent is possible but it will also mean a withdrawal of the service, but there are questions of how easy or desirable this position would be. Even if the consent form is separated from the giving of a service, if forms are signed at the same time there is still a potential issue of power that calls the consent into question.

Park (2003) quotes a CAT worker who says that clients rarely complain during assessments about repeated questioning, because they feel the process is too closely tied to them getting accommodation. If they feel this about complaining then it calls into question whether someone genuinely gives consent in a meaningful way. Ironically Park (2003) quotes the worker in creating an argument that we should extend information sharing between agencies. I would interpret it equally saying that asking for consent during the assessment stage has the danger of not being informed consent. We may want to ask for specific consent to contact specific agencies for reasons of risk, or simply for things like benefits, but perhaps the blanket consent form could wait until later in the relationship.

The *obtained and processed for specific purposes* clause is interesting as it could be interpreted to imply that we should not use information obtained in a key working session for purposes of risk assessment or housing management unless we are explicit about it. This could become interesting with subjects such as drug use. How to achieve this separation is a theme we will return to in the chapters on assessment.

Moral and ethical considerations

Most agencies say that, if the worker has reason to believe that a client is going to harm themselves or a third party, then confidentiality should be broken. Some of this stems from ethical propositions we mentioned in Chapter 3 namely to look to the interests of others as well as the client and to intervene when necessary. However, if we accept this exception to confidentiality what remains un-defined is what constitutes 'reason to believe' and 'harm'. They are also complex issues. People may often make worrying statements that they do not carry through, or they may routinely harm themselves directly or through damaging behaviour.

A person may not always be in a fit state to make a decision for themselves and cannot give consent. This can happen where there are mental health issues or when someone is sufficiently intoxicated to not be able to make a decision for themselves, but this again remains ill defined. There is some guidance for what constitutes someone being able to give consent such as the Gillick Competencies (DoH, 1999; Standing Conference on Drug Abuse, 1999). This is based on what constitutes consent from someone under 16, but could be transferred to the context of our client groups. There seems to be a piece of work to be done here that is unfortunately beyond the concern of this book.

Models of access to information

An ethical consideration is *how* we let clients have access to written information about them. As we mentioned before, many agencies see this as an important moral consideration in that it is underpinned by some of our ethics such as individual responsibility, conscientisation and internal attribution. In my experience there are three different ways of allowing clients access to their files: instant access, delayed access and restricted access. There are also many shades in between. Instant access is where a person can see their file immediately. Some agencies take this further and actively get clients to sign pieces of information and agreements as people go along. Notwithstanding my earlier comments about informed consent and power, this can encourage ownership and involvement from the client. To tell people they have a right of access, often done at the beginning of the relationship when they can often not remember much beyond the relief of getting a service, does not necessarily convince them. We need to have ways of showing and constantly reminding clients that there is truth in the assertion that they have access to their files.

A counter argument to instant access is that clients will not look at the material positively. If they ask for it in an aggressive way, and we give it to them when they are in this state, then that may cause risk. A delayed access model would say that it would be better to let them look at it later when they have calmed down. While true, we would still have to deal with the client's displaced anger at them not being allowed to look at their material until later. Many local authorities work to this model, needing notice of up to 28 days from a client before they can see their file. Clients often believe during this time, people doctor the file accordingly (Seal, 2004).

The impact of these models on practitioners is that they have to change the way they write and what they write. It has to be information that they would feel comfortable for a client to read and which they could justify having written to the client. An example is given below, taken from an agency's resettlement recording policy:

> *In all recording workers are to clearly distinguish when they are offering an opinion as opposed to stating facts e.g. 'in my opinion Yasmin may be having difficulty living in a ground floor because . . . etc. It is preferable to let the facts speak for themselves e.g. 'Yasmin said she was burgled in her last ground floor flat and felt unsure about moving etc'. When using opinions, justify them with relevant facts where this is possible. It is also good practice to record users opinions alongside those of the worker where this is possible.*
>
> (Whitechapel Centre, 1998)

Practitioners often say that they find this a difficult idea because some of their thoughts and speculations could be lost. A blunt answer is to ask what exactly would be lost. If we are not able to justify our thoughts to our clients then could we justify them to anyone, do they have any worth? The first justification for a restricted model contains some counter-arguments, however.

A restricted model will let clients have a look at certain information written about them, but not all. Access to the unrestricted information can be either immediate or delayed. We have covered the most common examples of restricted information, that of risk assessment and third party information. Another common justification for a restricted policy is when clients are not allowed access to the 'day book' or 'hand over book'. These devices are often used in hostels and day centres and they contain a running commentary on the day's events in the project and immediate concerns, which is then handed onto the next shift to bring them up to date. An unsophisticated justification for not allowing a client access to it is that the book has information about other clients in it, and their confidentiality needs to be protected. Where this reasoning fails is that this information could be given to them but in a delayed way, with information about others blanked out.

A more sophisticated response is that this could be information about something that has not happened, but that the worker thinks has the potential to, ie that a client is suicidal or violent and that the next shift needs to know. A counter argument could be that the agency should be making the assumption that everyone they work with may be potentially suicidal or violent case and their working practices should reflect this. More importantly, if this is not the case then workers are left in the position of trying to make judgements as vague and possibly labelling and identifying those who have the *potential* to be violent to others, or the *potential* to be suicidal. We will discuss later how difficult it is to make risk assessments identifying who is a risk, let alone those who have the *potential* to be. It also begs the question of what the team will do with this knowledge? Will they treat the person differently or be more vigilant with them?

Positively, the above arguments do make a case for adopting a group casework model for working with clients, in that the different people on different shifts will work with the client, taking over from the interventions of their colleagues. It does not, however, give a sound reason for having restricted access to the things we write about clients. Perhaps just stating the facts and qualifying our opinions, as we do in our case files, and then allowing colleagues to make their own assessments has more validity. Perhaps some information about potentially risky situations might be lost, but this needs to be countered by the risks caused by having a book that clients see the worker routinely writing things about them in and that they know they are denied access to.

Instrumental Considerations

The most common instrumental consideration for extending confidentiality beyond an individual is when a project adopts group confidentiality within an agency. This is where what a client shares with a worker is not confidential to that worker alone but could be shared with the staff team. Reasons for this sharing vary, the most common being the fifth reason given above for recording information: *To provide continuity of service to the young person in the event of the Personal Adviser being unavailable, ill, or changing role* (CSUN, 2003). While understandable, this approach does not give the client any choice in the matter of when and how they share information with people. A client might share some things with a particular worker, having built up trust and they may not want another worker to know about those issues until a time of their choosing. Some clients have told me that they would not want to engage with a worker if they felt that worker already knew something that they would want to share with them in their own time, if at all. One agency (Seal, 2004), in the light of this dynamic, took a more subtle approach, negotiating with a client what information could go on a common file and what would remain with the worker if they left.

A slightly different reason for group confidentiality is for the personal protection of the worker. The issue shared may not be something that they feel they can, or want to, carry, not because of any particular perception of risk, but because it is an emotional burden. The issue here is whom the worker should share their feelings with. If it is about advice or personal support, then perhaps the line manager or an external supervisor would be appropriate. However, for reasons we shall explore in the chapter on worker support, this sharing is often done with team members, simply because they are there. While human, it means that the team knows about an issue personal to the client because of the support needs of the worker and the failure of the support mechanisms of the agency, rather than the needs of the client.

The main reason for having group confidentiality is it fits how the team works with people. Individual confidentiality is tied to an individual casework model. However, as we saw in the chapter on working styles, this is not the only model in operation. The biggest expansion of group confidentiality is to include external agencies (CSNU, 2002). Current notions of confidentiality do not take account of this shift. As Park (2003) says:

> *Inappropriately restrictive interpretations of confidentiality are less of a problem than they once were, but the approach taken by many agencies is nevertheless outdated and requires revision.*
>
> (Park, 2003: 24)

Park (2003) makes these comments in the light of the current debate about information sharing between agencies. He shares a common current view that laws such as the Data Protection Act 1998 are difficult to implement and often unhelpful. The reasons given for wanting this change are largely to do with achieving more holistic assessment, more efficient co-ordination of services, and clients becoming fed up of telling their same tale to various agencies. These kinds of arguments are similar to those made in other contexts like Connexions (CSNU, 2003) and *Supporting People* (Randall and Brown, 2003). Many of the arguments presented by these authors are predicated on the idea that this expansion of confidentiality and information sharing about clients will make the services we provide for them better. While they make convincing argument for this view, we should also consider the losses that may happen from a weakening of the notion of confidentiality, as I feel that to date the argument has been a little one-sided.

One of the arguments for greater information sharing is that clients resent the retelling of their stories (Randall and Brown, 2003; Park, 2003) or feel alienated at having to repeat their tales when these are painful and difficult (Park, 2003). While this may be true for many clients, if one holds with narrative theory (May, 2000; Curran, 2002) it is equally true that some people find comfort in the telling and re-telling of their tales, it is how they make sense of their lives. A further criticism is that we need to ask what the other agency will do with this knowledge, if, as we discussed before, the client does not want to share this with another worker until they have built a relationship and chosen to do so.

Another view is that sharing information between agencies making for a more holistic and efficient service provision for the client (Park, 2003; CSNU, 2003). However, Jeffs and Smith (2002) argue, with regards to the Connexions service, precisely the opposite. In a situation where there are fragmented care services, something Park (2003) acknowledges in relation to homeless services, there is a positive advantage to the client in agencies not working together effectively. The client can play them off against each other and perhaps between them meet their needs; something that would not happen if services were 'joined up'. Admittedly this dynamic favours those in a position to take advantage of it, but it illustrates that the picture is not that clear cut.

Jeffs and Smith (2002) again talking in the context of Connexions, see the expansion of the demand for record keeping in governmental initiatives as symptomatic of a wider culture of surveillance. It is not the desire to create a more effective service that is the problem but the focus and context of the work, the fact that substantial use is made of material gathered on the person, rather than from them is the issue. This creeping process of gathering information on individuals renders them:

. . . more and more transparent, relentlessly reducing the private spaces into which people have traditionally been able to retreat for refuge and self-definition.

(Whittaker, 1999: 4)

To return to an example from our own context, the end of the Rough Sleepers Initiative was an interesting one. Right from the start the agenda was clear that for the third left after the initiative there would be less tolerance of people sleeping rough (Social Exclusion Unit, 1996). The street teams that have replaced them include joint working with police with extensive 'information sharing' and an explicit brief that, if people do not engage and move into accommodation after a certain point, other legal methods will be brought to bear (Pleace, 2000).

Conclusion

I hope I have not given the impression above that we should not re-examine and move on from a position which sees confidentiality as the sanctity of our profession. I would agree with Park (2003) in what he says in one of his concluding paragraphs:

Rather than place confidentiality at the core of policy, agencies should consider drawing up client information policies within which confidentiality in its literal sense of privacy and secrecy is one element, and equal or greater importance is placed on matters such as informed consent and information sharing.

(Park, 2003)

I am reminded of one discussion I had with a client. I explained that our relationship was confidential and whatever they said was between us apart from if it had anything to do with children, terrorism, treason, if they were a danger to themselves or others or if they were too out of it to make their own decisions. In addition, if I found what they were saying difficult I would share it with my supervisor, and the team, if I thought they had the potential to be dangerous to themselves or others. The whole of the team could look at the file anyway in case I fell under a bus. I remember the client turning round to me and asking if anything was left.

I do, however, think that we should not forget why confidentiality was considered central in the care professions for so long. Many authors when talking about confidentiality, see one of its central tenets as being about trust (Beauchamp and Childress, 1994; Ashleigh et al., 2001; Hoy, 1997). Rowe (1999) who researched what he calls the 'boundary transactions' between homeless people and workers, has this to say about trust:

Perhaps the overarching theme that I came across in the accounts of homeless people was that of a complete break in trust with others, an obliteration of any remaining shred of a social contract between them and others . . . Trust is a thread that is stretched and loosened and wound through the many moments of a relationship and it can break at various points. When the worker and the client have known each other for some time, trust is tied to an investment in the relationship and negotiations over long-term needs. In early encounters, though, trust is more of an all-or-nothing proposition.

(Rowe, 1999: 82–3)

Perhaps having greater information sharing between agencies has benefits, but considering Rowe's thoughts, we should consider our timing. Not breaking confidentiality, particularly in the early days, can be a concrete way of building trust with a client, because you demonstrate that you are not betraying it. Trust, as Michael Ignatieff observes, is a matter of human gestures, not of abstract values. While it may interfere with our interventions, even to the point that a care package is not put together as well as it could be, that may not matter if it means that the client has enough trust to engage with it.

On a final note, when I have asked clients whether they believe the worker who tells them about confidentiality, in response I have got a resounding 'no'. Perhaps with the erosion of confidence in, and the reality of, confidentiality we should stop saying to our clients that we observe confidentiality and say to them instead that: Yes, we will tell others some of the things that you tell me. We can go into the reasons why, but we will ultimately need to find a way of building up your trust in me that when I do tell people, it is not to abuse you or try and damage you, but to help you or because I have to (Seal, 2004).

Chapter 8

Assessment One: Principles, Eligibility and Risk

Traditionally social work texts have expressed agreement that assessment is a key element in practice because without it workers would be left to react to events and intervene in an unplanned way. Having agreed on the centricity of assessment, texts then dismiss the subject in a few pages. Apart from some brief homilies on counterchecking facts and hypotheses and the necessity of reassessing wherever appropriate, most writers make a list of information-yielding sources and then depart from the subject to other aspects of the process.

(Milner and O'Byrne, 2002: 8)

While this comment is made within the context of social work, and specifically about social work authors, resettlement workers have even fewer resources to help them with assessment (Seal, 2002). This is illustrated by the initial reactions practitioners make to some simple questions in the session on assessment. The difficulty people have in responding to the apparently simple questions of 'what we are we looking for in assessment' and 'how do we then assess', echoes Milner and O'Byrne's (2002) sentiments. Practitioners on my courses normally give a range of things they look out for in the form of a list of issues the client may want to work on. There are several potential dangers with this approach that we shall return to later; not least of which is that we have reduced a complex process to the 'list' that Miller refers to. Some workers say that they let the person identify their own issues. While showing a person centred approach that presumes that the client knows what is going on. As Egan (1986) illustrates below, many clients come to us precisely because they do not know, or they continue to make unhelpful choices:

Many times clients come to see workers because they cannot get their heads round a particular problem, they are confused about particular issues, or they do not have all the pieces for the full picture. Workers need to help clients to clarify the issues therefore enabling them to progress to the next stage of developing goals and strategies.

(Egan, 1986: 89)

Assessment has many levels in our work (Parker, 2003). Firstly there is assessment in terms of whether the service is appropriate for an individual i.e., of whether we should work with a person. Within that there may be components of risk assessment and assessment in terms of housing management. (We will return to the former later in this chapter.) Next there is assessment in terms of what needs to be done and worked on, often called a needs assessment. There is finally the process of assessment, how assessment is conducted and by whom. Park (2003) sees this process as having several stages, which I will later use for the basis of the discussion.

Assessment frameworks

Prior to examining these dimensions of assessment, I would like to consider the use of assessment frameworks themselves and the positions people adopt in relation to them. There does seem to be some resistance to them from workers. While this may be for various valid reasons that we need to take note of and seek to address, it can also be a culture that has developed among workers as Park (2003) noted in his recent research on assessment practice in homelessness organisations:

> *In some settings it may be necessary to take steps to encourage a positive approach to the learning of technique and the development of good practice. It is not unusual to encounter resentment at the suggestion that assessment practice might be improved. This is often the case where standards are particularly low, where spurious assertions about 'professionalism' are often voiced in contexts where the genuine professional would consider the matter barely worth a mention.*

(Park, 2003: 12)

A more philosophical division in assessment that I will now consider is whether it should be a positivist, structuralist activity or a relativist one. I will attempt to examine an outlook that marries the two.

Structural approaches

Many structural approaches to assessment, as Bucknell (2002) points out, have a positivist world view. In other words things can be tested, measured, and causal links can be shown. Many assessment frameworks in the care system have this tendency, from ASSET, used by Youth Offenders Teams to the Special Needs Assessment used by Social Services. The former is used to predict potential criminal tendencies, the latter for signs of abuse.

Within a homeless context it could be that the presence of drug use is by definition a problem, a history of being kicked out of a hostel is a threat, a history of broken tenancies indicates the client cannot settle or the presence of debt means the client cannot budget. Park (2003) notes that there is a tendency for workers to follow this approach even when the assessment or referral form does not. Often the presence of potential issues such as 'mental health' or 'drug use' may be intended as being an opportunity to open up a discussion on the matter, but may be used otherwise by workers. Park recounts the testimony of one worker's experience:

> *One of the things I had to design was a hostel referral form. I had to ask questions that relate specifically to what I know the hostels were going to require, because if I didn't have that information, then my referral would end up in the bin and wouldn't even be looked at, but I also know that if I had too many 'Has this issue, has that issue . . .' beyond three, there are certain hostels that wouldn't look at the referral. I'm quite conscious of that. So in actual fact it's one of the reasons I've stayed away from having a ticky-box assessment or referral form. Because I do think some workers look down and see how many ticks are present.*

(Drugs Outreach Worker)

Beyond this kind of laziness, there are several problems with such approaches. To think of assessment as a purely positive process ignores some of the debates about the limits of positivism that even the positive sciences are recognising (Everitt, 1995). Can we really predict with people that accurately? Taking on Gidden's 1987 critique of structuralism at an extreme, a structural approach to assessment takes away an individual's agency and role in the assessment (Edwards, 2002). The individual's opinion, and indeed that of the worker, is irrelevant. If the attribute is there then the assessment is done.

A further problem with a positivist approach is that it does not necessarily help with solutions. Indeed it is the structural approach that prompted the naming of solution based therapy (DeShazer and Berg, 1989). Even if we accept the structural premise, and believe that a certain aspect of a person's behaviour or character is demonstrably associated with being inclined towards criminality, being at risk or failing to sustain tenancies, does that then help us to work with the issue? At best it leads to a separation of identification and solution. Once an issue has been identified we then look towards some other intervention to move it forwards.

Relativist approaches

In attempts to move away from these approaches, one may go to the other extreme with a more post-modern individual approach. Workers on my courses commonly say that they should treat everyone as an individual and their problems as unique to them. While an understandable reaction to the disempowering nature of the structural services and positivist approaches, there are dangers in this approach. Taken to an extreme it could descend into relativism with every client's situation unique and without any commonality between the issues that homeless people face (Habermas: 1984). Far from treating people as individuals this can turn into a locating of the problems within the individual (Derrida's critique of Fukuyama, 1989) by focusing on the uniqueness of the situation and ignoring some of the wider political dimensions, in our case structural failures in the care system (Smith, 2002 in Wolfe and Richardson).

Practically, this places a great emphasis on the relationship between the worker and the client as there are often no external reference points. This gives a lot of power to the worker to come to conclusions about the ability and needs of the client, something we have explored the danger of in the previous chapter. Even if this power dynamic can be addresses and changed in the favour of the homeless person, that still assumes that the client can work things through. While not necessarily a bad thing, this approach is overtly humanist in its approach and perhaps needs to be acknowledged as such (Glassman and Kates, 1992). We will explore the limits of a humanist approach in Chapter 15 on cognitive interventions.

As we noted before people often come to us precisely because they cannot work things out for themselves. Another criticism of the individualistic approach is that to assert that we assess everything uniquely is a fallacy. We always have criteria by which we judge things (Milner and O'Byrne, 2002). Unfortunately, the rationale behind these judgements are often hidden, even to the assessor themselves, and explained away as 'common sense'. However, 'common sense' is often not common, allowing us to all agree on it, or sense, meaning that it is logical and stands up to scrutiny. The challenge is to make these hidden frameworks overt.

A final resistance to formal frameworks is what I would call 'the relationship building fallacy'. A point identified by some authors (Edwards, 2002; Smith, 2002) is that practitioners commonly identify the need to build some kind of relationship before the use of a formal assessment framework. This begs the question of how a relationship is built in the first place, as relationships are something people 'do, rather than just have' (Duck, 1999: 21). Within certain contexts such as youth work it could be claimed that a relationship is made in a context other than the intervention (Jeffs and Smith, 1998), but that simply shifts the question to how that relationship was formed. More importantly within a resettlement context the relationship is often more contractual from the outset and quite how a relationship can be built in this context remains unanswered. The process of building a relationship is not neutral and requires structure, as outlined in Chapter 4. As Perlman (1979: 2) argues, what we call a 'relationship' should be 'a catalyst, an enabling dynamism in the support, nurture, and freeing of people's energies and motivations toward solving problems and using help'. It is more than just a discussion with a person.

Bucknell (2002) provides a useful exposition of an approach that acknowledges the difficulties of falling into either a relativist or a positivist approach and points towards a solution. He locates the uniqueness of the situation being how that issue fits into the client's frame of reference, and its potential solution, rather than the issue being unique in itself as structurally it is not. This gives a useful bridge between a positivist and a relativist approach, as it acknowledges that there may be common characteristics to certain phenomena, but these need to be contextualised within the individual's situation both in their meaning and solution. This then leaves us with a further agenda for an assessment framework, in that it will need to:

- Be a catalyst for developing an appropriate relationship between a homeless person and a worker.
- Preserve the agency of the worker and the homeless person.
- Be an empowering approach allowing the young person to explore their own situation.
- Acknowledge that while the issues the person faces are not unique, how it is contextualised in their life and ways of moving it forwards are unique.
- Integrate the assessment of issues with developing solutions for them.

Assessing eligibility for resettlement

The historical context for assessment of whether homeless services are appropriate or not is largely a statutory one (Park, 2003), the emphasis having been on whether people were eligible for a statutory service as opposed to making an assessment of a person's needs. As an example, there are five criteria for eligibility for assistance from local authorities (Housing Acts, 1977/85/96; Homeless Persons Act, 2002); to have recourse to public funds, to be homeless, to be priority need, to be unintentionally homeless and to have a local connection.

As Park says, there is some legitimacy in this approach, but there are some dangers with it in terms of services like resettlement:

Housing assessments ... present few problems when used for their principal purpose of identifying eligibility and making appropriate allocations of property, but their weakness shows up where an agency has a parallel welfare function.

(Park, 2003: 4)

There is also a cultural danger in that this emphasis on eligibility rather than needs, duties rather than rights, can bring with it a culture of workers using assessment as gate-keeping for services rather than assessing the suitability of a service to meet the needs of homeless people. There have been few attempts to develop criteria for accepting people onto resettlement programmes (Bevan and Stretch, 1998). Those that have done so have largely tried to determine the level of needs of potential clients. (Randall and Brown, 1995, 2003). There is some merit in this project, and we will return to it when considering managing caseloads in Chapter 11.

As a starting point for assessment, however, such approaches fail to take account of issues discussed in Chapter 2, as not everyone is ready for resettlement and not all resettlement services are suitable for all clients. At best they seek to exclude some people not for their unreadiness for resettlement, but for having too high a level of need. At worst there was a combination of assessing people in terms of risk and suitability for a service, which did not take into account the different issues inherent in both, blurring the distinctions between these two forms of assessment.

Work that I did in collaboration with colleagues from a project in Liverpool attempted to develop a means of assessment that took account of other relevant factors. It had three dimensions, which were to assess a person's needs, motivation and ability, in combination.

Need

The assessment of need in homelessness is an interesting and contested field (Park, 2003) and something that we will return to both in Chapter 9 and in Chapter 11 on caseloads.

Motivation

Perhaps uniquely to resettlement in homelessness a second element that needs to be assessed is a person's motivation. This element has several components:

Is the person ready to make a change?

As change is fundamental to resettlement (see Chapter 2), a client must be prepared to make the necessary changes for their successful resettlement. Assessment of readiness to change is a subtle matter, a simple 'are you ready to make the necessary changes' is likely to elicit a 'yes response'. We will return to this consideration later when looking at the process of assessment. Some of the setting up of expectations will be covered in the chapter on referral so perhaps at the assessment stage the next question is the more fundamental one.

Is the person aware of what these changes may involve?

The referral stage should have established a basic level of motivation in a client and we will discuss later how the process of assessment should further assess and reinforce this. The client will need to be aware of what these changes may involve. In Chapter 2 we discussed a definition of resettlement and established the importance of the worker having a clear conception of this. The need for this understanding equally applies to the client. The assessment process should therefore have an educative role into the nature of resettlement. Again the process of assessment should take account of this.

When I run training on these issues some participants say that their clients would not be prepared to engage in this discussion, as they only want to know when they are going to get their flat. It seems reasonable to say, however, that if they are not prepared to debate the nature of the changes they will need to undertake, then they are not ready to make a change. We should not forget how hard a process this can be, particularly for people for whom homelessness has become an identity, as we examined in Chapter 2. The challenge is to allow the assessment and educative processes to happen while at the same time dealing with the loss of self-esteem and self-belief that this could entail.

Is the person willing to accept support?

Being ready to change, and even knowing the nature of the changes that need to be undertaken, does not necessarily mean that a homeless person is willing to accept support. To accept that you need support can be some way into identifying as a homeless person. Snow and Anderson (1993) again chart how in early stages of homelessness a person displays what they term 'emotional distancing', seeing themselves as different from other homeless people and viewing their own homelessness as an accident, a temporary aberration. To accept support, particularly in resettlement, is difficult as it entails an acceptance that your needs go beyond needing just a home, and that you cannot cope in other ways. As above, the challenge is to allow this to happen without totally disempowering the person. We will examine later in Chapter 15 on models of cognitive interventions that may allow this to happen.

Is the person willing to be an equal partner in that change?

A final consideration is whether, having accepted the need for support, the person is to be an equal part in that change. We charted in Chapter 3 how getting people to accept responsibility for themselves and their actions can be a difficult process. Later chapters in the book will examine ways of working that will enable this. However, this is difficult to assess at the start of a working relationship with a person and perhaps reinforces a later argument that assessment should not be a one-off process. At the end of the process of assessment people will need to be taking some responsibility for their changes or at least show a potential or will.

Ability

Ability may sound like the most judgemental and positive of the criteria, but that is not so. Ability can be described as the ability to reach the stage needed for the accommodation you can get for the person in the time frame you can work with them. Assessment should be seen as a functional process examining the agencies and its potential usefulness to the user, rather than about that person's needs (Rank, quoted in Smith, 2002). A practitioner needs to communicate to the client that they are not necessarily there to identify needs, and solutions, and it needs to be considered whether the service will be useful to the client. Following Smith's (2002) thoughts on Rank, we should perhaps worry about any service that claims to be holistic in its provision.

Unfortunately, many homelessness organisations make this claim, even if it is in the form of an aspirational statement such as, 'fighting to end street homelessness' or 'meeting the needs of the homeless people of . . .' While the motives for these aspirations are admirable, they carry the implication that they can, or will attempt to, meet all needs. This has an impact on clients, particularly where their needs are, in the end, not met.

For an example, an ex-client of mine described how on one occasion, he was waiting to be told to leave a hostel. He knew what he had done and that he would be required to leave as a result. In those final moments, sitting on his bed, with his bags packed, hearing the worker's footsteps coming down the corridor, he read the hostel's leaflet. Its mission statement was along the lines of 'we are here to meet the needs of homeless people at their point of need etc.' He found that ironic given that a worker was coming down the corridor to kick him out. He remembered feeling dehumanised as a result.

Although my client had broken the hostel's rules, his situation did raise the question of whether it is fair to put a person through a service that cannot effectively respond to their needs. As we shall explore in the chapter on the resettlement process, putting a person through that process is not neutral. If it fails it can lower their self-esteem and belief in themselves, entrench a destructive identity even further and take away options as the local authority would consider the person intentionally homeless or it might leave them with rent arrears or burn their accommodation bridges in some other way.

A word on risk assessment

A risk assessment is a statement about how likely a person is to harm whom and in what circumstances.

(CIH, 1997)

The aims of risk assessment and management are to protect service users, staff and the wider community from physical or mental harm, exploitation, or other danger, by identifying as accurately as possible the nature of the risk, the factors which contribute to eliminate or control the risk and the measures necessary to eliminate or control the risk.

(Bradley et al., 2004)

Within organisations risk is related to the agreed decision making processes. This is a growing emphasis on individual accountability, which is then closely linked to service accountability. Within most operational settings many small providers of services are forced to work with risk simply to justify their existence.

(Rogers, 1998)

Much work has been done of late on risk assessments in the contexts of homelessness (Bradley et al., 2004; Barker, 1998; NHA, 1997). These works are an invaluable source of information on how to structure assessment, the principles behind them and the legislative background. Bradley et al. (2004) note how many agencies still do not have risk assessment policies and they list reasons that agencies give for this:

- staff aren't comfortable about writing down sensitive information;
- resources, especially 'we haven't got time', 'there's already too much paperwork';
- staff do it informally in their heads;
- risks are low; nothing has happened here 'the risks are just part of the job';
- we like to give people a fresh start and don't ask them about their past.

Many of these are reminiscent of various aspects of working culture that we have talked about in previous chapters.

The first two opening quotes of this section are meant to mark another cultural shift from earlier risk assessments that concentrated on the client and the risk they pose, to a later concentration on the wider notion that everything, including ourselves, could contribute to the creation of a risky situation. The earlier manifestations of risk assessments, where workers perceive clients as the source of the problem and risk, are underpinned by a way of viewing clients that we covered more comprehensively in Chapter 4. The last quote illustrated another cultural aspect of risk assessment. The first half of the quote resonates with the feelings practitioners have expressed on courses, that they think risk assessments are as much about working out who to blame if something does go wrong as managing and reducing that risk. The second half of the quote resonates with another feeling from practitioners that certain aspects of their job are risky, but they carry on with them because they are expected to do so regardless of the risk.

In this section I intend to discuss some of the dimensions of risk that we should consider beyond what we already do, which our working cultures sometimes mitigate against us considering in detail. I will do this using some examples of the practices that we give perhaps a little less attention to than we ought, often through the aforementioned pressures to justify our existence.

In training I use the example of the Newby case (Simms, 1995) as a framework for discussion about risk, leading to an examination of the Newby Competencies. Briefly, Jonathan Newby began working for the Oxford Cyrenians as a volunteer in April 1993 and was the only person on duty when he was attacked by a resident John Rous, in the office. He was 22 years old when he died. Rous had several admissions to psychiatric hospitals and had lived on the streets for 20 years.

The competencies were developed out of lessons learnt from the case. I would divide the competencies that were developed into three broad categories:

- **Competencies of risk assessment of an individual.** This included an understanding of symptoms of mental illness and its effects on the individual, substance use and its effects, observation skills.
- **More general competencies of the worker.** This included the ability to communicate, knowing the roles of other agencies, networking skills, ability to follow procedures etc.
- **Organisational competencies.** These included planning and managing care, the development of guidelines and policies, the support of staff, the importance of induction etc.

The main point of this discussion in training is to illustrate that we are a part of the dynamic of risk, our skills, knowledge and attitudes as workers are as much a part of creating a risky situation as the client and their issues. Similarly the absence of policies and of an organisational culture of having policies and even the high promises that an agency makes to its clients that it then does not deliver, are other dimensions of risk that need to be taken into consideration. Positively, Bradley et al. (2004) recognise some of these issues, saying risk assessments should including examining situational factors such as how we give out warnings and exclusions. They also highlight that we should take account of the physical environment and should take into consideration things that have a positive impact on risk including the physical fabric of a building and how it is managed. Others like the Salvation Army (2000) have recognised that having too many rules or staff not communicating properly are possible triggers of aggressive behaviour.

In training, the above framework of individual, worker and agency factors were used in analysing risky situations that workers had been in. Of all aspects of a resettlement worker's job the one that seemed to come out as the consistently risky was visiting people in their own accommodation. Many of the physical considerations Bradley et al. (2004) recommend, such as retreat routes, panic alarms, etc. simply do not apply. The only consideration concession people had was to have a mobile phone, and they needed to call in by a certain point. This may stop a person being held against their will but it is unlikely to stop an immediate risk. Other identified risks were of not knowing what state the person will be in, or of who else might be in the accommodation. Some practitioners were able to take along another worker, but this was seen as under exceptional circumstances and it is unclear, beyond that person being able to escape, what advantage this has.

In the light of this a discussion might ensue about the purpose of visiting people in their homes. Reasons might be about a change in environment, the marking of a different stage in the relationship with a change in the power dynamic. While true, much of this could be achieved in a café or in a park, a potentially less risky situation. In the client's own accommodation the client has control of the environment, and this may be important, but it can also be a risk in itself. A common reason practitioners gave for going into someone's own home, that a meeting in a café or park could not achieve, was that the worker could check whether the client was telling the truth about whether they were coping or not. If the client is not telling the truth, the worker will be physically confronting them with their own deception, something from which the client cannot escape. This is a situation that could very easily be a trigger for aggressive behaviour. Salvation Army (2000) and Miller (1993) tell us how confrontation can push people into denial: if this is not possible because of the physical nature of the confrontation, aggression is another option.

This is not to say that visiting people in their own homes is not always worth the risk. It is more that it is a convention of how we work that perhaps needs to be thought through again. Most practitioners reported that it was a routine aspect of their work, and in the case of floating support, an expectation. Perhaps such working practices should become more of an exception and are an example of how 'providers of services are forced to work with risk simply to justify their existence' (Rogers and Freiberg, 1994).

Conclusion

In this chapter we have covered just some of the aspects of assessment. We need to have assessment and it needs to take account of the individual but in a social context. Within the context of resettlement it firstly needs to establish who resettlement workers should embark upon work with and more importantly who they should not. Risk assessment is one such other consideration. As stated before, the sources mentioned at the beginning are invaluable as ways to operationalise risk assessment. The cultural aspect we need to think about are what areas of our service delivery should we prioritise by looking at and then changing.

Chapter 9

Assessment Two: Needs Assessment

Needs Assessments . . . are constructed so that needs within a set of suggested domains are identified, such as health, finance, housing, daily living skills and social networks.

(Clifford and Craig, 1998)

. . . often using forms that restrict recording to summary details. This model has been widely copied by voluntary agencies, though the analysis of options to meet identified needs is rarely pursued with the rigour required of statutory services.

(Park, 2003)

Park (2003) notes that approaches to needs assessment are often based on social service models, normally for community care. He also notes that they are often badly implemented. One of the major developments in terms of homelessness has been the 'Common Assessment Framework' a set of forms produced by the Homeless Multiple Needs Partnership, a venture by Phoenix House, The London Connection, St. Mungo's, Riverpoint and the Department of Psychiatry at St.Thomas. It has been published as a computer disc accompanied by a set of introductory notes (Homeless Multiple Needs Partnership, 2001). Simply put, many of these approaches take a list of issues, or areas of concern, to discuss with the client or possible work, perhaps with prompt questions to explore or bring them up. As an example the common assessment framework asks the worker to elicit factual information under headings including housing history, family and relationships, childhood, education, work, health and legal problems:

Collection of standardised data has too often become a substitute for intelligent enquiry, which requires a skilled communicator who understands that most people's lives are a tangled web in which the right thread to follow is not always obvious.

(Middleton, 1999: 23)

Park recognises the danger that Middleton expresses, saying that a wholesale adoption of the common assessment framework would be inappropriate. He also recognises that the origins of such approaches comes from social work concerns that essential details might be missed when considering elderly people for domiciliary or residential care. A comparable thoroughness can be found in the system for assessing and reviewing the needs of 'looked-after children'. However writers such as Skyrme (1997) see a fallacy in identifying information with knowledge, thinking that if we know a lot of facts about a thing, or a person, that tells us something. In fact it merely gives us a lot more information from which to try and establish some knowledge and meaning. The challenge would seem to produce an assessment that is simple, yet generates the kind of information that gives us this knowledge and meaning.

Brandon's (1998) four magnet model

Even if these approaches discussed above are simplified and are used not in a positivist sense that Park (2003) identifies as often the curse, Brandon (1998) rightly identifies that they are deficit models, identifying what people cannot do rather than what they can. They see people in terms of the problems they have rather than their attributes. Brandon proposes that we need to use a model that examines needs in a wider context, one that acknowledges that everyone has needs. A client once in exasperation remarked to me that he was fed up of workers talking about his needs, he felt that everyone has needs and what he had was problems. Brandon's model concurs with this, identifying instead the idea of magnets, 'to one of which all the elements in the life history of a client will be attracted' i.e. that our behaviour and ways of thinking will be directed towards fulfilling this need. He goes on to say they are universal and are equally applicable to ourselves. He is at pains to stress that they are not to be seen as indicators of failure, but as a way of getting a person to start understanding themselves:

> *These four magnets can be equally applied to the life of anyone. They are not about symptoms or syndromes or medical conditions. They cross gender, disability, age, religious and racial divides reasonably easily. They are intended to be essentially unifying rather than devisive. They remind us that we are all human.*
>
> (Brandon, 1998: 5.6)

Brandon further defines these magnets and their implications as the need for control, the need to develop and use skills, the need for joy and pain and the need for contact with others.

The need for a sense of control

This will include things like feeling powerful, that we have influence, can make decisions, have real choices or are listened to by others who are relatively powerful. Interestingly Hutson (1994, 1998) charts how the hostel experience itself can be disempowering. We have covered before in the previous chapter how the language we use as workers, and the way we present things, may intend to be empowering but actually end up as blaming the victim.

To use and develop skills

Many homeless individuals are geniuses of contingency, mixing and matching scant resources and changing strategies at the dictates of chance.
(Rowe, 1999)

I have always found the term 'life skills', still commonly used in this field, faintly patronising. We should remember the ethic of conscientisation learnt from Chapter 3 are we really saying that homeless people do not have skills? If I went to a strange city where I knew no-one and had no money I doubt if I could get something to eat, find somewhere to stay that night and possibly have people to look out for me. Many homeless people could achieve that and yet they are told they need to develop life skills. That does not apply to everyone undergoing resettlement of course, but surely a better starting point for skills is to see what people can do rather than tell them what they cannot. Identifying skills is not as easy as asking people what skills they have, as they may not recognise those for themselves. This is where we have to develop skills in conscientisation and help people recognise what they can do. As an example, I used to do a skills inventory with clients asking them to name the roles they had led in their lives and the skills they had developed from this. One client replied that he had no skills, as his main role for years had been a drug dealer. That role required ability in negotiation, accounting, communication and versatility, which needed to be pointed out to him. Clients who have been lone parents, have survived the mental health system or been homeless will have developed some skills as a result it is important to see their positive applications.

Using Friere again (1968) he points out that it is not that marginalised groups have not developed skills in the roles they have had, it is that they are told by society that either these roles are not skilled or that they are not the skills that they need. This is a perspective that they then internalise. We need therefore to find imaginative ways of getting people to recognise how much they can do; the aforementioned skills inventory is perhaps a start.

To understand and cognicise the pain we experience

In relation to working with homeless people, Brandon invites us to ask some interesting questions of ourselves:

- What is the nature of suffering for all of us?
- How far are support and services a source of pain?
- What help is given to understand the nature of pain?
- What are people's sources of beauty, joy and pleasure?

He believes that we often shy away from this aspect of the work as it is too close to ourselves and our own pain. Sinason writes of the essential stupidity of staff, taking the meaning from the original word stupified – meaning numbed by grief: 'we are knocked silly by the grief we witness' (Sinason, 1992: 56). Given this difficulty there are implications for the way workers are supported, a theme returned to in Chapter 10. Our duty is to find out what a client feels about pain and joy, what are client's sources of pain and joy are and how they relate to each other. They may feel that they do not deserve joy, or that it is the only thing worth pursuing. Pain they have endured may have become a part of their identity, and this may be a negative or a positive thing for them.

The need to have human contact

Bayley (1995) says that human contact, 'fulfils our social needs for attachment and intimacy, social integration, nourishment, reassurance of worth and reliable assistance' (Bayley, 1995: 35). Such a need casts light on the aforementioned Dutch criteria of two positive relationships apart from the worker for ending resettlement mentioned in Chapter 2. Brandon's ideas are supported by recent research that identifies loneliness as the most common cause of tenancy breakdown (Dane, 1998; Radall and Brown, 2003). Brandon also talks about the converse need not to have contact, warning us of the danger of overexposure to people:

> *The fashionable emphasis on the social nature of human beings . . . can obscure the genuine need for being on our own. We also need some space for personal healing and reflection as well as being in proximity to others.*
>
> (Brandon, 1998: 15–27)

This sentiment has been catalogued with regard to people both within hostels, and as a reason for not going into them (Randall and Brown, 1996). In practice I have found people to be suffering from both phenomena. Often the person who identifies a loner and seeks solitude, once resettled reports feelings of loneliness.

The 'four magnets' model has interesting implications for resettlement. It implies that, as meeting these needs is a human condition, whatever situation a client is in they will find ways to meet them and their behaviour will tend towards one of these magnets. This way of thinking is useful in explaining certain phenomena in hostels. I will examine two of them; that there is always a top dog, or controller, and that people commonly increase their drug use, often to the level of the highest user.

Regarding the first, a precursory problem is that many hostels think of themselves as some kind of holding ground, a place people will treat as a bed on their journey to their own flat (Ham, 1994). In fact the hostel often becomes that person's home, and the people in the hostel become that person's community (O'Neil, 1996). As workers deny the community that exists in their hostel, means of meeting needs are not put in place. Some authors have noted that as well as not providing these skills hostels can actively take them away making people feel socially isolated and contribute to a loss of self-value and a loss of motivation (Commander et al., 1998). Denied of other forms of control, at its extremes including over when to eat, when to go to bed, and other daily activities, they turn to each other and hierarchies and fiefdoms develop.

Brandon's model is also useful in explaining why people's drug use tends to worsen in a hostel. The quickest way for people to meet their needs will be to join a drinking or drugs school (where people pool their resources to buy their substances in common, gaining from economies of scale) which will actually meet all the points needed on that magnet. Clients will have an instant place in the hostel's hierarchy, (drug use is also associated by some authors with clients having a sense of control), a way of developing and using skills (as a drug habit requires skills to maintain) a way of dealing with pain and an instant circle of friends. It might be that a homeless person should not do this because of the long term consequences. Daly (1996) charts how the experience of homelessness, with the fight for everyday survival, tends to leave homeless people with an immediate outlook, not looking to the medium term, and certainly not the long term.

Looking at the four magnet model in terms of worker interventions and assessment, the role for a resettlement worker becomes that of enabling people to make the transition from the old situation to the new situation. In terms of assessment, the worker needs to see how a person functions in their current situation and what they might have to change when they go into their new accommodation. Not withstanding the difficult situations in hostels we have just described, the way a person meets their needs there may or may not be usable in their new situation, as that may be radically different. The bully, or controller, often feels lost in their own flat because they cannot reproduce their way of having a sense of control in their life (Seal, 2002). Questions to consider are:

The old situation

- How is the client meeting their needs now if at all?
- Is the behaviour that meets their needs destructive to themselves or others?
- Is their way of meeting their needs sustainable in the new situation?

The new situation

- What new things will the new situation throw up?
- What needs to change in the ways of meeting their needs?
- What can we do about this?

A set of parallel questions can be put to the client: how have you met your needs in the past for control, to use your skills, to understand pain and to have contact with people; compare that to the new situation:

- What ways of meeting your needs can you keep as they are?
- What ways of meeting your needs have you got but need to change?
- What ways of meeting your needs do you need to develop?
- What ways of meeting your needs do you need to develop later when the worker has gone?

These approaches also have the advantage of meeting some of the standards for assessment that *Supporting People* regard as giving a good quality service:

> *The written procedures describe how service users' views are to be incorporated . . . Service users confirm that their views have been listened to and taken into account.*

(ODPM, 2002)

A case study may help here to illustrate the use of such a framework.

Bob is 54 years old and a powerfully built man. He describes himself as warm, friendly and easy going. In large groups he is mostly quiet. He spent time in a psychiatric hospital due to schizophrenia, and looks back on this time with a mixture of fondness for the other patients and resentment to the staff. He met his wife there and they have two children. Although they are divorced they still see a lot of each other – he refers to her as his wife. He worked as a gardener at the hospital. He spent most of the time in your hostel sitting in the lounge talking to whoever was there.

You moved him into his own flat two months ago as he wanted the peace and quiet. When you come around he keeps apologising for having to see you and has made a point of not ringing so as not to 'waste your time'. Despite this whenever you suggest ending the programme he comes up with more things he needs to work through. He has started going back to the hospital and has even been doing some of the gardening there again. He says it is where his friends are. He says that he does not like the evenings as he is 'alone to think about the whys, whens and maybes'.

(taken from Bevan, 1998)

If we examine this case study using Brandon's model we could argue that in many ways Bob is meeting his needs. He has a sense of control, particularly over something (the hospital) that controlled him for a long time. While he may be going back there it is on a slightly different basis, as a volunteer, marking a shift in the power relationship. He is also using and developing his skills in the gardening exercise. He has contact, with people who have been a large part of his life, and probably always will be. His ex-wife is a source of both pain and joy as were the staff and residents at the hospital. His feelings towards the staff at the hospital may give the worker insight into how he is reacting to them. The flashpoint seems to be the evenings and this is perhaps the area that needs to be addressed. When I have given the case study to practitioners without this assessment framework, I have often had very different reactions. People want to get mental health services involved, even to the point of trying to get him sectioned. People have often talked about engaging counselling services and there were definite worries about him going back to the hospital. This was seen somehow as failure rather than something quite natural to him and may explain some of his anxieties at night, feeling guilty because many workers tell him he is doing something he should not.

I have taken a very definite view here in describing Bob's situation and on exploration with Bob his needs may be quite different. The four magnets model explains that we can take an alternate view accepting that Bob may be doing many things that work for him. It also moves away from the aforementioned tendency to create needs in a person (McKnight, 1996). Yes, Bob may have issues to sort out, but the real question, as we shall return to in a later chapter, is whether he is probably alright enough to be able to sort it out for himself without the worker. Even if he is not quite right do we really need to create a multi-agency package involving numerous services for an indefinite time, a tendency Illich (1976) warns about? Perhaps Bob just needs a dog to walk in the evening, as one of my training groups concluded.

The process of assessment

There are only too many linear, prescriptive and stylised assessment formats that come nowhere near meeting the complexities, uncertainties and ambiguities of current social work practice.

(Milner and O'Byrne, 1998: 2)

Assessments are approximations, best seen as a process with constant readjustments, rather than an event.

(Bevan, 1998: 3)

These two quotes give us an interesting message, we should see assessment as a process rather than an event, but also that we should not reduce it to something that is too simplified and not understood or valued by practitioners. Interestingly the *Quality Assessment Framework for Supporting People* (ODPM, 2002) reinforces this perspective at several points in their standards, with an interesting equal emphasis on understanding as well as knowledge:

> *The assessment process is written down and staff can describe the procedures which are followed . . . Staff are able to describe the assessment and review processes and the rationale behind the key elements.*

(ODPM, 2002)

Taking referrals

We have examined in a Chapter 6 how we refer onto other agencies. Another consideration is about how we take referrals. Our referral process is important for three reasons; it determines users' expectations; it gate-keeps who accesses the service and it determines other agencies' initial impressions. On the first point, by the time a client is in front of the worker we would want them to have some idea about what resettlement will entail. On the second point, even before we apply our criteria for eligibility, we will want some inappropriate clients to have been excluded.

One agency I worked for took people straight from care and put them into their own flat. The referral process the client had to undergo was quite elaborate, an application form, two interviews etc. There was a deliberateness to this in that the agency took a view that the kind of person who would cope in their own flat straight from being in care, would need to be able to respond to this level of bureaucracy and demands. If they could not respond to this then they were judged not to be ready.

Some agencies have an 'open' referral system, as in people self-refer (common in direct access centres). While this seems initially to be a flexible approach, there are a number of problems with it. Firstly it is not an open system, a demand is being made on the client to know at what point they need intervention and be able to turn up and wait (drop in centres rarely see people immediately) and those who cannot are excluded. This may be legitimate, in that this demand is used as a test of their motivation and ability. However, I suspect that it is often done on the basis of organisational convenience, rather than having been thought through.

Some agencies run a waiting list for access to their resettlement service. Some do this on a date order basis, some when a place comes up, the worker will look down the waiting list and see who is the most appropriate client for resettlement. My problem with the former is that it is random, some people who would be appropriate for resettlement need a quick intervention, while some who are not can wait until their date comes up. The latter system makes sense as long as 'appropriate' is defined as much in terms of them being motivated and being able to respond to the service as them being 'needy.'

Timings

As Bevan (1998) says, assessment should be seen as a process rather than a one off event. On the other hand, there should also be a cut off point where a decision is made on whether the agency works with a person and the issues to be worked on. Agencies should not be afraid, given previous comments, about requiring the person to have the ability to respond to what the agency has to offer and to set a time frame for this. If a successful assessment cannot be carried out within that time frame it could be reasoned the person is not able to respond to what the service offers, or vice versa. Many agencies already do have set a time period; such as an initial 28 day assessment period in a hostel before moving them on elsewhere. However we need to make sure that the timeframe is based on the testing of this ability rather than organisational convenience, and that there is sufficient flexibility to take account of those at the margins.

An extended period would seem to be a more effective way to measure motivation, as it is not realistic to take it as given that a client is motivated just because they say they are in initial interviews. Some practitioners on courses reply that this just means that people comply up until the end of the 28 day period. However, as another practitioner responded, the very fact that they have been able to sustain some behaviour for this length of time says something in itself. It is then down to the worker to channel this motivation in a different direction.

Blurring of assessments

On a slightly different issue, there is often a blurring of assessment itself and putting its conclusion into action. There is a 'natural' dimension to this; it can be a means of building a relationship, as we will cover in the next chapter on support planning. However there is merit in seeing the two as distinct phases. In the 1990s, community care policy changed, requiring a split between the assessment of needs on the one hand and the planning of responses to those needs on the other (DoH, 1991).

The split is logical for a number of reasons. Firstly, people may start taking actions before they have built up a true picture of the situation. This is often because a client is demanding action or certain issues seem self-evidently critical (Park, 2003). A worker needs to hold to the boundaries of the relationship and remind themselves, and the client, that they are undertaking a planned process of intervention rather than crisis management. It is tempting to take action too quickly, but it is an illusion to think that we can make any meaningful intervention after knowing the client for a matter of hours, or even minutes, in a situation of complex and/or entrenched homelessness. One agency I worked with made it a rule that the worker would not take any action on behalf of a client until their third meeting in the belief that, until then neither party could have built up an accurate picture of the situation or established a sufficient relationship of trust. Furthermore to blur these stages can miss out the intervening stage of establishing a working contract, as discussed in the chapter on support planning.

The politics of truth

A final issue is that attention needs to be given to the dynamics that the assessment process may have set up. One consequence of those dynamics is that people may lie during the assessment process causing later difficulties in that relationship, when the fault may be in a flawed assessment process. This is important, given that many workers say that they think honesty is one of the crucial factors in a productive relationship (Seal, 2004). Going back to the most common form of assessment, one of the rationales for having a list of issues to bring up with the client is that raising something gives permission for it to be an issue of concern for the client (Milner and O'Byrne, 2002). The raising of these issues can also be as a result of a second blurring, confusing needs assessment with other things that have to be assessed, namely risk assessment and housing management issues. Suffice to say that a needs assessment, a risk assessment and a housing management assessment, while looking at the same pieces of information, are assessing for very different things.

As an example of these dynamics, clients are often asked whether they are using drugs. The worker may be asking the person if they use drugs from a needs assessment perspective, believing, quite rightly, that this may be an issue of concern for the client and they may need permission to talk about it. However this may have been done at the same time as explaining to the client that drug use is not allowed on the premises, giving a potentially contradictory message. To complicate matters the reasons for not allowing drug usage may be from a risk assessment perspective – heroin use is often not tolerated for this reason, or it may be from a housing management perspective. The use of cannabis rarely causes risk but, certainly for legal reasons, it certainly raises housing management issues (Flemann, 2004).

Even if the explanation of these contradictory policies it is not done at the same time the client, who may well have been through the homeless system before, might make the link themselves and assume that an admission of drug use might be damaging. This assumption may be true as the worker may use this information in a different context. Sometimes workers try and separate the issues by stating that drug use would not affect the client being accepted for the service. However this is often done before enough trust has been established to allow the client to accept this seeming contradiction between the dual resettlement, risk and housing management roles held by many workers. Sometimes we underestimate how much clients may distrust us initially. Rowe (1999) sees this as an all or nothing situation in the early days, often stemming precisely from a confusion over the workers intentions. He recalls a young man's comments to him:

> *Let's face it, I would trust a homeless junkie before I would trust somebody like you. The junkie, you know exactly what he's looking for – the next high, his next fix – and you could be his meal ticket – You're always on your guard. With you, I don't know where you are coming from. You can tell me a whole lot of shit and I could believe, leaving myself fucked.*

(Rowe, 1999: 83)

Rowe (1999) describes how clients are aware of the dynamics of the processes they undergo with workers and develop a pitch for workers in gaining access to services, seeing it in transactional terms. Seal (1998), in a survey of clients' attitudes towards workers, examined this transaction in terms of accessing resettlement services. A clients 'pitch' was often to admit to a number of issues to be worked on, believing that this was what made workers feel worthwhile, but they were careful to make their 'level' not too chaotic to be unmanageable. This is quite a human reaction and a parallel could be drawn with applying for a job. We will emphasise our successes but show ourselves willing to learn and develop. We downplay the negative and try not to draw attention to any gaps.

Given this context, it is not then surprising that the answer to the question 'are you using drugs' is 'no', but is it fair to then label that client as a liar, if we subsequently find out that this is not true? More significantly, this dynamic can set a precedent of deception in the relationship, with the client believing that it is necessary to lie about certain things. Perhaps rather than saying we expect clients to tell the truth, a more useful question to ask ourselves is what level of truth can we can expect, or do we need, in a given situation?

> *There are many, and often conflicting, truths about any one subject's situation . . . Since an analysis is making sense of a set of facts and it is possible to construct any number of accounts, we would argue that the most truthful analysis is the one that is the most helpful: the one that leads to the most useful understanding and to an intervention that achieves the service user's goals in the one that has the most truth.*

(Milner and O'Byrne, 2002: 77)

The above quote illustrates the point that truth is fairly subjective. Some clients may well be in the position where they do not know what the truth is, it is changeable, or they simply do not know how to tell the truth. Snow and Anderson (1987) chart how another aspect of a homeless person's identity can be the creation of fictitious histories and current narratives about their lives that do not add up. Other authors show this to be a common phenomenon with people who have a history of care or abuse (O'Riordan et al., 2003). However Milner and O'Byrne imply that this is perhaps just an exaggeration of how any person makes sense of their life. This stems from narrative approaches to working with clients (White, 1993, 1995, 1996; White and Epston, 1990; Epston, 1998) which hold that everyone has a narrative, it is the tale we tell ourselves to explain the events of our lives. We consolidate our inconsistencies, ambiguities and contradictions into a tale that makes sense to us; where the truth lies in this, according to White, does not really matter.

In a piece of research I conducted on inter-colleague conflict in care organisations (Seal, 2004) a common phenomenon of ingrained conflict in a staff team was that both parties felt compelled to tell any newcomer their version, or narrative, of the story; the versions were rarely compatible. One of my former clients explained how he had spent his community care grant with an elaborate tale about how he had cleaned himself up for his daughter's wedding, bought drinks for guests, going into detail about the speech etc. In fact he had spent it on drink but it was clear that my client was creating this narrative for himself and not me.

Conclusion

In conclusion, rather than outlining a definitive process, we have outlined criteria for what an assessment process should be. It should:

- Be educative while not lowering people's self-esteem.
- Build on what they can do rather than what they cannot.
- Test their motivation and ability to respond to what the service can offer.
- Have appropriate time limits for deciding whether we should work with a person and what that work may entail.
- Separate assessing for resettlement, housing management and risk.
- Appreciate what level of truth we can expect and need at given points.

Chapter 10

Support Planning

Planning is central to any real change like the chain on a pedal cycle. You can pedal as hard as you like but the wheels won't go round unless the chain translates your effort through the hub and on to the wheels . . . it is the major way of translating the individual wishes of the customers into individual services.

(Handbook of Care Planning, Brandon and Atherton, 1996)

The danger that planners face in looking so far into the future is that the link with the present is broken.

(American Planning Association, 1986)

This chapter examines good practice in developing support plans. As such it follows on from the preceding chapters on assessment. Once we have agreed to work with a client, and what issues to work on, the next questions are; the issues to start with, how to start breaking these issues down and identifying the first few steps we should make.

The above two quotes illustrate some of the concerns we should have at this stage. Brandon and Atherton (1996) remind us that it is crucial to make sure the first issue we work on has relevance, and that it relates to the picture as a whole. The American Planning Association (1986) reminds us to keep a focus on the present. In this chapter I will develop these themes, evaluating the relevancy of Egan's 1998 work *The Skilled Helper* and the idea of 'task-centred casework'.

Leverage

According to Egan (1998) clients usually seek guidance because they want to change something in their lives, but they may not be sure what this change constitutes or even what issues to focus on. It is therefore the role of workers to help them 'identify and work on problems, issues, concerns, or opportunities that will make a difference' (Egan, 1998: 98). Workers need to help clients focus on issues and to prioritise the order in which they are to be dealt with. In situations where clients are grappling with many issues at once, the guidance worker helps clients search for some leverage. He defines leverage as tackling one particular problem which is key to resolving some of the other problems faced by the client and will build their motivation.

Leverage therefore seems essential to our role as many of our clients face more than one issue and this fits neatly with Bevan's (2003) definition of resettlement clients. In a way these ideas will not be new for workers as, helping clients to prioritise has been identified by practitioners as a key component of their work in training (Seal, 2004). However, given that many clients are not able to draw an accurate picture of their situation, something we explored in the previous chapter, are they any more likely to be able to prioritise once this is attained? The question is how we help the client to identify the issue that will give us leverage. At this point, when asked, practitioners become more vague and say things like 'the most important one', the 'most immediate concern' or something specific like 'sorting out the benefits'. It seems that we need to establish more systematic criteria for leverage, or we may end up freewheeling on Brandon and Atherton's bike. As a stating point, Egan identifies four criteria for helping us identify the issue that would give us leverage. I will examine each of them in turn.

The issue the client sees as important

This seems an obvious starting point, and is a central tenet of the client centred approach (Rogers, 1968). However, this is not as simple when the client presents with an issue that seems to be a red herring, or what the worker would see as key. I once worked with a client whose assessment had revealed a multitude of interrelated issues. He was street homeless, an intravenous drug user, HIV positive, estranged from his family, had numerous outstanding warrants etc. When I asked him what he wanted to work on I got a very different answer to the one I would have expected. He replied that he used to be a printer, and that this was a profession he eventually wanted to return to. To remain a member of the printers professional association one has to keep up dues which for fairly obvious reasons, he had not been doing lately. He wanted me to make an arrangement so that when he was ready he could return to his profession.

To me this seemed to be the least of his worries and I said so, suggesting that instead we concentrate on a more concrete issue like his housing or his warrants. His reply was straightforward, and he said that I was not listening to him. I learnt two things from this. Firstly it made me realise that the issue we pursue, or try and steer our client towards, has to relate to their ultimate goal. Even if it feels like, or turns out to be, a red herring or an avoidance of the 'real' issue, we have to take it as the starting point. Secondly, given our previous discussion about the imbalance of power in our relationship with clients, it showed a lot of confidence for him to say I was not listening to him so early on in our relationship. It made me think of clients who did not have the confidence to challenge me when I suggested an issue to take forward, and outwardly agreed, but privately lost faith in me or lost ownership of the process.

In a way this is a qualification of the opening statement of the American Planning Association. It is saying that we should not lose sight of the future by over-concentrating on the present at the expense of future goals as this again becomes meaningless. Egan recognises this by saying that in general, we should 'work on a manageable problem or sub-problem'. The issue the client presents with may not end up being the thing we even work on, but links need to be made to the issue otherwise leverage is lost. The most common example practitioners give of a red herring issue is when a client says that if they just had a flat, 'it would all be sorted'. This statement in fact gives us some leverage as it opens up the possibility for a discussion on what it is that needs sorting, and what it is about a flat that will sort it.

The issue that they are willing to work on

This may seem easy, particularly if we have gone by the first criteria and are looking at an issue the client has picked themselves. However, practitioners identified a common phenomenon whereby people identify an important issue to them, but the moment the worker starts trying to engage with it the client shuts down or tries to change the topic of discussion. We will come back to this phenomena in Chapter 13, where we will examine how people are often reluctant to talk about an issue, even if it is a thing they have brought up, when they are moving between the stages of change of pre-contemplation and contemplation (DiClemente, 1991). Suffice to say, the reaction is also viewed by some authors as generally normal and human (Miller and Rollnick, 1991; Prochaska and DiClemente, 1986). As an example, when I have something difficult to say to my partner, I will rarely come straight out with it, I will normally have to change the subject or only go so far a couple of times before a proper discussion happens. As Miller and Rollnick (1991) say, 'ambivalence is normal', making decisions and having frank discussion is the exceptional behaviour for people. We will also consider Motivational Interviewing in the final chapter as a way of dealing with this reaction in a client.

The issue that seems to be causing pain

To consider the issue that seems to be causing pain adds a different dimension. Many authors (Tew, 2002; Bowlby, 1980; Kübler-Ross, 1974) have acknowledged that pain is a barrier and something that we need to overcome. What is worrying to us as resettlement workers is the concern that many of the issues that could be causing pain may also be at the edge of our boundaries, or in areas where we are not professionally competent. We should perhaps remind ourselves of some of the lessons of Chapter 2 when we explored the bridging role of resettlement workers. While we may not deal with the issue we also cannot ignore it. Within the context of working out the issue for leverage, we need to acknowledge the issue causing pain and make the appropriate links between it and the issue we will actually work on. This issue we choose may itself be an issue that achieves leverage for dealing with the painful one. Again, as above, the person may be actively avoiding dealing with this issue, or even acknowledging it. In the latter case it becomes something we note, with the aim of returning to it at a later stage. We will return to this in the chapter on cognitive interventions.

The issue that leads to an improvement of their condition

Egan (1998) sees this as particularly important in the earlier stages of an intervention and is a nice practical counterbalance to some of the more psychological criteria. It is based upon the idea that people will only engage in a thing if they see the benefits, if they can see a net gain from the experience. While there is a rich debate on whether people calculate such a cost benefit analysis in terms of their engagements with services, or indeed in terms of entering into any relationship, it does seem to have some relevance in the early part of a relationship.

I remember one particular initial session with one client, which I thought had gone well. We had, it seemed to me, worked on the issue that achieved the greatest leverage. The client had identified the issue, it was one that she was willing to work on and was the issue that seemed to be causing pain in her life. I was looking forward to the next session, but unfortunately she did not turn up and ceased to engage with the agency. Some months later she came back and I asked her why she had not turned up to our appointment, as I had thought the previous one had gone well. She replied that, from her point of view, it was also good initially. However, it had also opened her up to herself and left her thinking about difficult issues on her own for a few days. In the long term she felt the session had actually made her feel worse about things, so why would she come back for another?

It made me realise that, at least initially; people needed to have a short term net gain from their encounters with me as a worker. Later on in the relationship they could perhaps handle a session that they found difficult, trusting me enough to believe that it would have some longer-term benefit and that all sessions would not be like that. Positively in housing these early net gains are often easy to get. People will often have problems with social security or debt that can be at least alleviated fairly readily. What we need to remember as a worker, and even try and get our clients to realise, is that these gains will not make the big differences in the greater scheme of things. They are a part of building a trusting relationship that can deal with some of the issues that are really causing the blockages inherent to those undergoing resettlement.

Making sense of issues

Interestingly, Egan (1998) talks about the next stage of the process as being able to 'make sense' of the possibilities. It is only after this stage that we start making plans. Egan sees the importance of three tasks and three associated concepts. We need to initially *consider the possibilities*, asking ourselves what are the possible options for action, including all the less favourable ones that we could take. Secondly, we need to *develop an agenda* of what would it take for these to become realities and what would be the consequences. Lastly, we try and *develop commitment* to whichever of these possibilities we could build a reasonable commitment towards and appreciate how it relates to the other ideas and issues previously identified.

It is worth mentioning that Egan (1998) is often closely associated with the growth of task-centred casework. Throughout the 1960s in the USA and Britain, the effectiveness of more traditional psycho-dynamic casework was being questioned. There seemed to be little evidence that it led to any measurable change in service users or their problems, despite lengthy contact (Fisher, 1973). Reid and Shyne (1969) developed task-centred casework as a response to traditional casework, which focused on service users' problems and the tasks they needed to carry out to resolve them, rather than psychological causes. In orientation it represented a move away from the psychological and towards an emphasis on the practical. Cataloguing its development, Mayer and Timms comment:

> A clash of perspective existed, with social workers appearing to focus on psychological investigation and treatment, whereas service users were wanting practical help to change problem situations.
>
> (Mayer and Timms, 1970: 54)

While this was in many respects a positive move, as an orientation it could exacerbate the over emphasis on the practical already noted in the resettlement field.

From my training work, I find that practitioners are often familiar with the basic tenets of the task-centred casework model, associating it with a recent move towards greater setting of goals and targets with clients, and the need to meet outputs under *Supporting People*. However, the tasks practitioners set were also almost exclusively practical, i.e. the client will do this and the worker will do that, as this was their understanding of the model, or what they chose to draw from it. Ironically this was not necessarily the original intent of Reid and Shyne as their model drew on several psychological theories, including behavioural psychology and social learning theory (Hudson and Macdonald, 1986). Their aim was rather on moving from a focus on the past and possible causes of an issue to a focus on the present and possible solutions to the issues. This is a tradition that continues today in the form of 'solution focused therapy' (DeShazer, 1989) a subject we shall return to in the chapter on cognitive interventions.

Practitioners also seemed to apply task-centred casework almost exclusively at the planning and execution stage rather than, as Egan intended, seeing it as equally applicable at the stage of making sense of issues. It seems then that we need to rescue some of the original intentions of Egan and others. We need to see the tasks we set for ourselves and clients as being as much about people's emotions and thinking as about the practical, and as valid at the stage of making sense of issues as it is in planning future developments.

Doel and Marsh (1992) identify five criteria for the making sense of the issues stage of the process:

- Acknowledge the presence of the issue.
- Establish a working definition of the problem.
- Identify what needs to change.
- Identify where they want to get to.
- Agree on what is their motivation.

Below is a model I believe meets these criteria and helps the client to explore their issues. It is a practical tool and is presented in a format that I have used with clients. I will illustrate the model by talking through a common issue in resettlement, that of budgeting.

Before we can start making plans about any issue we need to break down and agree on what we are talking about. The phrase 'I want to learn how to

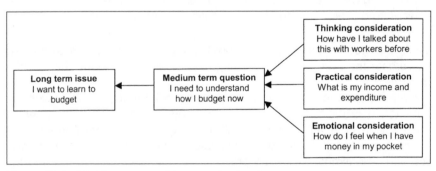

Figure 10.1 Making sense of issues – budgeting

budget', could mean a lot of different things. It could mean that the person wants not to be in debt, it could mean that they want more money, it could mean that they simply want to know how they are spending their money at the moment. Workers can make clumsy assumptions; a theme we will return to when exploring the 'thinking' consideration.

A medium term question, that could help us clarify the end issue, could be to understand budgeting at present. However, even that is a difficult question to answer. Personally I budget by spending money until I get letters telling me not to spend any more. What this does not give me insight into is my relationship with money, perhaps the ultimate question behind the desire to learn how to budget. Therefore this medium term question also needs to be broken down into smaller considerations. I define these as emotional, cognitive and practical considerations, mainly to ensure that the first two considerations do not get overlooked.

Cognitive considerations

It is important to ask clients to consider how they have talked about these issues with workers in the past. We have already explored how in resettlement this will often not be the client's first journey through a hostel, or indeed the resettlement process. It is therefore quite likely that this will not be the first time they have talked about an issue like budgeting. It is useful if clients can explore, and then avoid, unhelpful ways that the subject has been discussed in the past, or any fears they have about having the discussion. As a worker I often based my interventions on received wisdom of what issues were about, or made clumsy equations that made assumptions, tried to miss out stages or over-simplified issues.

A common reaction can be to make the equation that budgeting equals debt, necessitating a first step of filling in an income and expenditure sheet. This can be an important later step, and is given as an example of a practical consideration, but to start with it misses out on so many other possible dimensions. It can also be an invitation to lie as such exercises can end up being slightly embarrassing – gaps appear that people do not venture information about, or the worker suspects the answers given are not true. A client of mine, in response to the question of how this game had been done before with workers, relayed thinking that such exercises were really about finding out if people were engaged in illegal activity or working while claiming benefits. Developing the point, another client reported feeling an inward groan if the worker pulled out an income/expenditure grid. He knew that he would then have to go through a session that neither party believed in, or found useful, and in fact built up barriers between them.

Emotional considerations

The emotional consideration can either explore how emotional factors impact upon a clients thinking or intentions, or how it allows emotional dimensions, such as fears about the issue, to be explored or at least acknowledged. The question 'how do you feel when you have money in your pocket' is more about exploring the former, but can lead onto the latter. On one level the question explores a very human phenomenon, practitioners expressed that they had good intentions on the day before they got paid, often to change their habits and not be in the same position next month. However, on pay-day when they had money in their pocket, their priorities changed. This is useful to help humanise some of the reactions that clients also have. However, there is a difference with many client's situations, and it has to do with the relativity of money.

Practitioners have noted the common phenomenon of clients 'blowing' their community care grants or budgeting loans (discretionary grants and loans obtainable from the Jobcentre Plus for people undergoing resettlement) in spite of the fact that they then move in to a new home with nothing. I remember trying to explore with a client who had just done that, why he had done so and he was being quite evasive. It was only when I asked him how he had felt when he had the community care grant in his pocket (normally anywhere between £250–£1000) that he started to open up. He replied that he had felt 'like a king' for a week; he could go into any bar, buys drinks for everyone, stay in a hotel, go for meals, suddenly have lots of friends and people who wanted to know him.

He knew some of that was false but he did not care, it was a once in a lifetime experience for him as he could never have a sum like that in his pocket again. The alternative had been to spend the money on substandard furniture: on balance he felt that he would rather have the memory. This made me realise the difference in how my clients and I conceive money. I am more used to that kind of money in my hands, at least in theory, and can conceive of it happening again. He could not, and it influenced his behaviour and thinking on the matter. It was by taking a step back that I was able to ask my client whether it would be enough to 'feel like a king' for a weekend or four days as opposed to a week. In this way we were able to make plans for the rest of the money in terms of his flat.

Planning and achieving the tasks

It is not my intent to go through all of the other stages within Egan's 1998 model or the wider model of task-centred casework. Doel and Marsh (1992) and Egan (1998) identify further criteria for these stages. I have picked out ones that, from my training work with practitioners, seem to have relevance to some specific practice points to make:

- *Acknowledge all the possible options, including all the less favourable ones*
  This was seen as important, particularly if the 'game' had been broken and clients felt they could be more honest. The less favourable options for budgeting could include such things as theft, begging, prostitution or cash in hand work. Acknowledgement of these was seen as important as they are often the option of choice for many clients. In this way workers would not suffer the accusation of suggesting 'undesirable' options people had not thought of.
- *Examine and identify the necessary steps for each task*
- *Identify the skills that are needed for each task*
  Clients may have to learn new skills, although, as we explored in the assessment chapters, we should not underestimate the amount of skills people have. Practitioners also thought it was easy to underestimate how some client's may need many steps to achieve things. This was particularly so when it was a thing that the worker did routinely such as make phone calls, contact other agencies or complete forms. Practitioners had many experiences of clients who hid the fact that they lacked the skills, confidence or self-belief to take certain steps. Instead they used diversionary tactics such as questioning the importance of the task or trying to persuade the worker to do it for them.

When I worked on a youth drugs awareness project, a volunteer suggested we did some detached work on the back of buses as this was where many young people 'hung out'. This seemed a good idea and I asked him to ring the bus company and make an appointment for the two of us with the manager. When I questioned him a week later he said he had not got around to it, the week after that he could not find the number, a further week later he thought I should do it and the week after that that it was a bad idea anyway. It was only upon further questioning that it came to light that he had not made the appointment because he was scared to make the phone call. It had not occurred to me because he was always making calls on his mobile phone. He replied that this was different because it was 'important' and meant talking to someone 'more important' than himself. With some coaching he was able to do this and the appointment was made. Developing this point, practitioners thought it equally important to acknowledge that the client may have to learn skills and steps that many people do not. Clients needed some congratulating that they, perhaps unfortunately but nevertheless necessarily, had learnt these skills.

- *Establish who is to take responsibility for tasks*
  Who was allocated which tasks was seen as crucial. On a simple level, practitioners had to resist the temptation to take on too much, particularly

when clients are pushing. Initially workers may do more but by the end of the relationship the balance had to be the other way around or there were worries about the clients ability to cope once the worker had gone. On the other hand sometimes workers could put too much onto the client, creating a potential negative disempowering dynamic. One practitioner described actually talking about the process of task-centred casework with the client. They expected the client to be positive, seeing it as the empowering process that many authors described it as (Macdonald et al., 1992; Doel and Marsh, 1992; Reid and Shyne, 1969). Instead they replied that they actually found it disempowering, the weekly session where the worker started by telling the client all the things they had done as part of the agreement before they discussed why the client had not done theirs. On reflection the worker realised he had been a part of creating this dynamic. He tended to take on tasks he knew he could successfully do, not wanting to let the client down. At the same time he encouraged the client to take on tasks that would push him slightly, to help his continuing development. Instead of feeling empowered, the client had his feelings of inadequacy reinforced, particularly in the face of a worker who could do things.

- *Acknowledge difficulties including ones out of the worker or client's control*
This can be hard, and can leave one in danger of being negative but it is essential, particularly in respect of control. Many things, particularly many practical things, are dependant on the actions of others or, in the case of things like community care grants and housing allocation, are fairly random. Unpredictability can be difficult to handle, I remember working with one client where things were going unusually well. A flat was allocated, more or less where she wanted it, it came more or less at the best time and she got a decent community care grant without having to go to review. The day before they were due to move in the council's housing repairs department went on strike for nine months and she could not move in. The client found this very hard to handle and blamed me for the situation.

We have already covered how important a feeling of control is for clients and how they have often been in positions where they have been controlled. To be subject to random process and to be at the mercy of systems we cannot influence is difficult and there is a temptation to personalise things, to make it less random. Giddens (1996) concept of 'structuration' can be useful here. When people do not feel powerful, or are in situations where they are subject to control, they will find a way of regaining that control, to be able to influence things, even if it is an illusion. This can be equally true when the system is working for people. I remember another client who had a statutory entitlement to housing, but could not really accept this. He only did when he felt that I could 'pull a few strings' and that there were a few 'blags' he also had to pull for the flat to happen. I think this was partly because this was what he was used to, the world he knew, but it seemed also to be important because he then had some influence in the situation.

This tendency could explain the dynamic of the client blaming me for the council strike. In a way I had been party to the dynamic described as I also find it hard to think that I have little control over the situations of the clients. Previously the client had felt that I had got the flat for them, and I had been happy to take some of this credit, probably putting it down to it helping to build our relationship. Unfortunately this had then set up the precedent for these things being within my control. Perhaps practitioners should explore what their role is with clients in greater detail. Many clients of mine believed, or wanted to believe, that I could get them all kinds of things like accommodation, money, access to other services etc. In a way I wanted to believe this myself, as part of my identity as a worker. This helps explain further why there is a tendency in this work to emphasise the practical, because this is perhaps where I could feel powerful as a worker. As we explored in the chapter on worker-client relationships we need to explore our role with clients and find ways of continuing to communicate this to them.

Conclusion

To finish on a simple point, it is all too east to forget to congratulate ourselves on what we have achieved as we go along. The problem with a list of tasks is that that they can end up being just that, a list of things to get through and tick off. People need to see movement and be given a little encourage-ment as they go along. We also need to know how these small things relate to our ultimate goal and it is worth revisiting the process as we go along, lest we fall victim to the phenomenon in the opening quote from the American Planning Association and Brandon and Atherton.

Many other aspects of support planning will be dealt with in other chapters, particularly the chapter on how to record information. Suffice to say that planning is more than just agreeing what needs to happen, its starting point is trying to understand what has gone on and the options that we have open to us.

Chapter 11

Caseloads and Approaches to the Work

The issues around resettlement caseloads have been a source of constant discussion, and little work has been done around good practice in this area . . . Other care models do not cast much light on the subject, having caseloads varying between four and eighty.

(Bevan and Stretch, 1998: 4)

Caseload management sets out the kind and volume of work undertaken by the supervisee. A head count of case files or even of individual service users or families is not usually a good indication of the actual work involved. You will need a consistent and clear weighting system for each case and therefore each worker's case load.

(ELCS Practice Guidelines, 2003)

These two quotes illustrate common concerns expressed by practitioners on courses: how many cases should they hold and how do they differentiate between them? Part of this anxiety may stem from a lack of clarity about how this should be done. The quotes also illustrate two different concerns, one about numbers and the other about volume of work. When practitioners express the above concerns to me, they say firstly that the number to be worked depends on what they are trying to achieve and secondly that how you differentiate between the people making up a caseload depends to a large extent on the worker whose workload it is, not the client. It is these themes that I will expand upon in this chapter.

First though I want to consider the preliminary question of how workers are allocated clients, as this often determines the later questions. In my experience homeless projects have three broad ways of allocating cases, each with various pros and cons.

Caseload allocation

(1) Demand-led

A demand-led system is one where a client in need of a service is allocated to a worker regardless of the existing caseload. This method is most commonly used in day centres and advice centres, but also occasionally in hostels that support people after they have moved into their own accommodation. These projects generally take the view that they respond to resettlement needs as they arise. Workers do not have a set caseload but respond to what presents.

A disadvantage to this approach in resettlement is that we are normally talking about a long-term sustained piece of intervention. As such, a worker's caseload could increase indefinitely as more and more clients engage on this longer-term basis, but do not leave. In reality people need to find a way of prioritising and managing clients. Practitioners (Seal, 2004) may do this by using the aspect of the process that they have some control over, that of being able to close client's cases. Ironically in trying to make our entrance to the resettlement process open, we simply shift the need for control and manageability to another part of it. We will return to the issue of the closing of cases in Chapter 12.

(2) Fixed

Fixed caseloads are most commonly found in hostels where there are a fixed number of people living there. Workers may take on clients from a fixed number of rooms in the hostel, or when the worker next has a space in their caseload, due to closure of an earlier case. This system has the advantage of having a clear numerical amount of clients to work with. However, unless the project has a very distinct target group, and that target group presents with the same level of need, or perhaps more importantly creates about the same level of work for the worker to meet their needs, the predictability disappears. Peaks and troughs in workload may still arise depending on the level of need among the clients.

(3) Flexible

This is becoming a more common model in all settings, and one that can take the best, (but sometimes the worst) from the open and fixed models. Clients are normally classified by the level of support they are likely to need, typically high, medium and low levels of support. There are then, typically, two models of holding cases. The first is where the worker has a fixed caseload with a desired number of each type of case; say 10 low, five medium and three high support need. A second model is where the number of cases is flexible and varies according to the different levels of need among them e.g., 20 low and five medium support cases will be equivalent to 10 medium and five high cases. The choice between the models is often determined by the organisational setting. Hostels often use the former, having a fixed amount of clients while day centres often use the second, as they do not.

Generally this seems to be the most flexible and responsive way to allocate cases. However, it does demand a sensitive allocation policy that will need some human resource invested in it to get the balance of cases right. It also means that a client will need to be assessed before allocation, meaning that the client who does the assessing will not necessarily be the client who takes them on as a case. We will return to the dangers of this approach in the chapter covering referral.

The main question that arises with this method is that it still begs the question of how to decide what constitutes a case being given low, medium or high weighting.

Determining case weightings

Returning to the source of our opening quote, Bevan and Stretch (1998) identify the only attempt at weighting caseloads as having been work in the context of the Rough Sleepers Initiative by Randall and Brown (1996). More recently their criteria were developed further for *Supporting People* (2003). They list their suggested criteria in the appendices to this later report.

- **Low support needs:** requiring mainly practical help such as moving in, finding furniture, connecting utilities, sorting out benefits, initial settling in, contacting local services and identifying social support networks.
- **Medium support needs:** in addition to the practical help listed above, help or advice with other problems, not necessarily needing intensive professional help, but possibly some emotional support or referral to other specialist agencies. It may also involve support on money management to ensure the tenancy is sustained.
- **High support needs:** includes, for example, people with serious mental health problems requiring medication or professional psychiatric involvement, people having substance abuse problems or recovering from abuse, people with a recurring pattern of crisis leading to loss of home, or households with children having serious behavioural problems.

In addition Randall and Brown (2003) say that we can weight our cases in terms of the length of time we work with people. *Short term* is defined as being for up to six months; *medium term* as up to a year and *long term* as being continuing support for at least a year and possibly indefinitely.

The main criticism of these criteria, particularly in their RSI form, is that the mistake is made of equating the presence, prevalence and extent of the needs of the client with the amount of effort a worker will need to expend on them. It is the latter that should determine a person's caseload, as that will impact most on the worker. Practitioners report that their agencies often miss this point. To say that low support needs equate to the client having largely practical issues can miss the point and fall into the positivist trap we explored in Chapter 8 on assessment. These practical issues may end up being a lot of work for the worker, particularly if this is someone who has not been through the experience of being homeless before. The client may not know the ropes, may not have survival skills and will not have relationships with other agencies. The emotional impact of 'becoming' a homeless person may be a very difficult for them to come to terms with in terms of their identity (Snow and Anderson, 1987). Conversely, some clients in Randall's high level criteria will have many agencies involved with them, dealing with their mental health, children, etc. who may actually be able to help on many of the practical issues that will still need to happen. They may also have been around the process a few times and have become adjusted to being homeless, which may or may not be a hindrance.

Further criticisms are that these approaches do not take account of many other factors, subtleties and, crucially, individual variance. These factors might include people's functioning and aspirations within the context of their issues, their journey through the process and interaction with other agencies, the unpredictability of a client's development, the impact of the kind of intervention we have and the impact of local demographics. Randall (2003) has elements of these considerations, but his schema still seems to be outweighed by asking us to look at our clients 'needs'.

To illustrate some of these points, a client of mine had many of the issues that under Randall's (1995, 2003) criteria would indicate a high level case. He was street homeless, HIV positive, an intravenous drug user, estranged from his family etc. However, his functioning within these issues was high and his goals for my intervention were low. He was aware of what issues he faced, of what he needed to do and of what role he wanted me to play. In terms of my intervention he was a low level case. Another case of mine would have scored very low, initially, in that she was already housed, had no debts, had high levels of education and presented with only practical needs. In reality my involvement in the case was both intense and protracted.

The ELSC model

It seems necessary to develop a model of caseload weighting that starts from the very different point mentioned earlier, at looking at the impact of the client on the worker, rather than the more abstract 'needs' of the client. We will examine one such attempt by the consortium ELSC to do this, within the context of field social work. Their criteria are quite different from those of Randall and Brown (1995, 2003) and result in very different weightings:

Complexity: *this includes the number of other professionals the worker is involved with. It recognises the worker's role in drawing together profes- sional networks, for example in child protection case conferences and* *plans, or when helping a family to make decisions about the care of vulnerable or frail family members:*

Low level case: *Contact with other agencies either minimal or operating regularised/unproblematic or standard.*

Medium level case: *Contact with other agencies changeable, requiring initiation or maintenance.*

High level case: *Multiple or complex contact with other agencies requiring careful negotiation/advocacy/development or other high input.*

(Adapted from ELSC Practice Guidelines: Managing Practice, 2003)

A refinement for our context would be to take into account the existence, or non-existence, of agencies in the locality such as BME groups, refuges, mental health services, something with enormous regional variation (DfES, 2003). This seems to be particularly important for homelessness projects as the lack of presence of agencies often means the work falls to the homelessness agency, particularly when the project provides the client's accommodation. Even with statutory agencies, ease of access and levels of provision are just as variable across different regions and often depend on the policies of particular boroughs. This again needs to be taken account of:

Risk: *this considers the professional judgement required of the worker: are decisions to be made based on risk assessment; is the picture a fast changing one; is the work at a stage where professional anxiety is heightened because of lack of information.*

Low level case: No current risk involved or risk assessment known and understood by all parties, with consequent decisions and actions, including contingency plans negotiated.

Medium level case: Risk assessment in process of being undertaken, with options for action and decision ready to be put into place.

High level case: Current risk not assessed or there is a change of circumstances requiring new assessment.

Their approach to risk is interesting and something we touched on in a previous chapter. For them the absence of a risk assessment makes a case higher in its weighting due to unpredictability. This applies on a wider level; we should see unpredictability as a weighting factor generally. This should be both clients where we know there is unpredictability and where we have little knowledge of a client.

Even if there are no support needs identified on admission to a hostel, it is well known how personal problems can come to light as time goes on, if only because of the stressful environment that many hostels present, which in some cases can be considerable.

(Scanlon and Wigglesworth, 2001, quoted in Parkes, 2003: 5)

A second consideration in terms of risk is the impact of a lack of a risk assessment on the stress levels of the worker. This links in with the chapter on support mechanisms for workers. If the practitioner is working with clients with complex needs, and is expected to engage with these needs, rather than signposting other agencies, that worker will have different support needs than one who largely works with clients on a practical level. This is irrespective of whether the case weightings are similar. We need to move away from a view that support for a worker that consists of supervision every four to six weeks is sufficient, regardless of the different client groups they work with. Even if people have the capacity to work for difficult clients in terms of their caseloads, if they do not have the requisite experience, training and support then it is not safe or appropriate to engage with the client.

Travel: *does the worker have to travel appreciable distances to undertake the work with a particular individual or family; for example, placements in another part of the area.*
   Low level case: No travelling outside usual agency area involved.
   Medium level case: Regular, planned travel, no more than once a month.
   High level case: Unexpected travel on an occasional basis or regular travel more than once a month.

While relevant and practical, travel needs to be expanded upon and take account of other aspects of the working context. As an example we need to look at the style of our engagements with people – do we engage with them on an ad hoc basis or do we have an appointment system? More generally we should look at how our context impacts on people psychologically. The intensity of an accommodation project is quite different from that of a day centre and different again for floating support (Bradley et al., 2004).

Limitations

What the ELSC model generally seems to miss out on is the crucial aspect of how the client functions within all of these issues. A client who will engage with the worker and has insight into the issues facing them is very different to one who does not. Also, going back to the previous case studies, we should take account of what the client actually wants us to do. Some clients may want the worker to engage in all their issues and do not trust other workers, some may want to involve other workers but see one as the lynch pin. Others may see the worker as one part of the myriad of care professionals involved in their lives and they have very specific interventions in mind. An adapted version of the ELSC's weighting could look like this:

Table 11.1 Weightings

Criteria levels	Low level case	Medium level case	High level case
Other agency involvement	Minimal, unproblematic or standard involvement. Appropriate agencies exist and are useful.	Contact with other agencies changeable, requiring initiation or maintenance. Some appropriate agencies exist and are accessible.	Multiple. Complex or problematic contact requires careful negotiation/ advocacy/ development or other high input. Many needed agencies do not exist.
Risk and predictability	No current risk involved/risk assessment known and understood by all parties, with consequent decisions and actions, including contingency plans negotiated.	Risk assessment being undertaken, with options for action and decision ready to be put into place. Mainly predictable work, needs reviews.	Current risk not assessed or change of circumstances requiring new assessment. Work changeable and unpredictable.
Client engagement/ capability	Client will engage, takes responsibility has insight into issues and worker has a distinct role.	Client mainly engages, has insight into some issues, role of worker needs reviewing periodically. Worker seen as central.	Client periodically engages and only with that worker. Has flashes of insight, role of worker needs constant negotiation. Reluctant to take responsibility.
Working context	Work happens in project appointment system.	Work happens in a variety of places. Loose appointment system.	Mainly home or street visits off site. Work happens when client will engage.

In theory a numerical weighting system could be applied to this schema (low = 1, high = 3). If this is done weightings could vary from 4–12 which, while complex, is probably a fairer representation of the clients we meet and our varying work loads.

Morse's model

Finally, I would like to challenge Bevan and Stretch's (1998) quote about other care sectors not giving us insight into our practice on caseloads. Morse (2003) has written a fascinating article called *Review of Case Management for People Who Are Homeless: Implications for Practice, Policy, and Research*. In it he examines American approaches to homeless people and the way in which they structure their interventions. He identifies seven approaches to working with homeless people, and goes on to list their structural characteristics. One of these characteristics is how caseloads are held, Morse looks at this within the context of the agencies' whole approach from their philosophies to the length and intensity of their interventions. I have drawn parallels with the structures of services in this country as I think there are some lessons to be learnt. We should try and think a little more widely about the factors that impact upon caseloads incorporating it into the whole working style of our agency and project.

Intensive case management

'The emphasis is on outreach, assisting clients to access needed services and providing advocacy as needed.' He makes a distinction between whether these services are delivered with a large or a small caseload. He thinks either can work, it will just change the shape of the work that is then done with clients. With large caseloads, workers assess clients' needs, plan, link with services and monitor. With medium caseloads they link clients to services, monitor, have a fair involvement, and assist clients in problem-solving and recovery strategies. With small caseloads workers can do aggressive outreach, develop trusting relationships, undertake counselling and give practical assistance. This model seems to have parallels to floating support in this country, with the same emphasis on outreach and a care planning approach.

Assertive community treatment

'The emphasis is on providing intensive treatment and support services in vivo, for an ongoing, open-ended period of time. Staffing is intensive, utilizing an inter-disciplinary team that includes psychiatrist and nurse and a shared caseload.' This model seems to be very close to how CAT teams operate, with multi-disciplinary teams and an emphasis on relationship building, the importance of trust and going at the client's pace.

Clinical case management

Emphasis is placed on an individual therapeutic relationship between the worker and the client. Attention is also given to resource needs and linkages.

Services are provided both in the community and office-based. While not a total match, there seems to be some parallels to day centre work in this country, particularly in the setting and the emphasis on long term ongoing work.

Social casework management

Emphasis is placed on increasing the capacity of the clients' social networks to interact and support each client while also performing functions of outreach, and service linkage. Interestingly this approach seems to be particular to the United States. It seems closer to a community work approach and, as discussed before, there is no tradition in Britain. It would seem to be closer to some of the emerging self-help projects such as those among the Groundswell Network (2004).

Brokerage

Emphasis is placed on assessing, planning, referring and helping clients to access needed services and resources delivered by other providers elsewhere in the community, and monitoring ongoing needs. Contact tends to be office-based and less intensive. This would seem to have a definite parallel to many advice workers approach to working with homeless people, epitomised by the housing aid network of Shelter.

Advocacy

Emphasis is upon providing case-specific advocacy to facilitate clients gaining needed resources and services while promoting client involvement. Staff are generalist with training in mediation, negotiation, and mental health law. Advocacy services are designed to be on-going, as needed. In this country we often see advocacy as a narrower focus around court representation (Shelter 2000), whereas American models have more of an emphasis on community and peer advocacy, again drawing on the community work field (CSNU, 2002). Perhaps this is again an area of further investigation for services.

Critical time intervention

A key feature of critical time intervention is that services are time-limited to a 'critical period' during and after the transition from shelters to housing (limited to nine months). Activities are otherwise similar to Intensive Care Management, but with a special focus on assisting clients to develop stable, ongoing relationships within their natural and service support systems. While there are again some parallels to floating support here, there is again more of an emphasis on developing clients' own natural networks, something not given much emphasis in this country. Interestingly, as discussed in Chapter 2, authors such as Neale (1994; 1996) think we should have much more emphasis on developing clients' own support structures networks and build on their own informal networks.

It is worth noting that two of these models do not work on an individual basis with workers, but take a group approach. Single working, with a client having a dedicated 'key worker' is a model adapted from clinical psychiatry (Watts and Bennett, 1991). This approach has grown over the past 20 years with 71 per cent of hostels in London using the model by the mid 1990s (Harrison, 1996) and anecdotal evidence suggests that that has continued to go up. This can be seen positively, Warnes and Crane (2002) note how it is a model particularly suited to the hostel environment, ensuring certain clients are not neglected and allowing for the development of a more in-depth relationship that ensures consistency for the client.

However, individual working is not the only way on ensuring consistency; in fact a group approach can be more appropriate for some clients (Lehman et al., 1997; Morse et al., 1997). In hostels some clients may not like the formality of an individualised approach or prefer to tell different aspects of their life to different individuals. A group approach also means that clients are exposed to a variety of styles and expertise, which, while there is a danger of confusion, could also be enriching. In a way people will inevitably be exposed to more than one worker style, particularly in hostels. Acknowledging this and adapting a team approach to working with individuals will at least highlight the importance of consistency and perhaps lead to the development of mechanisms to ensure it. Oxford Night shelter has recently adopted a team approach, with any one client being worked on by up to three workers. There are implications for confidentiality and how we record information (discussed in Chapter 7 on recording information). The importance of the flexible approach, taking account of the nature of the clients you work with, rather than simply adopting a key worker approach for organisational convenience is enshrined in the *Supporting People Quality Framework* (2002):

> *Records show that, when necessary, assessments and reviews are carried out by more than one member of staff so as to broaden the skills/ knowledge base.*

(ODPM, 2002)

Conclusion

While there would be merit in further exploring the parallels and lessons to be learnt from American models of structuring work, this is not the scope of this book and this chapter. What is useful here is that Morse produces a schema examining issues of caseloads and highlighting some of the factors and criteria discussed earlier in this chapter. Below is an adapted version of that model that I will leave for the reader as food for thought (and further reading) about a more holistic way to think about caseloads and our approach in general.

Table 11.2 Models of case management

	Intensive Case Management (ICM)	Assertive Community Treatment (ACT)	Clinical Case Management	Social Network Case Management	Broker Case Management	Advocacy	Critical Time Intervention (CTI)
Parallel to British models	Floating support	Streetwork CAT team	Day centre	None or self help	Advice and drop in	Advice and advocacy	Floating support or self help
References	Rog et al. (1987) Wasylenki et al. (1993)	Lehman et al. (1997) Morse et al. (1997)	Kline (1993)	Kline et al. (1991) Bebout (1993)	Morse et al. (1997)	Freddolino and Moxley (1992)	Susser et al. (1997)
Intensity of work	Intense or minimal	High	Medium	Medium	Intense	Intense	Some
Work with other agencies	Extensive	Some	Some	Some	Some	Extensive	Extensive
Service duration	Limited – medium	Ongoing	Ongoing	Medium	Medium	Brief	Time limited
Case-loads	10–15:1 or 25–40:1	10:1	15–20:1	15–20:1	50–80:1	5–10:1	7:1
Service location	Community	Community	In project	Mixed	Office	Mixed	Community
Staffing pattern	Individual	Team	Individual	Individual	Individual	Individual and group	Individual
Staff skills	Generalist	Mental health	Generalist	Community work	Advice	Advocacy	Community work

Section Four
Developing Practitioner Skills, Working With the Process of Change

Chapter 12

An Operational Model for Resettlement Revisited

Doing resettlement work is very often a 'taken for granted' aspect of the work, everyone assumes that everyone else knows what the project does and how the individual workers go about it. In practice, these assumptions seem to have very little justification, even though they apply to the central task of the project workers. We found different and potentially conflicting models of resettlement work, and of the resettlement task.

(Coleman et al., 1990: 28)

Bearing in mind the above quote, it seems that while we have established that resettlement is a process, it is equally important to spend some time exploring what this process looks like. This chapter will concentrate on developing a more generic model of the process. This will be done by examining and deconstructing the 14 stage model of resettlement as outlined in *The Resettlement Handbook* (Bevan, 1998). We will then expand on the theme of resettlement as a process in the chapters examining change in an emotional and a cognitive context.

The National Resettlement Forum (NRF) developed the model in the period 1996–1997 having come to the same conclusion as Coleman that there was a lack of consistency amongst workers as to what their work entailed, and what the process of resettlement was that their clients went through. The forum undertook a mapping of workers perceptions of the stages of the process, exploring what was important within them and any good practice (Bevan, 1998). These perceptions were brought together into a framework with a set of aims, standards and good practice for each of the 14 identified stages: referral, introduction, assessment, housing options, resettlement plan/care plan, referral on, gearing up for change, preparing for the move, the move, settling in, post-move on support, flying solo, evaluation and safety net.

I will be concentrating on three stages; gearing up for change, the move and flying solo. This is for two reasons, firstly because other stages, such as assessment and referring on, are covered in greater detail in other chapters. Secondly of those remaining stages, these later ones have been recognised as needing the most attention and development in evaluation (Randall, 1996) and in my experience have caused the most contention and discussion in training. The lack of attention these stages have received was used as a justification for the splitting of the resettlement task between two teams in the Rough Sleepers Initiative, the Contact and Assessment Teams (CATs) and the Tenancy Sustainment Teams (TSTs) (Social Exclusion Unit, 1997). *Supporting People* also acknowledged the importance of attention to the later stages with substantial investment in floating support schemes. Practitioners have generated much of the material in this chapter. In training I asked practitioners to review these stages using four questions as a framework for the review:

- What is realistic and what is unrealistic about the standards?
- What relative importance do practitioners place on the various stages?
- What emotional reactions do practitioners observe in clients in these stages?
- What are the arising implications and issues arising from these questions?

Gearing up for change

This is the stage where clients have been made, or are about to be made, an offer of accommodation and are waiting to move in. The three identified standards at this stage are:

- to ensure that the client understands appropriate tenancy agreements;
- to ensure they are clear about furniture grants and that the appropriate lifeskills are developed and
- to ensure that issues around cycles of change are explored.

Three issues arose from this stage; what people need to know about tenancy agreements; myths that people create about their impending accommodation and emotional reactions at the stage, leading to a consideration of how much priority it should be given.

Early models of resettlement covered legal aspects such as a basic understanding of tenancy agreements (Randall, 1994). They were often structured in the form of 'lifeskills courses', lasting several weeks that clients were encouraged or given incentives to attend. Bevan (1998) says in his evaluation of resettlement that we should, 'go through a specimen tenancy agreement. It is very important that the client knows what the main sections are before they sign it'. However this still begs the question of what is it important that people understand.

I asked a client who had attended one of these courses what he thought of it. He said that if he had to know all this law just to get a flat then he was not sure if it was worth it. This reaction illustrated to me a fundamental flaw of these courses in that people do not need to know all of these things to have accommodation and to give this impression can intimidate people.

When I lived in a council flat some years ago the majority of my neighbours did not know what a tenancy agreement meant. They knew that they had a flat from the council and that there were certain basic rules of survival that went with it. Firstly, that if they made a nuisance of themselves too much or did not pay the rent the council would get rid of them eventually. Secondly, if they got a letter they did not agree with they went to 'the office' and talked to someone about it. Finally, if they did not understand the letter they found someone who did and then went down with them. Are there no parallels between what my neighbours knew and what clients need to know?

It was interesting to examine what constitutes nuisance with clients, as practitioners had worked with many clients who had been evicted for this. Bevan (1998) expresses this area as understanding a tenant's rights and responsibilities. Practitioners on my courses did this in different ways, many simply telling people their rights and responsibilities and some getting them to explore what they thought those were. Some practitioners described taking a step back in an attempt to understand why clients had become a nuisance. One way of eliciting this was to ask clients what the flat represented to them. A common reaction for people who had been in a hostel for some time was that it was freedom, a freedom to do what they liked free from interference, in a way that they could not do in the hostel.

This approach therefore combines this first standard with aspects of the third standard, exploring issues of change, which is in many ways more fundamental. We covered in the assessment chapters how privacy in hostels was minimal and the impact this could have on people. Smith (1995), talking to rough sleepers found that their reason for not going into hostels was a desire for more freedom, less constriction and interestingly, that the street afforded more privacy. It is important to explore ideas, such as being able to do whatever they want in their own flat, with clients, as they have dangers. However, these ideas are touching on some fundamental needs (Brandon, 1998) that clients have emotionally invested in the flat. As such those deserve as much attention as the task of exploring tenant's responsibilities.

We will return to other emotional reactions at this stage in Chapter 13 on Prochaska and DiClemente (1990) and on transitional theory, as they are linked to these models. Suffice to say at this point that practitioners often identified two common, but opposite, reactions. People either were not really interested in thinking about the change they were about to face or they were very worried about it, sometimes to the point of obsession. Both are understandable and documented reactions to impending change as we shall later explore (Selye, 1956; Bowlby, 1961; Kübler-Ross, 1969; Klinger, 1975).

In explaining the phenomenon to clients or practitioners I draw a parallel to the reactions my students have and which I used to have to assignments and exams. As a child I never did homework until the last possible moment, finding creative ways of avoiding thinking about it. In later years when I came back to education my reactions were different, I worried about my assignments and what was being asked of me. I remember going to my tutor and asking many times for clarification about a particular criterion of the assignment or how exactly to do a bibliography. It was not until he asked whether there was anything that he could say that would take away my fear of doing the assignment that I realised the real significance of my behaviour.

This calls into question much received wisdom about resettlement that preparation is all (Randall, 2002; Dane, 1998). Many of these studies make a mistaken logical leap. Their premises are based on the fact that homeless people have said that they did not feel ready for their move and were not prepared for the reality of it. From this the researchers conclude that people should be better prepared, avoiding the reality that many people cannot face things until they happen or become paralysed with fear about the change (Bowlby,1982). In these cases Bevan's (1998) standard that we should 'explore the consequences of change' with clients becomes problematic. Some cognitive interventions can help in this matter, and we will explore them in the final chapter. However in cases where we cannot break through to people, the question becomes how we can support people when they have to face things, bringing us to the importance of the move.

The Move

This stage is rightly identified by Bevan (1998) as being key in the resettlement process. Practitioners identify it as a flashpoint for clients. Practitioners note a common client mantra during assessment: 'the flat will make things sorted'. For clients the move can be the first time that they face the reality of moving into their flat and the deception of their mantra. This is a natural reaction for all of us, but for our clients it can be more acute. To seek and even identify a simple answer to the complexity of problems we face is noted by many authors as common (Derrida, 1974; Miller and Rollnick, 1993; Pratt, 1992). This is a very human reaction, I often identify the new job I have got, or the holiday I need or the house I am moving to as the answer to my problems. With clients it is just that the deceptive nature of this common fallacy hits them at a particularly vulnerable time. This is exacerbated by the realities practitioners identify about the move, as we will now discuss.

While Bevan (1998) suggests standards of 'making sure the property is ready for the move' and that 'furniture has been secured'. In reality, when clients are moving into public housing, rather than other forms of supported accommodation, they are often made an offer without notice, have to view within a few days and sign for the tenancy just as quickly, possibly on the same day as the viewing. This means that the preparing for change and gearing up for change is often condensed into a matter of days, which can be consumed with practical issues. It used to be possible to claim dual housing benefit for a period of up to four weeks, but this option is now severely restricted (NHA,1998). People will rarely have a community care grant (if they receive them at all) before they move. Restrictions in terms of health and safety (Randall, 1994), has at the same time meant that furniture resource projects are limited in what furniture they can give people. Consequently people often move in with little or no furniture.

Many authorities also do not do carry out repairs until a person had moved in, fearing vandalism or squatting (Reeve and Coward,2004). Finally, homeless people are often given one offer of accommodation (Smith,1995) and the impact of housing policy in the last 20 years (Balchin, 1998) has meant that housing stock, particularly in the south, is often hard to let accommodation where people did not want to take up the right to buy. Put that together and we can see how facing the reality of an unfurnished 'hard to let' in a state of disrepair, far from friends and all that is familiar, and certainly not the solution to all their ills, is indeed a difficult thing to confront.

Given this stark reality, it is surprising how often practitioners do not give priority to this stage. This is partly to do with the structure of agencies; much resettlement work is still done by hostel workers (Bevan and Williamson, 2002) who do not have the capacity to support people in the move, due to the need for cover in the hostel. I presume that it is for this reason that Bevan (1998) stresses the importance of handing over to another worker in the standards. Even when workers have the theoretical capacity to help clients with the move, whether they do or not is often determined by what other appointments they have that week. Given the lack of notice as to when clients get flats and the relatively short timescales involved this can easily mean that they will not support their clients. Perhaps workers need to prioritise this stage, even if it means disappointing or annoying other clients because of cancelled meetings. Perhaps they would be consoled by the knowledge that they will receive similar priority when they themselves move. It may also show them how important a stage the move is.

The standards of this stage start by saying how important it is to give both practical and emotional support on the day of the move. Given time constraints it is more important to consider what it is realistic to achieve and perhaps whether emotional or the practical support is more of a priority on the day of the move. I would argue that it is the former as one practitioner memorably said on a recent course:

> . . . there are probably many people they know, or we could get, to help them practically in their move, but how many people could they be honest with about the mixed emotional reactions they may be having.

On one memorable occasion I remember moving a client into his flat one morning and leaving him sitting in his chair surrounded by boxes and looking content. For some reason I felt that I would just check in on him on my way home that night. When I got there his door was open and when I went into his room he was still sitting in his chair, holding the same cup of tea; he had not felt able to move. This incident changed my practice to only supporting people in their practical move if I had time, but I would normally go and see them the afternoon after their move and support them emotionally. This did not always make me popular with clients as they wanted practical help and as we have said could often not face the emotional side of the move until they were experiencing it.

Resettlement workers often do not have a lot of ground to negotiate with social landlords over when people can move in, but perhaps we could persuade them to make it Monday morning instead of Friday afternoon or, at worst, Friday morning rather than the afternoon. One agency I worked with used to routinely move people in on a Friday in the belief that it would be positive that the clients would have the weekend to settle in. After the course they did indeed re-negotiate this to being Monday morning and found that their rate of failure in the first few days halved.

Another area of standards Bevan (1998) mentions is around furniture. The standards are 'whether the person(s) have the basic household items, and/or did they have the wherewithal to have a meal and bedding on the first evening'. There is some realism to this in that it recognises that people will often not have a full complement of furniture. However, it still begs the question of what basic household items are and whether the ability to have a meal and bedding is the most crucial aspect of this.

Seeing these items as a priority could be seen as following the priorities of Jobcentre Plus, as the items they consider a priority for a Community Care Grant are a bed, bedding and a cooker (NHA, 2001) Strangely this has entered the consciousness of workers and when I ask their opinions of what the essential items are on courses; these items are the most common replies. Interestingly when I have asked the same question of clients on courses the priorities are often very different. Often with single people it is things like televisions, books, radios, company and drink that are seen as priority items.

This brings me to an important consideration about the move, it goes back to the question of what the stage represents, something perhaps not emphasised enough by Bevan (1998). There are both conceptual and practical dimensions to this and it is important that we get them both across to the client. Conceptually we need to emphasise that the move represents a stage in the process and not the end of it. There will also be a change in both the circumstances and the nature of the relationship with the worker, possibly a change of worker.

Given the flashpoint nature of the move in practice, it is also important to redefine what we think that means practically. In this sense the move represents a return to bare survival as the client will often be materially worse off. Hopefully that will not be permanent, but this stage could quite easily continue in the medium term. For resettlement clients this may not be as difficult as we might imagine. Many clients will be used to survival, either on the street or in a succession of temporary accommodations. The danger is when they or the worker have built the move up to being something more. Returning to the themes in our chapter on definitions, the move represents a move to a house, but not to a home. The home will be the end result of a process of building, of which the achievement of accommodation is but the start.

Returning to the question of priority items, and bearing in mind what the move actually represents, when considering the move my question to clients changed from 'what do you want in your new home' to one of 'what is the one thing that will help you not pack it in, when you are trying to survive for the first few days'. The answers I got were interesting, and quite personal. One woman, who had been through domestic violence, felt that as long as she had the wherewithal to wash she would be ok. This is a far cry from the bed, bedding and cooker that I would prioritise.

Flying Solo

Finishing or closure is seen by most authors (Anthony and Pagano, 1998; Epson and White, 1995; Gutheil, 1993; Robb and Cameron, 1998) as a crucial part of the process of working with a client. The standards in *The Resettlement Handbook*, as stated, seem fair enough and reflect the sentiment that this is an important stage. It states that when we finish we should, 'review their initial needs and reasons for support', 'reinforce their achievements, the changes they have made and the support that will follow on'; 'clearly list the reasons for closure, as they do not want to feel rejected'; 'list future considerations: rehearse lapse or risk situations and develop strategies for handling them, looking to refer for alternative support if needed'.

However, practitioners' experience was that most of their endings did not happen like this. Most relationships were reported as having finished with either a 'bang' or a 'whimper', the relationship ended following an argument or a misdemeanour or the relationship simply faded, the worker eventually stopped knocking and/or the client stopped answering. A third variation of the ending was that the client sought to perpetuate the relationship, even when objectively the task was done. Whenever the discussion turned to the idea of the worker withdrawing support the client presented with a crisis that perpetuated the relationship. In my own practice I remember discussing with a client about why our previous relationship had ended with an argument, his reply was that I would not go away and so he got rid of me in the way that he ended many things, by creating that argument.

This made me realise how unclear I was about when I think an intervention is over. Practitioners reported that they were similarly unsure of what criteria they had for ending relationships with clients, beyond people being able to practically manage their households. It seems that practitioners also lacked a way of having effective closure, either for themselves or clients. The aforementioned Dutch model of resettlement, emphasising other relationships beyond the worker as a criteria for withdrawing support, starts to make sense. To achieve this we need to return to some other authors' thoughts about the ending process.

Developing this further, Meyersohn and Walsh (2001) identify three considerations for a worker regarding endings. The first of these, to assess factors that are likely to influence the client's response to endings, seem to be broadly similar to Bevan's standards (1998). However there is more of an emphasis on looking at levels of dependency and attachment of the client to the worker. Anthony and Pagano (1998) see having another agency involved with the client as easing this transition with an individual worker; unfortunately this is often not the case with resettlement. Interestingly they identify a second consideration, developing the ideas of Robb and Cameron (1998), as the worker needing to consider their own attachment and detachment to the client. While this thought initially puzzled many workers they agreed that to have impact was a significant source of motivation. This is not unusual amongst care workers and invokes Brandon's (1998) four magnet model once more, as the need for control.

Bevan (1998) talks about the relative merits of three types of ending styles:

- **Open:** when people's needs have been met.
- **Fixed:** a set time frame.
- **Flexible:** a set time frame that can be re-negotiated.

When asked for their preference practitioners invariably thought the open style was most responsive to client's needs. When practitioners considered their own feelings on endings, they saw that this choice was often for mixed reasons. Sometimes it was so that the client did not feel rejected, sometimes it was because the worker needed closure and was insecure about whether their intervention had been right or not, and sometimes because the worker themselves would miss their interactions with the client.

Interestingly client reactions were mixed; while many did indeed find this style reassuring, as it meant they were not being abandoned, as many found it disempowering as it implied that the process would never end, that they would always be in deficit, or that they could not be trusted on their own. Meyersohn and Walsh's (2001) third consideration is at this emotional level, saying we must attend to and validate the client's feelings about the end. This can include the sharing of our own feelings, reinforcing the concept of purposeful expression of feelings and controlled emotional involvement (Biesteck, 1961) discussed in Chapter 4:

> *Natural unsettling feelings for the client may include sadness, relief, loss, anger, guilt, inadequacy and anxiety . . . feelings of satisfaction may include pride in accomplishments, an appreciation of the relationship and excitement about the capacity for other attachments. Most clients have mixed feelings, but the worker can frame the ending as a positive episode in the client's management of separation. Near the end of the relationship the worker may share some of his or her own reactions . . . this highlights reciprocity in the relationship.*

> (Meyersohn and Walsh, 2001: 6)

Of interest here is the phrase that the end of the relationship is but an episode for the client. It seems therefore important to give consideration to the meaning of the end of the relationship for both client and worker.

Returning to ending criteria, practitioners were asked how they would know when the intervention was over and how this was expressed to the client. Many practitioners answered along the lines of 'when the client's needs had been met', particularly when an 'open' style of ending had been adopted. This statement begs the question of what needs we are talking about, and practitioners thought it was predicated on the field's centricity on practical issues. If we are to include cognitive, emotional and practical needs, then this is a strong statement, and perhaps an unrealistic one. A more realistic notion could be that we will work with them until they no longer need us and that the needs and issues that they still have, can be met by themselves or with others. More starkly, given issues of resources and attachment, the debate could centre on how the client and the worker are going to cope with the fact that the intervention may well have to end before both parties feel that it should.

Meyersohn and Walsh (2001) offer four strategies for having this discussion with a client. The first three are topics to reflect on: that everyone's life includes continual oscillations between togetherness and parting; a review of the client's methods of coping with separation, dependence, and anger and finally a review of the client's past, present and future, so that they can help form a coherent sense of identity. The fourth strategy is a series of rituals to mark the ending of a relationship. Many of Bevan's (1998) standards are a form of this, other suggestions are in the form of art work, diaries and even graduation ceremonies. Perhaps though, it is worth remembering that sometimes endings will just be messy, or they may simply fade. College graduation ceremonies are strangely surreal affairs that many graduates, including myself, avoid.

Conclusion

Phillips (2001) notes how friendship groups often end messily and simply disintegrate when their time has gone. Given this, it may be worth reassuring clients and workers that this may be how their relationship ends, and that if this does happen, then this is alright too.

As I stated at the beginning, I have only covered certain aspects of the resettlement process as outlined by Bevan (1998). If the reader has time I would recommend that they review the other stages for themselves, using the questions I set practitioners if that has seemed like a useful framework.

Chapter 13

Prochaska and DiClemente and the Cycle of Change

The fact that it (the process of change) is a wheel, a cycle, reflects the reality that in almost any change process, it is normal for the person to go round the process several times before achieving a stable change.

(Miller and Rollnick, 1991: 15)

When I first became a worker my natural inclination was not one of a theoretician. It seemed to me that academics made up stories about other people's lives. Yet as many authors have said (Wolfe, 2000; Richardson, 2000) the process of theory making is simply one of someone trying to explain what they have observed. In this sense we are all theoreticians as we all have a sense of how things are going to go, or at least thoughts about it. This is often labelled 'common sense', the problem being that it is often not 'common', as in it is commonly held, and does not always make sense, as in coherent. The main issue here is that the model, with its assumptions and ideas, will not be explicit, and being implicit will not be contestable. By this token it means that our clients will have a theory, an idea, of how the process of resettlement will go. What we need, therefore, is a method of bringing their ideas about how things are going to go to the fore and examining them, as they often will not make sense.

We acknowledged in Chapter 2 that the process of change is rarely a linear model. However, many of the clients I worked with assumed it would be. People rarely enter into a process of change, at least consciously, with the idea that this time it will not work but it will be about learning, rehearsing, for the time it does. However, returning to Miller and Rollnick (1992), the process of change rarely follows this pattern and the person will often not make it first time. This fact has been noted in many other change situations, in dieting (Moore and Shepard, 2002), drug use (Klein, 1993), and domestic violence (Burman, 1993). With drinking a person will often attempt to stop drinking four or five times before they stabilise (Miller and Rollnick, 1993). There has been no systematic research into entrenched homelessness, or resettlement, as to how many times people go through the process before they are successfully resettled, but indications are that it is rarely once (Big Issue in the North, 1998; Crane, 1997; Randall and Brown, 1994).

I remember one client I worked with, let us call her Sinead. She was in a situation where I thought the flat we obtained for her could work out, but that realistically, it could just as easily not. To compensate for this, when working with her I placed great emphasis on the fact that things do not necessarily work out first time and that she could come back to me if she felt she needed to. At the time this did not seem to be a message she wanted to hear, she seemed more concerned with knowing when her flat would be ready. Things did not work out when she moved into the flat and it eventually broke down. Unfortunately, she was not engaging with me at this point.

Three months later I saw her walking towards me in the street. Seeing me, she turned around and walked the other way. This being my days of less than best practice, I ran after her and asked her what the matter was; we had agreed that we could talk about things if they broke down. I remember the look in her face, it was a mix of shame, guilt, remorse about what had happened and anger: anger at herself for having let herself and other people down and anger at me for being a reminder of this. It made me think that I had to find a more effective way of talking to people about the process of change and to engage with their 'models' of how they thought things were going to go.

Prochaska and DiClemente developed a model in the 1980s that offers us some insight into the process of change. There are several versions of their model (Miller and Rollnick, 1993) but broadly there are six stages:

- pre-contemplation (not thinking about it)
- contemplation (thinking about it)
- decision/ determination (deciding on a course of action)
- action (starting off)
- maintenance (where you have changed but have not got used to it) and
- the final stage where you have either changed or you have relapsed (evaluation).

The statements in brackets are the translations I have used with clients in explaining the model. I am not happy with the term relapse. It seems to imply a model of abstinence, i.e. a person has relapsed into drinking with abstinence as the only alternative. It seems an odd choice of a word given that it was developed in the context of alcohol use and sought to challenge the notion of dependant drinking and the primacy of abstinence (Prochaska and DiClemente, 1985).

What the term relapse does not take account of is that the initial decision could have been wrong. Relapse implies that the decision was right, but the person needed to change their behaviour, their thinking or their reactions to their emotions. Indeed it could be that their emotional and cognitive reactions have led them to choose a course of action that is not right for them. Perhaps a better term would be 'evaluation', that is, evaluation of both the decision and the actions and feelings that accompanied it, following Bisteck's (1961) notion of 'purposeful expression of feelings and controlled emotional involvement'. It could be beneficial for a worker to find an example from their own life that illustrates the feelings of going through a change. It would need to be one with sufficient ambiguity in the decision stage to allow for the possibility of the wrong choice having been made. My example is about the process of becoming a vegetarian.

Initially I spent a long time flitting between the pre-contemplative and contemplative stage of change, a phenomenon we will return to later. The decision stage was interesting in that I decided to go straight to becoming a vegan. DiClemente (1991) identifies a common reaction to change as making an extreme decision, 'If I am going to make a change then I may as well make it a big one' or, as was the case in many clients I worked with; deciding to change everything, accommodation, relationship, drug use etc. Unfortunately DiClemente also recognises that these decisions are often the least likely to stick.

Similarly DiClemente says that strength of determination to change is not matched by a similar success rate. He went as far as to say that 'being adamant about a change can be a sign of a weak rather than strong determination to change' (DiClemente, 1991: 197). Other authors such as Alexander and Ruggieri (1998) feel that determination is the most important factor in a successful transition. Unfortunately, and by their own admission, they concentrate on examining successful transitions and this would not preclude determination being an equally important factor in unsuccessful ones. In unsuccessful change DiClemente (1991) says that to make determined statements can be an indication that a client needs to convince the worker that the change will happen as they have not really convinced themselves.

Coming back to my example, in the action stage I felt great, I was starting to re-learn cooking, my friends and family were supporting me and my sense of self-righteousness about my choice was probably insufferable. It was in the maintenance stage that problems started to occur, another stage we will explore in greater detail later. I started cheating. I had developed cravings for milk and cheese and eventually acted upon them. What was interesting was my behaviour. I felt exceedingly guilty about what I was doing, harbouring fantasies that people would reject me. Logically I knew this was not true but it did not stop how I felt. I became secretive, going to cafes out of town for tea and sandwiches.

Eventually a friend of mine did catch me out. Afterwards I asked him how I had looked when he had 'caught' me. He replied that my face was a mix of guilt, shame and anger, in fact very much like Sineads from my earlier example. At this point I was tempted to give up and go back to eating meat. Instead I chose to become a vegetarian, something I thought was a little more realistic but that did not represent giving up completely. This change worked and went on to become a lifestyle I sustained for many years. Importantly it meant that the initial change had not been a failure but a part of the process and that it took more than once to go through the process before a change became real.

We could examine many of the stages of change in more detail. However two stages, or more accurately the borders between two stages, seem to be particularly pertinent to resettling homeless people. These are when people are moving between the pre-contemplative stage and the contemplative stage and when people in the maintenance stage are at the crossroads between making the change 'real' and 'relapsing'.

Maintenance

Maintenance is not an absence of change, but the continuance of change.
(Kent, 1993: 314)

In terms of resettlement interventions maintenance is normally when someone has moved into accommodation, has got over the initial shock of the move, but then things start to become a little more complex. As the quote above indicates, this stage takes time and this is a surprise as people often think, or want to believe that the process is over as soon as the change happens. It is in this stage that people are vulnerable as they may be thinking that they have failed because their feelings are ambiguous and their behaviour and thoughts are not fitting their model of how things should be going. Kent (1991) identifies three common reactions:

- ambivalence and premature self-efficacy
- rigidity and fear and
- reluctance to engage.

I will examine them in turn.

Ambivalence and premature self-efficacy

Some clients may believe they have gone as far as they want to or need to when they reach the actions stage. They may be reluctant to consider that they need further help, because they expect counselling or treatment to finish once they have made initial changes.

(Kent, 1991: 315)

Kent (1991) is talking about premature self-efficacy; thinking you have got there before you actually have. Kent says that this is a very human reaction, and one just wants the change to be over. With resettlement clients it often takes the form of thinking that once they are in their flat, the process is over. They may want to end their relationship with the worker or see all those other issues and goals that had been agreed in the action plan as somehow not so important.

Interestingly, Kent (1991) locates the source of premature self-efficacy as being just as likely to come from outside sources as from the individual. This can be from the expectations of others, such as family or agencies, or from the structure of the services, with their implicit assumptions. For an example, many homeless agencies are structured on the assumption that people have been successfully resettled once they have moved (Harrison, 1996). Some of this may be for funding reasons; *before Supporting People,* many hostels could not support people after the move because the support they were given was funded through their housing benefit, so once they moved out the money stopped. There is also the legacy of housing being seen as the solution to homelessness, so once the client has a place a worker's job is done.

Rigidity and fear

Clients who have achieved what they have for so long desired, may at first feel extremely pleased with having done so. They may appear to be almost superstitious in how they act: Nothing must be altered, they believe, lest it break the 'spell' of their new behaviour pattern.

(Kent, 1991: 315)

The above quote illustrates the reaction of rigidity and fear in the maintenance stage. When a person first moves into their flat they have a way of dealing with the things they face that works. However they do not work to a model that sees change as a continual process (DiClemente, 1991) and feel that if they stray from their initially successful pattern everything will fall apart. I remember discussing with one client about what he would do when he moved into his own premises. He identified several things that he saw as positive steps. He could eat out, and not have to eat the food at the hostel. He wanted to go swimming as he was aware that he had not been fit for a lot of his life. He did not mind the occasional pint of beer as he felt he could control this now and had previously been denied the opportunity, as the hostel was a dry one. Finally he was looking forward to choosing what to watch on television in the evening, as he had not been able to do so in the hostel.

When I visited him a few months after he moved in, he quite carefully and insistently relayed how he spent his days. He would get up in the morning, go for a café breakfast, then for a swim, he would have a pint on the way home and spend his evenings watching television, but was starting to feel as though the walls were coming in. He confessed fear at moving away from this pattern as it had worked well so far, although cracks were starting to show.

Perhaps the most common manifestation of the phenomenon is what Kent (1991) calls 'rescue me'. We mentioned in the previous chapter practitioners have reported a common experience that when the task of resettlement is coming to an end, and nothing more needs to happen, some clients do not want to let go. Practitioners went on to describe how when any discussion is had about the worker leaving, or the relationship ending, the client will create another 'crisis' to perpetuate the intervention. Perhaps in this case we have become a part of the pattern of their behaviour, or routine, that they are afraid to move away from.

This final letting go is identified as very difficult in other fields, particularly the dependency field (Allsop and Saunders, 1991). In my working career I knew many people who were on relatively small amounts of methadone for years. If they were taken off suddenly they would often go back to using street drugs, and often a lot of them. We cannot explain this behaviour as them meeting a chemical need but the methadone fulfilled a psychological one. The problem is when resettlement workers become a client's metaphorical methadone, with the client feeling that as long as the worker comes round every few weeks then he will be all right.

Reluctance to engage

The final maintenance reaction is the opposite of this and the client does not ask for help. I have found that some clients would lose accommodation for reasons where I could have usefully intervened but they did not tell me. When I asked them why, a common reaction was that 'I had done so much for them already that they did not want to be a burden.' This was despite my constant telling them that I was paid to be with them and they could bring up other issues. While there could be many reasons for this behaviour, Kent (1991) says that sometimes it can be put down to a lack of self-esteem and self-belief, coming from a perception that they were not worthy of having an intervention. A slight variation of this is where people do not think they are worthy of success and consciously, or unconsciously, sabotage their initial success. In many ways these are the most difficult reactions to respond to as, given their nature, they will often be happening when the client is are not engaging with the worker. We will return to this question, and the more general question of what to do with all these reactions in the conclusion to this chapter.

Pre-contemplation/Contemplation

This stage is of particular interest to resettlement workers as we have acknowledged that a client will probably go through this stage several times before making change stick. DiClemente (1991) sees it as one of the most crucial stages that often sets the tone for people's reactions in later stages. Operationally this stage is often when someone is starting to re-engage with the project after a failed attempt or when a client engages with an agency having been through a different one.

The latter case would seem to need particular sensitive handling as the worker will be inheriting legacies from the client's previous engagement with services, about which they will have little if any knowledge and will take some time to gain a picture of. In the former it would be worth reflecting on practitioner's feelings about clients' re-engagement with their service. Workers may feel anger, sometimes feeling that they let the client down, and sometimes at the client for letting the worker down. Even if we accept that a person may not succeed in their goals the first time round we may still find this difficult. As the client hopes that each time will be successful so may workers, feeling that a 'failure' is a reflection on them, and the effectiveness of their interventions.

Bevan (1998) reinforces this perception, for while he acknowledges the reality of needing a safety net (one of his identified stages) he still portrays it as a crisis situation, an unfortunate occurrence, rather than a natural part of the process. That our clients are first time successes is something we are judged on by our funders. The numbers of people 'successfully resettled' is a criteria for *Supporting People* (2002) as it was for the Rough Sleepers Initiative before it (DoE, 1997). It is justifiable to measure us by the impact of our interventions. However, we need to argue for a subtler approach and criteria that are more reflective of the nature of change and the fact that statistically, many people are not likely to make it first time.

Judging workers by the criteria of 'successfully resettled' also assumes that the power to change lies within workers and not the client. While we are undoubtedly a significant part of the equation, clients need to go through the change process themselves. Criteria like re-engagement with services, a change in the time periods between attempts, a change in entrenched destructive behaviour or a change in choices that have historically not worked would seem to be more appropriate measures.

DiClemente (1991) documents four common reactions in this stage:

- reluctance
- rebellion
- resignation and
- rationalisation.

Reluctance

Reluctance is where someone does not want to engage with the service or talk about their unsuccessful attempts to change. One could say that this is reflected in the fact that people are not there, however internally another characteristic of these reactions is that they are not necessarily logical, or consistent which is helpful to distinguish them from genuine considerations. The reactions have elements in them that are inviting the worker to re-engage with them. In the reluctance stage this can be that people come to the service but withdraw when you try and talk to them. They want you to know they are there but are not ready yet to engage. Drawing a parallel with my own smoking, when I have not succeeded in giving up again, I say that I do not want to talk about it. However I will feel the need for others to understand that I do not want to talk about it, talking at some length about the fact that it is something that I do not want to talk about. Some clients would ring me up to tell me that they did not want to work with me or come back to the service. One wonders why they felt the need to ring me and tell me rather than voting with their feet. Sometimes it could be that they felt the need to give me this feedback, but sometimes I think they were trying to tell me something else.

Rebellion

Again drawing a parallel, rebellion is where I as a smoker have thoughts like, 'why should I pack in smoking, I enjoy it', 'why is everyone putting pressure on me to stop' (even when they are not). For homeless clients it can take the form of accusations that we did not keep our side of the bargain, or forced them into making a decision when they were not ready or that they were perfectly happy where they were and we were trying to get rid of them. Again a need is felt to come and tell us about this rather than just talking about it to others. Similarly I feel the need to tell people who may encourage me to stop again rather than sharing my thoughts with more hardened smokers. (I may talk to the latter in the pre-contemplation stage, but that changes when I am on the boundaries between pre-contemplation and contemplation.)

Resignation

Resignation is a difficult reaction to respond to as the person will say that they can never change and that the situation is hopeless. As a smoker I may feel that I cannot stop smoking. Others may be able to, but I do not have the sufficient will power, motivation or ability to do it. Sometimes we can put a client's contradictions to good use, for while they are saying that they cannot change, the fact remains that they are saying it to the worker, the person who will encourage them to try again. Their very presence demonstrates that they have some hope, even if they do not recognise it at the time. If they really had no hope, why were they there?

Rationalisation

The final reaction, rationalisation, is perhaps the most difficult as it appears to be rational and can be hard to distinguish from a genuine rational explanation. It can take two forms, a half-rationalisation and an over-rationalisation. A half-rationalisation is a reasoning that does not stand up to scrutiny. As a smoker I will often use half-rationalisation like, 'it is more dangerous to cross the road' or that 'I could get run over by a bus tomorrow'. If I were to follow the first statement through to its logical conclusion I would have to say that I will therefore smoke but will never cross the road again, but I do not. The 'bus argument' is linking two unrelated truths, I may get run over a bus tomorrow, but it will not stop me killing myself through smoking. For clients half-rationalisations are normally about why accommodation failed. Practitioners on my courses have identified a multitude of different manifestations of this from practical reasons like, 'I did not have all the furniture', 'it was not in the street I wanted', 'I did not have any curtains'; to more emotional reactions like, 'I just felt it was the wrong place', 'my neighbours looked at me in a funny way'. Again, as we acknowledged before the difficulty is distinguishing these from other genuine reasons. The difference can be that people become resistant to thinking these reasons through and being challenged on them, as I do when people challenge my smoking half-rationalisations.

Over-rationalisations are when we make the issue so complex, intertwined and intractable that change seems impossible. For clients that may take the form of an attachment to life on the street, or the hostel and their friends there, that becomes their tale against change. It can also be associations with accommodation, like Jimmy in Chapter 2 identifying his reasons for not sleeping in his flat became his flat reminded him of his mother's house. I would not want to deny that sometimes things are very complicated for our clients and the issues they face, but it must be a consideration that it could also be an elaborate reason for why change is not possible.

Critiques and uses of the model

With all of these reactions we have examined, the question that remains is how we can respond to them. On one level it can be enough to simply point them out, to give a name to them. People may not have realised how they were reacting or may feel ashamed of their reactions. We can point out to the client that they may be creating crises because they fear the worker leaving. It may also change our discussions with clients – instead of dealing with the crisis we can say that one happens whenever we, as the worker mention leaving Then we can focus on whether the client has noticed this and why they think it might be happening. Some of the discussion mentioned in the previous chapter around endings might then perhaps then become possible.

Conclusion

Whether clients are aware of their reactions or not, it may be worth pointing out that these reactions, may not be logical, but are none the less very human and common (Inglehart, 1991). Importantly, we can point out that the client's reaction is not because the client is inadequate or stupid (a conclusion many clients with very low self-esteem may be quick to jump to). To this end, this may be another legitimate area for disclosure of our own personal reactions to a change. This fulfils our earlier criteria for disclosure as we are sharing the emotional content of our experiences rather than their detail (Biestek, 1962). Just pointing these things out may be enough for clients to open up and discuss their reactions and feelings about them. Sometimes this will not be enough as people's reactions are more deeply rooted. In these cases we need to have more systematic approaches to working on people's thinking. We will return to this in the final chapter, where we will examine a variety of cognitive interventions that we could make.

Chapter 14

Working with Emotional Reactions to Moving Accommodation

Most people resist change. Any change. Especially, big changes and changes which they cannot understand or see the consequences of. Very few enjoy changes because of the change itself. Resistance to change in people's lives is as natural as is change to life itself (in order to improve). Most people experience a big change as being dragged away from a warm, familiar, comfortable and controllable environment and being thrown into a cold, unfamiliar, hostile one.

(Craine, 2001: 45)

This is an important starting point for this chapter, which is centred on the emotional reactions of clients to a move in accommodation: people find change difficult and resist it. This concept may seem simplistic as reactions are more nuanced than that. Personally some moves I have been through have been critical and significant, while others have merely inconvenient or even enjoyable. The question for us then becomes how much clients will resist the changes they are going through and how stressful that will be for them.

Several authors have made a distinction between the normal changes of life and 'critical life events', with the reaction to the latter being quite distinct (Ingelhart, 1991; Klinger, 1988). The question is whether for homeless people, and people undergoing resettlement in particular, moving home constitutes such a 'critical life event', and if it does, what that signifies.

When one asks the lay person to define the concept 'critical events', one frequently gets a listing of various critical life events. Usually, the events listed are undesired events such as the loss of a family member, the loss of employment, a serious illness or a divorce. Psychologists by contrast, generally consider not only undesired events to be critical, but also positive or neutral events.

(Inglehart, 1991: 7)

In a way it seems self-evident that moving home for a homeless person would be a critical life event. More generally moving home is one of the more stressful events a person can go through (Holmes and Rahe: 1967). However it is worth looking at this more closely as it has a bearing on the emotional reactions we are likely to observe, one of which can be to deny the significance of the event (Kübler-Ross, 1969). When asking what constitutes such an event Inglehart (1991) does not attempt to define objective criteria for an event being critical. For Inglehart (1991) 'critical' is whatever creates a significant change in the pattern of a person's life or, to put it another way, something that significantly challenges a person's world view or concept of self. By this token moving accommodation would seem to be a very significant event for our clients, as by being labelled 'homeless' they are being defined by their lack of accommodation. They can choose whether to embrace this identity or fight against it; either way it is significant.

Accommodation is also the aspect of a client's life that defines their interaction with us. For people undergoing resettlement the worker and the client have identified problems around their housing as needing attention and thus having significance. This is not to deny that for some people accommodation is not the fundamental issue in their situation but, even here, this realisation will make the move a critical event. It is the realisation that obtaining accommodation is not as significant as they thought it would be, facing the deception of their own cry of, 'if I just had a flat it would all be sorted' that challenges their world view and concept of self.

The study of the significance of critical life events and our reactions to them has a long history in psychology (Inglehart, 1991). A number of researchers have taken their observations of reactions to specific events and developed stage-centred theories. Such events are, for example, rape (Sutherland and Scherl, 1970), miscarriage (Zahourek and Jensen, 1973), becoming blind (Fitzgerald, 1970), losing a spouse (Parkes, 1972), having a life-threatening disease such as cancer (Gullo, Cherico and Shadick, 1974), the separation or loss of a child's mother (Bowlby, 1961; 1980; Horowitz, 1976; 1985), bodily problems (Shontz, 1965; 1975), or death and dying (Kübler-Ross, 1969).

While many of these theories are about reactions to things that are seen as negative, or that we have no control over, parallels have been drawn with events that we perceive, at least initially, to be positive (Inglehart, 1991; Klinger, 1975). This has been done particularly in the sphere of management, often in the context of organisational change (Institute of Management Studies, 2003) or job change (Employment Assistance Programme, 2004). Some authors (ITP, 2004) have argued that these reactions are actually far more common than has been surmised, stating that any significant change of circumstance can cause us to go through these processes. What varies is the intensity of these experiences. According to Inglehart's criteria this initial

Author	Bowlby (1969, 1973, 1980)	Kübler-Ross (1969)	Shontz (1975)	Fitzgerald (1970)
Event	Separation loss	Death and dying	Bodily impairment	Becoming blind
Stages	shock protest despair detachment	denial anger bargaining depression acceptance	shock encounter (helpless, disorganised) retreat psychological growth	disbelief protest depression recovery

Adapted from Inglehart (1991) *Reactions to Critical Life Events: A Social Psychological Analysis*

Figure 14.1   Event-specific stage theories: an overview

perception of positivity could mean the event is even more likely to be critical, because the challenge to our world view will be greater if the event turns out to be more problematic than we thought it would be.

Below is a summary taken from Inglehart (1991) of the various stages that have been observed in reactions to different critical life events.

Stages of reaction to critical life event

I will examine an adapted version of the stage model, developed by the Liverpool Resettlement Forum in the mid 1990s, with credit going to the St Helens Accommodation Project in particular. It is mainly based on the ideas of Worden (1984) who adapted the Kübler-Ross (1969) model of grief reactions to bereavement. This version is a six stage model that also seeks to identify the general pattern of emotional ups and downs that people will experience. I will examine each stage drawing on practitioner's experience of reaction from clients, as described in training. I will also talk through an example from my own experiences, that of moving to new employment.

Shock and confusion

Looking at my own example, this stage happened when the organisation rang to offer me the position I had just applied for. I had hoped that it would happen but when it did my reaction was still one of shock, and the reasons not to take the job came to mind. Given I had put emotional investment into this job application, this could appear a strange reaction. I had decided to change jobs, worked on the application form, worried about the interview, then went through the stressful experience that a job interview can be. Yet my reaction was still one of shock and confusion when I was offered the post.

As Bowlby (1969) notes in reference to bereavement, while we may know the change is coming, we have not taken account of the full significance of

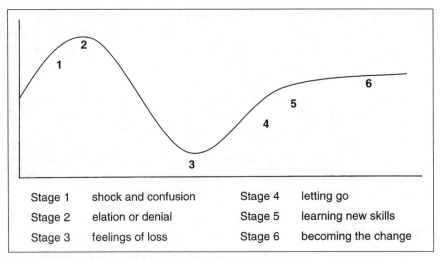

Stage 1	shock and confusion	Stage 4	letting go
Stage 2	elation or denial	Stage 5	learning new skills
Stage 3	feelings of loss	Stage 6	becoming the change

Figure 14.2   The six stage model of grief

the change. We do not face the reality of the change until it is upon us, only thinking about our myth of what it represents. It could be that we have attached great significance to a change and think it has the power to right the other ills in our lives or have underplayed its significance, seeing it only as a slight interruption in our lives. In the case of resettlement we examined how true this can be in Chapter 10, where the accommodation is the solution to everything but people do not want to examine that idea.

Practitioners have reported that some clients pretended change was not happening, or that they did not understand the offer letter they had received, even though it had 'tenancy' written all over it. Some practitioners reported people rejecting the flat at this point, but for irrational reasons such as they just had a 'feeling' that this flat was wrong for them, or for reasons that had suddenly become important and had not been mentioned before. There are parallels here with the half-rationalisations we discussed in the previous chapter, and these reactions can happen at the same time and compound each other.

Elation or denial

My reaction on getting the job quickly moved to elation later that day, having accepted the position. A characteristic of this phase is being unrealistic about the significance of the change (Waldon, 1992). I thought about the positive side of the change, thinking that it would be the dream job with no politics and enormous autonomy. For clients there can be a similar lapsing back to the idea that the new flat will solve everything. This can feel like a step backwards if the worker had got the client to face that myth and made contingency plans, or planned further steps for when the client moves in. Unfortunately, they suddenly no longer see the relevance of either; it represents a return of the old myth but in an exaggerated form.

The other reaction of denial is probably more common for those who did not see it as a big significance in the first place, Practitioners reported that clients would fail to sign up saying that they had forgotten or were busy. This can be frustrating for the worker when previously the client had seen the gaining of accommodation as fundamentally important, if not a problematic change. This still represents a return to this old myth, but it has now been exaggerated to a belief that the change is not actually happening at all.

Feelings of loss

For me this stage occurred when I had been in my new employment for a short while. It was a point where I felt lost, I was new; everyone else seemed to know what they were doing and there was a working culture that I was not a part of. There is some truth in this being the actual process of how people become encultured into work, Wenger (1999) describes similar process of how 'communities of practice' develop. However I started to think about my previous job, seeing it through rose coloured spectacles, remembering and concentrating on the things I had liked about the job. It also affected my behaviour; I would phone former colleagues for the flimsiest of reasons, I would go out with them socially and catch up on any gossip. While there is, again, a natural element to this (we take people with us in our lives) it seemed to be more than this. I was probably socialising with them more than when I was actually working there and forgetting why I had left there in the first place.

Clients can have similar reactions, constructing their previous accommodation in particular ways and letting it affect their behaviour. Clients may start visiting old haunts, going back to their previous hostel and talking about their time there fondly, even though a matter of months or weeks ago they saw things very differently. It would be a mistake to see any return to a client's old life as a negative thing, as they will also carry people from their old existence. However, there will need to be a discussion about whether this is a reaction to their new situation, or simply them keeping in contact with old friends. In my own experience, as my feelings and worries about my new job faded, I was left with a set of genuine friends and memories from my old job.

Kübler-Ross (1969) identifies an interesting stage that for us probably lies between stages three and four, that of 'bargaining'. This is where we have all but accepted that the change has happened but we are reluctant to go that final step. Our reaction is to try and bargain for a compromise. Personally I would often comfort myself that I could always go back if I wanted to. For clients this can take the form of trying to bargain with us, 'can I come back for a couple of nights a week' or 'will you visit me just occasionally'. Conversely, it can be with themselves, 'I will stay but only for the summer' or more negatively, 'unless they fix that then I will leave by next week'. It is hard not to rationalise with these reactions, either in the form of entering into the debate about whether they are possible or expressing exasperation at their creation of them. We should recognise them as what they are, emotional reactions.

Letting go

These stages represent the stages of moving on. Initially there is the importance of acceptance that change has happened and that it cannot be reversed, or in the case of accommodation, not easily. In most of the models outlined in Figure 1, this seems to be the final stage of acceptance, detachment, recovery etc. I would contend that this aspect of the change occurs earlier in that people can accept the change has happened but still remain angry about it (Kübler-Ross, 1969), or feel helpless (Scontz, 1975), or depressed (Fitzgerald, 1970). In the case of my own move, this is where I accepted that I had moved jobs and would not go back to the last place. I was starting to look forward but had by no means developed a positive attitude towards it. Practitioners reported similar reactions in their clients, people accepted that they needed to let go, but fear remained about what the future would look like. In this sense people can feel lower at stage four than they do at stage three, even if it is more realistic.

Learning new skills

The next stage is significant, that of learning new skills. There is a parallel between this stage and a moving away from the maintenance reaction of reluctance and fear (DiClemente, 1992) as discussed in the previous chapter. This is where we develop an early coping pattern, but then become afraid to move away from this behaviour. For me, it was when I realised that I could no longer preface my ideas with 'as someone new' in work, as I was no longer this. I remember feeling resentful towards someone who started after me, as they had greater claim on that statement. For clients it can be where they recognise the changes they have been through and start to see some worth in them. If they were not letting you leave, this can be the point where you can discuss what would happen if you left them and that perhaps everything would not collapse as they start to see that they are indeed coping.

Becoming the change

The final stage is where there is acceptance and an embracing of the change. The term 'becoming the change' involves an acceptance that we are indeed a different person now. The change is significant, if perhaps not the solution to all our problems. For me it was when I realised that I was now a lecturer rather than a front-line worker and that this was more than just a change in job title. I had a different role and responsibilities, but also different interests and perspectives. I had not lost my previous knowledge and experiences, but I was seeing them through different eyes. For clients it is to accept that, previously, they were a different person, they might still have friends in the homeless system but they now have a different status as a person with a home, and that that also had legitimacy.

Critiques and uses of the model

Before examining the problems with the model it is worth acknowledging its positives. As Ingleman (1991) says, stage models tend to communicate a positive life philosophy to clients and to persons indirectly involved, such as family members, friends, or workers. He outlines three ways in which these theories do this:

- Firstly, all of the stage theories postulate an end result that is, at least psychologically, positive. Kübler-Ross (1969), states that the last stage of reaction to dying is acceptance, and Bowlby (1980) points out that a detachment from the lost object or person and a re-organisation of life will finally occur. Our model says that people will eventually become the change they were seeking to achieve. This relatively optimistic outlook may help one to endure the negative stages such as feelings of loss or denial.
- Secondly, negative reactions such as denial or feelings of loss are seen as a normal part of behaviour (see Kübler-Ross, 1969, for example) and not as an indicator of an underlying pathology. It can be used to help the client realise their reactions are normal, similar to those of other people, and not a sign of mental disease or that the person is somehow inadequate or on the wrong track. It may help the worker to be more accepting and less judgmental about these reactions.
- Thirdly, these models may help to integrate a critical life event into a person's world view and this may help them understand their reactions to subsequent critical life events. I find, personally that knowledge does not stop me going through these emotional reactions to critical events in my life, but it does mean I recognise them for what they are, normal and temporary.

The first positive Inglehart identifies is also the model's potential downfall, however. For some people there will never be a positive outcome because they either made a wrong choice or they will not make the change stick this time. The emotional change model is linear, and as Prochaska and Diclemente (1984) have outlined, people and their changes rarely are. For this reason the model should not be used in isolation, but in combination with other models of change. It is important to keep checking on the prospects of a change sticking, otherwise encouraging people that they will get to stage four, five or six soon may be deceptive.

Another consequence of people's changes processes not being linear is that clients may not experience all of the stages, or may oscillate between different ones or different types of reactions in the same stage. As an example of the first oscillation is that some clients got stuck oscillating between stages three and four, sometimes feeling loss and sometimes accepting the need to move on. Regarding the second stage practitioners reported some client's oscillating between elation and denial, one day seeing the move as the thing that will solve everything and the day after denying its importance. Some authors think these oscillations do not really matter and are normal manifestations of the process (Harrowitz, 1965; Scohtz, 1975). However, other authors (TLC, 2004) report how some grief counsellors expressed anger at clients if they did not experience the stages sequentially, or perhaps more worryingly saw deviation from the stages as a sign of pathological reactions that needed professional intervention.

A complication is that people may be experiencing more than one critical life event at any given time. We noted in the previous chapter a tendency for resettlement clients to want to change a lot of things in their lives at the same time, some or all of which could constitute a critical life event. The problem is that they may be at different stages in their change processes for each event, and may have different reactions to each one. They may be at stage one in terms of their drug use, stage three in terms of their accommodation and stage five in terms of repairing their relationships with their family.

Another failing of the model is that it does not tell us the intensity of the experience, or the timescales involved. Later versions of the model did this (Klinger, 1975; TLC, 2004), saying that the intensity and duration of the reaction depends on how significant the change-produced loss is perceived. In other words it is relative to the person and how important the change is to them. As earlier discussions indicate, it is likely to be a significant reaction for those clients undergoing resettlement. Beyond this it is hard to map the emotional reactions over the physical changes people go through. Practitioners reported some clients going through all these reactions before actually visiting the property, while for many most of the stages three to six will occur once they are in the property.

This brings us back to the consideration of how and when we use the model. Similarly to the reactions identified in the last chapter, there is merit

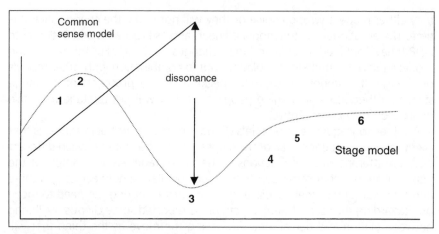

Figure 14.3 Common sense model

in simply pointing out to clients that people can have these reactions and to challenge the model the client may have in their heads. Practitioners reported that clients often have a model whereby when we change, things just keep getting better and better. Rationally it should, we chose it, know it is good for us and is the right decision. However this is where dissonance can occur with reality.

Operating on this common sense model, at point two when the client felt great, there is no reasons to believe that their reactions and feelings will not just keep going up. However by point three the dissonance between a client's expectations and their reality will often be at its greatest. While individual's realities will vary from this stage model, it will rarely look like their common sense model.

Conclusion

I found the model to be of most value, at least initially, as a retrospective tool, to help the client examine and try and make sense of what happened last time they made a change. It is not particularly positive for a client at stage two to be told that they will be feeling bad soon. It is also quite hard at stage three to believe that there will ever be a fourth, or at four that one can start coming back up the hill. As a retrospective tool the model becomes a thing that might help them evaluate their own feelings and reactions to change. In this way it may enter into the client's world view (Inglehart, 1991). This is perhaps most important because it is at stages three and four that they are often not answering the door to the worker or engaging with services. Knowledge of the model may be just enough to start them answering the door again.

Chapter 15

Cognitive Interventions in Resettlement Work

I do not understand my own actions. For I do not know what I want, but I do the very thing I hate.

(Romans, 7:15, Revised Standard Version)

Work with the homeless may be based on feelings of worthlessness, inadequacy, guilt and oppression. In the latter case, it may be a way of acting out an idealised image of self; of manipulating and dominating others in the name of 'doing good'; or of vicariously venting unacknowledged feelings of frustration and self-pity.

(Brandon, 1980: 65)

People change in many different ways and for a multitude of reasons. The psychology of change is a broad and fascinating subject in its own right. In one sense, in fact, psychology is the science of change.

(Miller and Rollnick, 1993: ix)

These three quotes are meant to illustrate the aims of this chapter, but also the ideas behind it and its limitations. The first quote reiterates some of my statements in earlier chapters that many of our clients undergoing resettlement come to us precisely for a cognitive intervention. They do not know what they want, why they do the things they do, and what they need to do to make change in their lives. Hopefully they may just have an inkling that something has to give. Later authors we will consider (Miller and Rollnick, 1993) will argue that this is probably the state most of us are in most of the time.

The second quote from Brandon (1980) while somewhat dramatic, is meant to illustrate the burden the first quote puts on us as workers. As we discovered in the chapter on support planning, helping people to make decisions is not as simple as laying out the different options they could take and then expecting them to choose between them. Many clients will change their minds, want us to take the decision for them or want to keep going over and over the same options. How to talk to our clients and help them to make decisions is a much neglected aspect of our work, especially if you take the view, as I do, that this is actually where we have greatest impact. Unfortunately communication can get relegated to a two-day course on listening skills. Worker's can come away deluded that, because they think they know what 'active listening' means, have done a role play on reflection and probably worst of all, picked up some pop-psychology about body language, they can now effectively communicate with clients.

Finally, the final quote illustrates the limitations of this chapter in that we will be exploring the first half of Miller and Rollnick's quote. It is not my intention to look at all the possible cognitive interventions we could undertake with clients; this has been done comprehensively elsewhere (CSNU, 2001).

I intend to explore just four examples of intervention strategies that seem relevant to resettlement workers. They are specifically concerned with change and may be the training courses that workers are most likely to encounter. I will call these brief interventions and the ones I will cover are:

1. Solution Focused Therapy (sometimes called Brief Therapy)
2. Transactional Analysis (TA)
3. Motivational Interviewing (MI)
4. Neuro-linguistic Programming (NLP).

I also do not intend my coverage of them to be comprehensive. By the end of the chapter, I hope the reader will have some idea of their principles and ideas, their applicability to their work and some of their limitations. As such these are easily 'skippable' sections if they are interventions the reader is already familiar with, or has already decided not to use. I hope workers realise how long their journey will probably be to intervene effectively in how people think, and how they think about thinking.

A cartography of interventions

Although I will not cover all the possible cognitive interventions, I think it is useful to give a very broad overview of some of the main schools of thought. This is mainly so that we can see how the four interventions we are considering sit in relation to them. There are many ways one could categorise the schools of thought on cognitive interventions and mine is not definitive. It is meant to illustrate something about the four brief interventions I am examining rather than to illuminate the reader about the schools of psychology. I have divided the schools into three:

- psychodynamic approaches
- cognitive-behavioural approaches and
- person-centred approaches.

Psychodynamic approaches

One of the key tenets of the psychodynamic approach is that people's emotional problems have their origins in childhood experience (CSNU, 2003). It is associated historically with Freud and more recently with Erikson (1948; 1977), Hollis (1964), Berne (1978) and Bowlby (1982). A distinction is made between the conscious and the unconscious mind, which is constitutes the ego (largely our consciousness, the thinking part), the super-ego (the internalised rules we have learnt about society and ourselves) and the id (our animal instinct, largely the *libido*, the sex drive and the *mortido*, the drive to violence) (Berne, 1978). A third central tenet is in how the personality develops. Freud was particularly interested in early development and the sex drive; Bowlby was more interested in the social and emotional development in this time. Erikson developed both themes to cover the whole of a person's life span (Milner and O'Byrne, 2002).

It is not without its critics, for a variety of reasons: for being a disempowering medical model (Ingleby, 1985; Barber, 1991), for being sexist (Hearn, 1995; Kline, 1972), for being racist (Devore and Schlesinger, 1991), and for simply not working (Hilsenroth et al., 2001). It may help to have these ideas in mind, even just to be aware of what we may be referring people at times. However, only a trained psychoanalyst will really be able to tackle this area effectively, another perspective that is normally integral to its philosophy, that only a trained professional therapist can help people.

Cognitive-behavioural approaches

Cognitive-behavioural theory can be considered a branch of behaviouralism (Milner and O'Byrne, 2002). Behaviouralism examines our behaviour traits and tries to establish how they were established, learned and are maintained. It believes that as these behaviours were learned, they can be unlearned and replaced with other ones. Consequently many behaviouralists concern themselves with how these patterns are learnt and how we can unlearn them. Its main proponents are Pavlov (1960), Skinner (1958) and Bandura (1977). The cognitive branch holds that our thoughts are also behaviours, and we develop unhelpful ways of thinking, that positively can also be unlearnt. It holds that behaviour is also mediated through how we think, that it is not just physical reactions to certain stimuli (Cigno, 1998). Three of its main proponents have been Ellis (1962), Beck and Tomkin (1989) and Seligman (1992).

Importantly CBT holds that our emotions are essentially cognitive in nature, they are a reaction to our thoughts and what an event has come to means to us, i.e. I lost that flat, I will never get another one, I am depressed. We need to break the link between the first event (activating event) and last (emotional consequence) event, by changing the middle reaction (belief) (Ellis, 1962). These belief reactions are sometimes called cognitive distortions (Ellis, 1964; Burns, 1992) and are ideas like 'I will always fail', 'I feel it so it must be true' etc. It is the worker's job to challenge them.

Again, there are critics of the intervention. Firstly some view that there is again a reliance on the worker as expert (Milner and O'Byrne, 2002), although some variants teach self-help techniques (Maguire, 2002). The main criticism is over what counts as 'cognitive distortions' rather than rational reactions and beliefs, with potential again for discrimination (Milner and O'Byrne, 2002; Renzetti, 1992).

Person-centred approaches

Otherwise called humanistic approaches, these approaches are closely asso-ciated with the work of Rogers and Freiberg (1994) and Maslow (1954). While still originally from a psycho-therapeutic perspective they differ very much in how the therapy is conducted. The person-centred approach views the client as the best authority on their own experience, and that the client is capable of fulfilling their own potential for growth (self-actualisation). However, it recognises that achieving potential requires favourable conditions and that under adverse conditions individuals may well not grow and develop in the ways that they otherwise could.

Taking the view that every individual has the internal resources they need for growth, person-centred interventions aim to provide three 'core condi-tions' which help that growth to occur. These are:

- unconditional positive regard (as it says, accepting the person and not being judgmental of them)
- empathy (the attempt to understand the situation from the client's point of view, rather than getting the client to understand the worker's perspective) and
- congruence (being 'genuine' and 'present', not aloof or detached)

Criticisms are that there is no basis in saying that people can self-actualise (Skinner, 1972; Matson, 1973) and in this sense, its presumptions have no more foundation than those of Freud and the psycho-dynamic theorists. Stemming from this, even if some people can self-actualise, can everyone? People who have been psychologically damaged or have been through extreme trauma may not be able to do this. There are questions of whether the conditions are actually achievable (Ryan, 2003), Rogers being very vague on how we achieve things like congruence. Finally there are criticisms that insight does not necessarily mean that people change their behaviour (Sheldon, 1982).

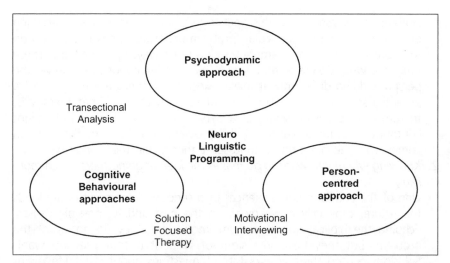

Figure 15.1 The relationship of brief therapies to schools of cognitive interventions

Above is a diagram of how the brief therapies could be seen to relate to the wider schools of cognitive interventions. We will explore why I have placed the brief interventions where I have, and the significance of this is when considering the interventions themselves.

1 Solution Focused Therapy (SFT)

SFT was developed in the 1960s as a reaction to perceived failures in more psychological interventions. Its main exponent's were DeShazer and Berg (1985; 1988; 1991; 1994). It is a theory that has been called atheoretical, postmodern and social constructionist (Milner and O'Byrne, 2002), rejecting the idea of an overarching theory that can tell us everything and saying that many of the ways we see clients and the solutions to their problems are social constructions that pathologises them. Given this, many of its advocates would not appreciate me placing it where it is in Figure 1, but I have done so because it shares with the person-centred approach the idea that it is the clients who must work out their solutions. Some cognitive approaches also draw on social constructivism, in that the scripts and behavior patterns that people internalise can be both socially and personally determined.

Two basic ideas underpin solution focused therapy:

1. *We are not the problem, the problem is something we are in* (Thompson, 1995).

Nothing is consistent and this applies to problems as well as everything else. A person with a particular 'problem behaviour' does not always do their problem well, for example they do not always drink or fight. These times are what DeShazer and Berg (1988) call 'exceptions'. Whatever the person is doing differently at these 'exceptional' times are the basis of a potential solution. Part of the task of solution focused brief therapy is, therefore, to discover whatever a person is already doing which might contribute to the resolution of the problem. The basis of the solution comes from the client rather than some theory that the worker has.

2. *Knowing where you want to go makes the idea of going there much more likely.*
   One of the common consequences of a serious problem is that it clouds the future, especially if we dwell on the past and its possible causes. Echoing the biblical quote, a client knows that they do not want the problem, but they have lost sight of what it is that they do want. Solution focused therapy asks lots of questions about what life might be like if the problem was solved. As the answers to these questions gradually unfold, a picture of where things are heading becomes clearer. The clearer the picture becomes, the greater is the possibility of change happening.

Assumptions

Milner and O'Byrne (2002: 67) outline some assumptions that underpin this approach:

- Problems do not necessarily reflect a deficiency.
- The future is more significant than the past; an understanding of what will be happening when the problem is ended avoids the need to understand the cause of the problem.
- The explanation for events is that they just happen; blame for what has happened is avoided but responsibility for what happens in the future is encouraged.
- Change is constant and inevitable – there are always exceptions.
- Meanings and changes are constructed by talk.
- Staying on the surface of the words is important in hearing what the service user is saying – looking beneath the surface is looking at one's own theory and thus finding what the worker expects to be there.
- Unless there is a goal that is salient to the service user there will only be confusion and drift – for a yacht without a destination port, no wind is a good wind.
- As long as the goal is legal and morally acceptable, no limits are put on service user aspirations for a joyous future.

Techniques

These are fairly simple and consist of the miracle question, scaled questions, coping questions and pessimistic questions. The most commonly known of these is the miracle question, which can be phrased as:

Suppose tonight, while you were asleep, a miracle happened and the problems you have to-day are gone in a flash, but because you were asleep you don't know how this happened. What would be the first difference you would notice in the morning?

The idea is that is gives a glimpse of the future without the problem. The worker then follows this up by exploring the aforementioned techniques, with the idea that this shows them that some aspects of this future are happening already. They are able to:

Describe what they want without having to concern themselves with the problem and without traditional assumptions that the solution has to be connected with understanding or eliminating the problem.

(DeShazer, 1994: 273)

Another technique of particular interest to resettlement is the 'spectrum of change' (Client Positioning). This technique is more about making an assessment of a person's situation within the change process. There is a series of questions that can give the worker a 'picture' of where the person is at with regard to the whole process of change. The worker needs to, and is given aid in being able to, assess the following components of change:

- Wants to change/Does not want to change.
- Knows what to change/Does not know what to change.
- Knows how to recognise signs of change/Does not know how to recognise signs of change.
- Knows how to change/Does not know how to change.
- Aware of obstacles to change/Unaware of obstacles to change.
- Confident about making changes/Lacks confidence about making changes.
- Ready to make changes/Not ready to make changes.

In terms of assessment this would seem to be an invaluable asset to resettlement work. SFT also makes claims to be effective in quite a short space of time, hence its alternative name of brief therapy. Positively there have been over 30 outcome studies (see Parton and O'Byrne, 2000 and Milner and O'Byrne, 2002) that have shown that the technique are as effective and long lasting as any other technique in the field.

Criticisms

The main criticism is that SFT requires a degree of insight; studies with older people with dementia have shown less success (Milner and O'Byrne, 2002).

Other authors have made accusation that the language of success, strengths and competence has a gender bias (Dermer et al., 1998). Milner and O'Byrne (2002) warn against using it clumsily or thinking that it is a quick fix or easily mastered solution. A particular warning is to think that we can ignore the problem, we still need to work with it, just not to get hung up on understanding completely its causes.

2 Transactional Analysis

TA was first coined by Harris (1970) and then developed by Berne (1978) and is a direct descendant of psychodynamic approaches, hence its place on Figure 1. It essentially looks at how communication operates between two people, seeing it as a transaction. It says that the nature of the transaction will depend on whether the participants are communicating as an 'adult', a 'child' or a 'parent'. Haynes calls these ego states, and all three states make up aspects of our personality (Jacobs, 1999). These states can be seen as negative and positive, and these aspects constantly override each other (Steward and Jones, 1999). In this way you can be a nurturing or a controlling parent, a free child or an adapted or selfish child, and a rational or cold clinical adult. Hopefully these states should be in balance, but sometimes there are negative 'transactions'. Harris (1970) thought that certain ego states could 'contaminate' each other and block other states. For example if someone is prejudiced or racist then it could be their parent, with certain learned beliefs, negatively contaminating their adult state of being rational. This may also be accompanied by a blocked off child, which means you have difficulty developing empathy with the group you have prejudice against. We can see how the theory grew out of the psycho-dynamic tradition with parallels between adult and ego, parent and super ego and child and id.

Berne (1978) talked about 'life scripts' whereby early experiences mean that in certain situations our parent or child state can take over, for example many parents find going back to school difficult and behave like children. In dysfunctional people it can be an all-encompassing script that becomes a 'life-plan' (Berne, 1978). The writing of the story begins at birth. By the time a child has reached the age of four the plot lines have been decided upon. By the age of seven the main details of the story have been written. Between the ages of seven and 12, a few extras are added and the story is refined. In adolescence the story is slightly revised and new real-life characters are added.

Berne (1964) also talks about how certain 'games' can be played when two parties play out their scripts together. Karpman (1968) suggested that whenever people 'play games' they step into one of three roles:

- **Persecutors** generally put other people down and belittle them, sometimes in the name of 'tough love' or 'being straight with people'.

- **Victims** feel they are put upon and sometimes search for either a 'persecutor' to put them down, or a 'rescuer' who will offer help and confirm the 'victim's' belief that they cannot cope.
- **Rescuers** believe they have to help others because they are not able enough to help themselves.

Techniques

The main techniques in TA are various ways to recognise and become aware of the states, scripts and games either party adopts in their 'transactions'. Other techniques intend to free up blocked aspects of a person in their transactions. For example their free child, or their nurturing parent, with a sense of rules and morals. Both Harris and Berne, saw 'normal' transactions between two people as; parent-parent, child-child, adult-adult and occasionally child-parent. Other transactions are mismatched, meaning communication can stop or one party tries to force the other into another ego state. Sometimes I have felt a client, who is perhaps acting like a child and avoiding responsibility, trying to force me into being a parent and telling them what to do. Some of what Harris (1970) and Berne (1978) call 'normal' reactions are not helpful and have dangers.

James (1973) has suggested a series of questions to analyse the stages in an individual's script:

1. Describe (the behaviour) what keeps happening to you over and over again?
2. How does it start?
3. What happens next?
4. And then?
5. How does it end?
6. How do you feel?
7. How do you think the other persons feel?

Transactional analysis also has a series of exercises and games designed to help people explore their emotions and states at different points of their transactions and how they relate to their various scripts and behaviour patterns. Others exercises look at whether any of our ego states are blocked or stuck in the negative aspects.

Criticisms

Criticisms of TA are similar to those of psychodynamic approaches in general. It is not person-centred as it is the worker who defines what state a person is in. This then begs the question of what constitutes an adult or child state, or the difference between a free and a selfish child. If a client complains about conditions in the hostel are they being a rational adult or a selfish child and more to the point, who decides? Milner and O'Byrne (2002) feel that it has an advantage over other forms of psychodynamic approaches because it is 'more user friendly for busy social workers'. It has also been accused of being pop psychology (CSNU, 2002). I find the idea of someone exploring something as sensitive as a clients childhood memories without proper training worrying, or perhaps I am falling into the psychodynamic trap that one has to be a trained expert to talk about such matters (De Shazer, 1988).

3 Motivational Interviewing (MI)

MI was primarily developed by William Miller and Stephen Rollnick in the early 1990s. It was developed in the context of working with problematic drinkers. More generally it has been applied to those who are going through problematic change and has since been extended to use with drug users (van Bilsen, 1993; Saunders et al., 1993), young people (Cox et al., 1993), HIV risk reduction (Baker and Dixon, 1993) and sex offenders (Garland and Douugher, 1993). It theoretically draws on two sources. The first influence was work on ambivalence and the conflict between indulgence and restraint by Orford (1985). He explored the psychology of people who do not change when they know their behaviour is destructive. He said that if the idea of change was entirely positive, it would be easy to carry out, hence we are ambivalent.

A second influence is research on 'self regulation' (Kanfer, 1987; Miller and Brown, 1991) which stems from the person-centred approach. It builds on the model of change by Prochaska and DiClemente (1982) we have already explored. The position of MI on Figure 1 is where Miller and Rollnick place it themselves, saying it draws on several strategies: client-centred counselling primarily on Rogers humanistic approach; cognitive therapy; skills training strategy where a young person's motivation is assessed and systems theory (Upton, 1990).

Key ideas (adapted from Miller and Rollnick, 1993)

- *Worker style is a powerful determinant of client resistance and change*

Miller and Rollnick are emphatic about worker style being very important and powerful. This departs from Rogers and Freiberg (1994), who would maintain that we are more of a mirror and should concentrate on maintaining the 'core conditions'.

- *Confrontation is a goal not a style, argumentation is a poor method for inducing change*

  Confrontation as a worker style or technique was a key concept in early dependency work (Yablonsky, 1989) and remains prevalent in America

(Miller, 1993). MI says that our aim is to get people to face their issues, but to confront them will push them into denial. A key concept is 'cognitive dissonance' which is the tension between what people say they want and how they are behaving. It is what happens when people face their issues. The key to resolving ambivalence is to skillfully play with this dynamic, again a significant departure from Rogers.

- *Even relatively brief interventions can have a substantial impact on problem behaviour*
  This is the idea that people are constantly thinking about change, even if they sometimes avoid it (not the same as denial as people know they are avoiding things, it is an active process). Many people make changes on their own without interventions, therefore our interventions can be small and brief, setting a seed that can make the difference. This seems relevant to resettlement as many of our interventions are brief and not the solid delineated hour that counselling often demands.

- *Motivation emerges from the interpersonal interactions between worker and users*
  Motivation is often thought of as a something people have or they do not. Practitioners sometimes ask me how they can motivate their clients as though it is a commodity. I answer 'talk to them' echoing Miller's claim that motivation is created by interaction with others, with workers and clients talking.

- *Ambivalence is normal, not pathological, but the key to change*
  Ambivalence, the see-sawing between thinking about a thing and not, facing it or not. Miller says ambivalence is a very normal reaction and probably something we are all stuck in most of the time. To make a decision is the fleeting moment when ambivalence is resolved, while ambivalence is the normal state of affairs. Consequently we need to work on this ambivalence. This work can be pronounced with problematic change, and means that the worker needs to have a little more patience. Laying out options or facts is not the key to getting people to make decisions. I know smoking kills me every time I pick up a cigarette packet. The fact that it tells me so on the packet does not make me stop.

Techniques

Miller and Rollnick outline five general practice principles:
1. *Express empathy*
   - Remember, acceptance allows change.
   - Use skilful and reflective listening.
   - Remember, ambivalence is a normal reaction not a personality trait.

2. Develop discrepancy
- Make them aware of the consequences of their behaviour.
- Focus on the discrepancy between present behaviour and future goals.
- Let arguments for change come from the client.

3. Avoid argumentation
- It's counter-productive, but easy to fall into.
- It breeds defensiveness and no-one wins an argument.
- It can be a way of either of you avoiding talking about things.

4. Roll with resistance
- Don't run from it, its momentum can be used positively.
- Perceptions can be shifted, remember to spin.
- Remember the client is the best resource for finding possible solutions.

5. Support self efficacy
- Foster belief in the possibility of change.
- Let the client choose and carry out change.
- Foster hope there are many possibilities to try!

Many specific techniques are similar to those encountered within counselling or 'listening skills' courses. They include reflection, summarising, restructuring, re-framing etc. Other techniques are more of a departure and include:

Cost benefit analysis

When discussing ambivalence a 'decisional balance sheet' is built up. It should tell the worker a number of things ranging from how committed a person is to change, to whether a person really understands the consequences of their behaviour. This approach is usually received in a positive manner due to there being a discussion of the positive reasons for the person's behaviour and not just the negative aspects of it (CSNU, 2002).

Describing concerns in 'worst case' scenarios

This can sometimes help people to see that things are not as bad as they may have initially thought. Questions that could be used to evoke a response include:

- What concerns you most?
- What are your worst fears about what might happen if you don't make a change?
- What do you suppose is the worst that might happen if you continue with the way you've been going?

Looking back

Sometimes it is useful to have the person remember times before problems emerged, and to compare these with the present situation.

Looking forward

Helping people to imagine a changed future is another approach for eliciting self motivational statements. Here the individual is asked how things might be if they were to change

Exploring goals

This approach can look at a number of issues. Ask the person to tell you what things are most important in their life (this can overlap with previous approach). The worker tries to find out what values or goals the person holds most dear.

Handling resistance

Motivational interviewing includes many more techniques for handling and decreasing resistance

Use of paradox

This is using the aforementioned fact that confrontation pushes people into denial to the worker's advantage, in that you are trying to elicit an oppositional reaction, ie perhaps the client shouldn't change, perhaps they should just stay in the hostel.

Criticisms

MI, as it says itself is, 'one approach, not the only correct and proper way to proceed with clients' (Miller, 1993: x). It presupposes that people can have insight into their situations which, as we have discussed, is not true of all resettlement clients. It also assumes that people want to make a change and that change will be positive, which again, is not always the case. It is also somewhat time consuming and involves a long term commitment to the client (Harper and Hardy, 1998) as opposed to its main alternative SFT. More generally Harper and Hardy (1998) think that the organisation needs to be clear whether it can fit into the philosophy of MI. Can it move at the client's own pace? Can it allow the person to fail a number of times before success is achieved? Can it support people intensively at the crucial times of change, such as when they move into their accommodation? If these things are not possible, the dangers of only using MI on part of the process are clear – you could open a person to their own contradictions, but are not there to catch their consequent fall.

4 Neuro Linguistic Programming (NLP)

John Grinder, Linguistics Professor at University College Santa Cruz and Richard Bandler, a graduate student in mathematics developed NLP in the mid-1970s. It draws upon four theoretical sources:

1. The notion of the unconscious mind as constantly influencing conscious thought and action.
2. The interpretation of metaphorical behaviour and speech patterns, especially building upon the methods used in Freud's interpretation of dreams.
3. Hypnotherapy as developed by Milton Erickson.
4. The linguistic works of Gregory Bateson and Noam Chomsky (Carroll, 2002).

It is because of this very mixed heritage that I have placed it where I have Figure 1. It is a very eclectic theory that draws from whatever it perceives to work (Grinder and Bandler, 1988).

Its name gives insight into its underpinning model. It believes that our understandings of ourselves and the world are created through a dynamic process between the nervous system (Neuro), through which experience is received and processed through the five senses, our use of language (Linguistic), non-verbal communication and others' language, and how our beliefs and behaviour are programmed in order to achieve results and goals (Programming). Another way of explaining this is:

> There is a relationship between perceptions, thinking and behaviour that is neuro-linguistic in nature. It is about how information is processed and stored according to our own highly subjective 'maps' of reality. The relationship is operating all the time, no matter what a person is doing. It can be studied by exploring a person's internal or subjective experiences of an event or behaviour.

(CSNU, 2002)

It has a set of underpinning assumptions, as outlined by the CSNU:

- People respond to their own view/map of reality and not reality itself.
- The mind and body are part of the same system.
- No person should ever be written off.
- People must feel that they have a choice.
- Anything can be accomplished if the task is taken in small enough chunks.
- Seek first to understand the person before being understood yourself.

- If a person is not responding than the 'fault' will lie with the communicator to change the way the message is put across.
- All behaviour has a purpose.
- There is no failure only feedback.
- If something does not work use it as feedback for future work.
- All information is processed through the senses.

Another core belief is that people have Primary Representative Systems (PRS) which are preferred ways through which people interpret the world via their senses. The language they use, and workers should use to tune into them, will reflect their preferred system. The main three PRS are:

- **Visual:** people tend to visualise their concepts and ideas. They will probably enjoy visual images, symbols and designs. People operating in this field will benefit from visual stimulation and will usually respond well to visual imagery exercises. Language to use should be visual: 'I **see** what you are saying'.
- **Auditory:** people tend to listen to the words a person says and responds to sounds and verbal communication. They may particularly enjoy music, drama and talking. They will find it difficult if a lot of noises are going on at the same time. Language to use should be auditory, 'I **hear** what you are saying'.
- **Kinaesthetic:** people respond and relate to things on a feeling level. Here people may enjoy physical and practical activities. They will understand points made with a feeling dimension such as the use of anecdotes. Language to use should relate to feeling, 'I **feel** what you are saying'.

Techniques

Workers train to be able to take clues as to the representative system that their client is using and to help them communicate in this system. The techniques are designed to help us to understand a client's behaviour and what may have caused it, relating to the aforementioned components of NLP. It includes knowledge about neurological processes (Neuro); listening skills training to know how to use rapport, body language and language skills to communicate more effectively (Linguistic); and behavioural techniques to help the worker know how to help the client understand what is driving them (Programme).

In summary, it allows people to understand their own programming with an aim to be able to re-programme their brain to become the person they want to be, and to achieve they goals that they want to achieve. In this respect NLP claims to have studied the thinking of 'great minds' and the behaviour patterns of successful people and have extracted *models* of how they work. 'From these models, techniques for quickly and effectively changing thoughts, behaviours and beliefs that get in your way have been developed' (Grinder, 1998).

An example of a technique that links to the physical 'neuro' aspect of the body, is to observe people's eye movements:

- **Visual remembered:** (eyes up to the right) Seeing images of things seen before.
- **Visual constructed:** (eyes up to the left) Imagining images of things never seen before, or seeing things in a different way.
- **Auditory remembered:** (eyes to the right side) Remembering sounds heard before.
- **Auditory constructed:** (eyes to the left side) Imagining hearing sounds never heard before.
- **Auditory digital:** (eyes down to the right) Talking to oneself i.e. remembering a favourite song
- **Kinaesthetic:** (eyes down to the left) Feeling emotions, tactile sensations (sense of touch).

Other techniques owe a debt to gestalt (Perls, 1972) with ideas like *Meta Mirror*. This technique is all about finding a different perspective on a situation. By physically stepping into different positions it may help the client to discuss their feelings and explore other perspectives. Others like persuasion engineering and trancing are close to the self-hypnosis idea of authors like Erikson.

Critics

The main critics of NLP have focused on some of its 'scientific claims' Heap (1988) conducted a meta analysis of the various scientific research papers and clinical trials of NLP with regard to its three main hypotheses on a Primary Representational Systems (PRS). He found that the hypothesis that a person has a PRS which can be observed in their choice of words has been found *not* to hold by the great majority of researchers. The hypothesis that a person has a PRS which can be determined by the direction of eye movements found even less support. The third hypothesis that we can improve our relationship with a client by matching their presumed PRS was again found to be erroneous. There is no evidence that focusing on the presumed modality adds anything to the relationship between worker and client (Heap,1988). One researcher, Cody (1988), found that therapists matching their clients' language were rated as *less* trustworthy and *less* effective by the client.

Other critics have attacked the notion of adopting more 'successful' programming patterns from successful people. Apart from the presumptions that great minds have something in common, and the debate about what constitutes a great mind, Carroll (2002) thinks we are coming down very hard on one side of the nature/nurture debate:

I think most of us intuitively grasp that even if we were subjected to the same experiences which Einstein or Tolstoy had, we would not have become either. Surely, we would be significantly different from whom we've become, but without their brains to begin with, we would have developed quite differently from either of them.

(Carroll, 2002: 3)

Carroll (2002) also feels that the techniques are philosophically flawed, claiming to be studying people's subjective experiences and yet concentrating on the 'meaning' of their behaviour by using objective criteria. The 'eye movement' notion is an example of this and the way body language is used is not taught subjectively but objectively. Some trainers claiming that using the techniques will mean you can read people's unconscious minds, to the point of being able to tell if they are telling the truth or not. Finally he says that this project, of speaking to the unconscious mind, is erroneous in itself, concluding that, 'all the scientific evidence which exists on such things indicates that what NLP claims is not true. You cannot learn to 'speak directly to the unconscious mind' as Erickson and NLP claim, except in the most obvious way of using the power of suggestion' (Carroll, 2002: 4).

Conclusion

In conclusion I would just like to reiterate that cognitive interventions are crucial to our work and are probably where we will have any lasting impact on our clients and how they conceive of themselves and the world. As such we should make developing our skills in them an essential aspect of our continuing professional development. This is also important because it is a developing field. The strategies we have examined in this chapter will develop and be challenged, and ultimately be surpassed by new ones. Workers will always be changing their thinking about how we help people with their thinking.

Conclusion: Resettlement Work with Homeless People: A Synthesis of Knowledge and the Emergence of a New Profession

The power and status of professional workers depend to a significant extent on their claims to unique forms of expertise, which are not shared with other occupational groups.

(Eraut, 1994: 21)

In the preface I talked about the three themes of this book: the need to define and delineate resettlement work, that the work is distinct and unique and that there should be a synthesis of practical, emotional and cognitive interventions. It is to these themes that I wish to return, as it is the links between them that constitutes resettlement's claim to be an emerging profession. Resettlement workers claim, uniquely, to be able to intervene with clients to address their entrenched homelessness. Eraut (1994) says that resettlement's claim to be a profession is contingent on our claims to unique knowledge. Three questions follow from this:

1. What is the nature of our professional knowledge and its acquisition?
2. Can we identify any criteria for what constitutes this professional knowledge?
3. Does resettlement meets these criteria for professional knowledge?

Eraut (1994) says that professions make three public claims about their knowledge; that the knowledge is identifiable, sufficiently complex to justify high level protracted training and is unique to that profession. In a professional context this acquisition of knowledge is, 'a rite of passage involving the acquisition of enough knowledge and qualifications to acquire an adult station in life' (Leadbeater, 2000: 111–2).

While we will come back to some of these ideas, it is important to explore what is not explained by these criteria i.e. the nature of the knowledge and how it is acquired. Eraut, drawing on a long legacy of educational writing (Aristole, 1976; Oakenshott, 1962; Ryle, 1949 etc.) distinguishes between

two types of knowledge: 'propositional' knowledge which underpins professional action and is learnt through training and 'practical' knowledge, learned
only through experience and practice. The relationship between the two is not
simple and needs elucidating. Taking the example of teaching, several authors
(Solomon, 1999; Shulman, 1987) write of the danger of simplifying their
interactive relationship, reducing teachers to being technicians with knowledge of a subject and practical 'tricks to get it across' (Solomon, 1999). I see
parallels with practitioner's desire in training to be told 'what works' and their
impatience at being told that a professional will continually need to synthesise
their knowledge with their judgement. Agencies seem to be developing a
similar obsession with developing competencies for workers, rather than with
developing professional frameworks for them.

Shulman's (1987) typology-PCK

Within teaching, Shulman (1987) thought that professional knowledge was
definable and, ultimately, could be made into propositional knowledge. He
identifies several dimensions to a teacher's knowledge: content knowledge
(of the subject), pedagogical knowledge (of learning and teaching techniques)
and contextual knowledge (of the learning environment and the learners). He
calls the synthesis of these, pedagogical content knowledge (PCK) and saw
them as the unique domain of teachers. For him, PCK represents a 'blending
of content and pedagogy into an understanding of how particular topics are
represented and adapted to the diverse interests and abilities of learners'
(Shulman, 1987: 8).

This typology could be useful in catagorising the knowledge base of
resettlement. However before attempting to adapt this model to resettlement, we need to evaluate how transferable it is to our profession. It is not
the concern of this paper to analyse the aim of teaching. I will assume that it
is about enabling the student to learn (Shulman, 1987). Neither is it my
concern to examine what we mean by learning, as there is an equal amount
of literature on that topic (Maslow, 1968; Rogers, 1996; Freire, 1968).

I will take the view that learning represents a change, not necessarily
in behaviour but in how the learner thinks, feels or behaves (Smith,
2002). Not all care professions, or aspects of them, see this internal
change in the client, or learning, as important for their work. For statutory
services such as social services and the probation service their concern
may not be internal change in the individual but in their circumstances
or external behaviour e.g. children going into care or compliance with
a probation order. Internal change may be desirable, but it is not a
necessity. Any transferability seems therefore to be in professions where
the goal is internal change in a person. As we established in Chapter

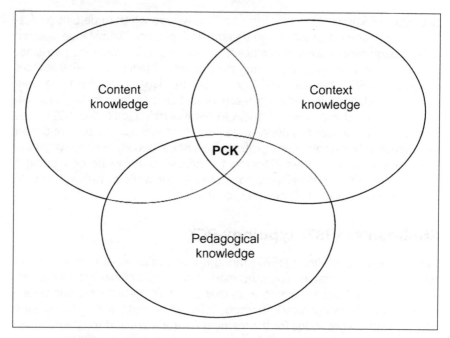

Figure 16.1   Pedagogical content knowledge (Shulman, 1987)

2, change is paramount in resettlement. This distinguishes resettlement workers from other roles in the homelessness field. Advice workers, hostel workers, soup run operators etc would not necessarily see change as important to their endeavour (Ham, 1994). They are there to provide a service, and change is not necessary. These services play vital roles, but if they are to make a claim to being professional it will need to be through a different route than PCK.

ICK

Adapting Shulman's (1987)framework to resettlement, content knowledge becomes impact knowledge, knowledge that the worker will need to know about the nature of homelessness and of the change the client will need to go through in undergoing resettlement. Pedagogical knowledge becomes intervention knowledge, knowledge the worker has of interventions that will get content knowledge across to the client. Contextual knowledge remains as it is and Pedagogical Content Knowledge becomes Interventional Content Knowledge (ICK). Combined, the framework could look like the figure below:

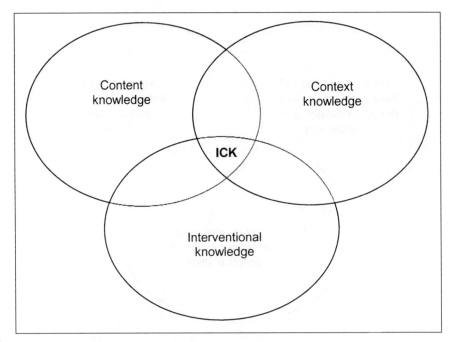

Figure 16.2   Interventional content knowledge

We can now start to see what a map of resettlement knowledge might look like. We established in Chapter 2 resettlement work's interventional knowledge (Stretch and Seal, 1992; Bevan, 1998). We established three levels that a worker needs to be able to intervene with a homeless person at: the cognitive, the emotional and the practical. In subsequent chapters we mapped out techniques that are associated with each level.

A considerable amount of academic literature exists on homelessness and working with homeless people that could inform both content and context knowledge. This can fall into several camps: the subject of homelessness as a policy issue (e.g. Burrows et al., 1997; Daly, 1996; Hutson and Clapman, 2000), how it is socially constructed (Hutson, 1996; Gaimo and Grunberg, 1992; Eungjun, 1999), the experience of being homeless (Wright, 1997; Dean, 1999; Dordick, 1997; Glasser and Bridgeman, 1999; Ruddick, 1996; Passaro, 1996; Hagan and McCarthy, 1997). There is some literature about homeless provision and people's experience of it (Crane, 1999; Kennet and Marsh, 1999; Satyamurti, 1981; Hugman, 1992; Humphries, 1999). We mapped out specific knowledge we need on the resettlement process in Chapter 2. In addition there is knowledge workers will need to acquire about the dynamics of specific issues with specific client groups such as drug and

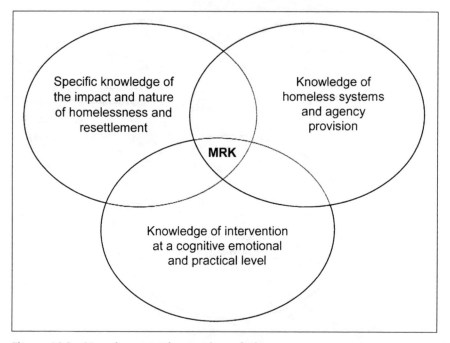

Figure 16.3   Mapping resettlement knowledge

alcohol problems; mental health problems; physical health problems; poverty and debt; unemployment; literacy and educational difficulties; childhood histories of abuse; the trauma of being a refugee and the dynamics of multiple needs. The impact of these issues on a client's identity will form the basis of a subsequent publication.

Context knowledge is both a combination of knowledge about services and their functioning and about the contexts of our own agencies and interventions. The former is readily available knowledge and the subject of many of the short courses provided by organisations such as Shelter, Homeless Link and SITRA. However there is a need to consolidate this knowledge and make it consistent across the field. As such this may also form the subject of subsequent publication. The later aspect of context knowledge was covered in the section on Structuring Our Work, the section on Working Relationships and the chapter on worker support. In summary, it seems that resettlement is a developing field of knowledge but one that could fit with Shulmans' criteria for what constitutes professional knowledge. A map of resettlement knowledge would look like this:

Shulman saw Pedagogical Content Knowledge as the source of teacher's uniqueness:

PCK is the category most likely to distinguish the understanding of the content specialist from that of the pedagogue . . . it identifies the distinctive bodies of knowledge for teaching.

In a parallel way it is ICK that defines the distinctive body of knowledge for resettlement workers. As the claim to knowledge is instrumental, it is this combination of knowledge and its application that can successfully and uniquely intervene with clients to address their entrenched homelessness. Finally, given our relative autonomy, our ethical stance (as covered in Chapter 3) is our guiding light in the making of difficult decisions and in the application of ICK.

On-going professional development

While positive, embracing professionalism leaves us with an agenda to develop. It also leaves us with developments to react to. Returning to the issue raised in the first chapter, we need to ensure that the things we are measured on remain relevant to our work and our clients. We need to ensure that the 'evidence base' upon which we base our practice does not get reduced to a series of 'set' interventions that do not take account of the complexities of our clients and of our working contexts. Rowlands established criteria for ethical evaluation in community organisations (1991). Adapting this, we need to ensure that our approach to evidence based practice and evaluation:

- Deconstructs stakeholders ideas and concerns around evidence based practice and evaluation.
- Creates an approach to evaluation and the establishment of evidence based practice that is critical rather than positivist.
- Creates evidence based practice and outputs that acknowledges the qualitative process of work as much as the quantifiable outcomes.
- Incorporates the views of the stakeholders in evaluation and the establish-ment of evidence based practice in an on-going way.

A second thing is that we will need to continue to develop our knowledge base. Eraut (1994) talks about how this is most commonly embodied in a course. We explored in the first chapter how moves are being made in this direction. These courses will need to cover the knowledge that makes us unique (our ICK). They will need to cover and test both propositional and practical knowledge, and most importantly their interaction. Finally we may, in time, want to consider developing another hallmark of professionalism (Dingwall and Lewis, 1983; Torstendahl and Burrage, 1996) that of the professional association. This will continue to develop standards and practice and be something that all practitioners are ultimately answerable to. While it is a start to have a code of ethics that we attempt to adhere to, is it ultimately enough to be answerable only to our consciences?

References

Alexander, K. and Ruggieri, S. (1998) *Changing Lives*. London: Crisis.

Alsop, R. and Saunders, B. (1993) Reinforcing Robust Solutions: Motivation in Relapse Prevention with Severely Dependant Problem Drinkers. In Miller, W.R. and Rollnick, S. (1991) *Motivational Interviewing: Preparing People to Change Addictive Behaviour*. 2nd edn. New York: Guilford Press.

American Planning Association (1996) *Principles of Planning in American Businesses*. www.apa.com/principles.htm

Anning, A. (2001) *Knowing Who I am and What I Know: Developing New Versions of Professional Knowledge in Integrated Service Settings*. Paper presented to the British Educational Research Association Annual Conference, University of Leeds.

Anthony, S. and Pagano, G. (1998) The Therapeutic Potential for Growth During the Termination Process. *Clinical Social Work Journal*, 26: 281–96.

Argyris, C. (1990) *Overcoming Organisational Defences: Facilitating Organisational Learning*. MA, USA: Allyn and Bacon.

Argyris, C. (1990) *Overcoming Organisational Defences: Facilitating Organisational Learning*. MA, USA: Allyn and Bacon.

Aristotle (1976) *The Nicomachean Ethics*. Harmondsworth: Penguin.

Ashleigh, M.J. and Stanton, N.A. (2001) Trust, Key Elements in Human Supervisory Control Domains. *Cognition, Technology and Work*, 3: 92–100.

Baker, A. and Dixon, J. (1991) Motivational Interviewing for HIV Risk Reduction. In Miller, W.R. and Rollnick, S. (1991) *Motivational Interviewing: Preparing People to Change Addictive Behaviour*. 2nd edn. New York: Guilford Press.

Baker, A. and Seal, M. (2002) *De-mystifying Dual Diagnosis*. HLG: Nottingham.

Balchin, P. (1998) *Housing: the Essential Foundations*. London: Routledge.

Balint, M. (1991) *The Basic Fault: Therapeutic Aspects of Regression*. Chicago: Northwest University Press.

Bandler, R. and Grinder, J. (1982) *Reframing: Neuro-Linguistic Programming and the Transformation of Meaning*. Santa Cruz: NLP Comprehensive.

Bandler, R. and Grinder, J. (1990) *Frogs into Princes: Introduction to Neuro-Linguistic Programming and the Transformation of Meaning*. Santa Cruz: NLP Comprehensive.

Bandura, A. (1977) *Social Learning Theory*. Englewood Cliffs, NJ: Prentice Hall.

Banks, S. (1995) *Ethics and Values in Social Work*. Basingstoke: Macmillan.

Bannister, J., Dell, M., Donnison, D., Fitzpatrick, S. and Taylor, R. (1993) *Homeless Young People in Scotland: The Role of Social Work Services*. London: HMSO.

Barber, J.G. (1991) *Beyond Casework*. London: Macmillan.

Beauchamp, T. and Childress, J. (1994) *Principles of Biomedical Ethics*. 4th edn. OUP.

Bebout, R.R. (1993) Contextual Case Management: Restructuring the Social Support Networks of Seriously Mentally Ill Adults. In Harris, M. and Bergman, H.C. (Eds.) *Case*

Management for Mentally Ill Patients: Theory and Practice. New York: Harwood Academic Publishers.

Beck, A. T. and Tomkin, A. (1989) *Cognitive Therapy and Emotional Disorders*. London: Penguin.

Bentley, T. and Gurumurchy, R. (1999) *Destination Unknown. Engaging with the Problems of Marginalized Youth*. London: DEMOS.

Berenson, K.R., Bingham, L.E., Griffing, S., Martin, A.J., Mandry, L., Primm, B.J. and Sage, R.E. (2000) The Process of Leaving an Abusive Relationship: The Role of Risk Assessments and Decision – Certainty. In *Journal of Family Violence*, 15: 2.

Beresford, P. and Croft, S. (1997) *Citizen Involvement: A Practical Guide for Change*. London: Macmillan.

Berne, E. (1978) *A Layman's Guide to Psychiatry and Psychoanalysis*. London: Penguin.

Berne, E. (1978) *Games People Play*. New York: Grove Books.

Bevan, P. and Williamson, D. (2002) *The Direct Access Centres Handbook*: London: National Homeless Alliance.

Bevan, P. (1998) *The Resettlement Handbook*. London: National Homeless Alliance.

Bhugra, D. (Ed) (1996) *Homelessness and Mental Health*. Cambridge: Cambridge University Press.

The Big Issue in the North Trust, (1999) *What Makes a Sustainable Tenancy?* Manchester: Big Issues.

Biestek, F.P. (1961) *The Casework Relationship*. London: Macmillan.

Bines, W. (1994) *The Health of Single Homeless People*. York: Centre for Housing Policy, University of York.

Birch, J. (1999) *We'd Love to Help But . . .* London: Shelter.

Bowlby, J. (1982) *Attachment and Loss*. London: Hogarth Press.

Bozarth, J. and Evans, S. (2000) *Person-Centered Casework*. International Paper presented at the Eastern Psychological Association, Baltimore.

Bradley, T., Cooper, A. and Sycamore, R. (2004) *Day Centres Handbook: A Good Practice Guide*. London: Homeless Link.

Brandon, D. (1995) *Advocacy Power to People with Disabilities*. Birmingham: Venture Press.

Brandon, D. (1998) Care Planning. In Bevan, P. *The Resettlement Handbook*. London: National Homeless Alliance.

Brandon, D. and Atherton, K. (1996) *Handbook of Care Planning*. London: Routledge.

Brandon, D., Wells, K., Francis, K. and Ramsey, E. (1980) *The Survivors: A Study of Homeless Young Newcomers to London and the Responses Made to Them*. London: Routledge and Kegan Paul.

Brody, S. (1996) *The Children Act and Homeless 18 and 17-year-olds: A Practical Guide to Assessment, Accommodation and Support*. London: CHAR.

Buchy, C. (2005) *An Ethnographic Study into Rough Sleeping in Oxford*. Unpublished PhD Thesis, Oxford Brookes University.

Bucknell, D. (2001) Supervision in Social Work: Messages for the Connexions Service. In Edwards, A. *Supporting Personal Advisors in Connexions: Perspectives on Supervision and Mentoring from Allied Professions*. Canterbury: Centre for Career and Personal Development, Occasional paper.

Bucknell, D. (2004) Assessment in Social Work: Solution Focused Approaches. In Edwards, A. and Seal, M. *Multi-agency Perspectives on Assessment and Assessment Frameworks*. Canterbury: Centre for Career and Personal Development, Occasional paper.

Burns, D., Hambleton, R. and Hoggett, P. (1994) *The Politics of Decentralisation*. London: Macmillan.

Burns, D.D. (1992) *Feeling Good.* New York: Avon.

Burrows, B., Pleace, N. and Quilgars, D. (1997) *Homelessness and Social Policy.* London: Routledge.

Cameron, A., Lart, R., Harrison, L., McDonald, G. and Smith, R. (2000) *Factors Promoting and Obstacles Hindering Joint Working: A Systematic Review.* SPS, University of Bristol.

Cameron, A., Harrison, L., Burton, P. and Marsh, A. (2001) *Crossing the Housing and Care Divide.* Bristol: Policy Press.

Carroll, M. (2002*) Neuro-linguistic Programming: A Sceptics Guide* www.skepdic.com

Carter, M. (1999) *Falling off the First Rung: Tackling Exclusions from Birmingham's Direct Access Hostels.* Birmingham: Birmingham's Homeless and Roofless Partnership.

Challis, D., Chessum, R. and Chesterman, J. (1990) *Case Management in Social and Health Care.* Canterbury: PSSRU, University of Kent.

Christian, C. and Kitto, J. (1987) *The Theory and Practice of Supervision.* London: YMCA National College.

Cigno, K. (1998) Cognitive-behaviour Practice. In Adams, R., Dominelli, L. and Payne, M. (Eds.) *Social Work: Themes, Issues and Critical Debate.* Basingstoke: Palgrave Macmillan.

Coleman, D. (1997) Contribution to 'Unfinished Business'. ROOF, April.

Coleman, G., Higgins, J., Smith, R. and Tolan, F. (1990) *Training and Development for Resettlement Staff.* London: SAUS.

Commander, M., Davis, A., McCabe, A. and Stanyer, A. (1998) *Keeping a Lid on it? Youth Homelessness and Mental Health.* Birmingham: University of Birmingham.

Cooper, P. *Ecosystemic Approach to Emotional and Behavioural Difficulties in Schools.* London: Macmillan.

Cooper, P., Smith, C.J. and Upton, G. (1994) *Emotional and Behavioural Difficulties: Theory to Practice.* London: Macmillan.

Cox, W.M., Klinger, E. and Blount, J.P. (1991) Alcohol Use and Goal Hierarchies: Systemic Motivational Counselling for Alcoholics. In Miller, W.R. and Rollnick, S. (1991) *Motivational Interviewing: Preparing People to Change Addictive Behaviour.* 2nd edn. New York: Guilford Press.

Craig, T., Bayliss, E., Klein, O., Manning, O. and Reader, L. (1995) *The Homeless Mentally Ill Initiative: An Evaluation of Four Clinical Teams.* London: HMSO.

Craine, K. (2001) *Managing Changes in Organisations.* London: Sage.

Crane, M. (1999) *Understanding Older Homeless People: Their Circumstances, Problems and Needs.* Buckingham: Open University Press.

CSNU (2000) Module Four: Networking and Working with the Community. Distance learning material for the Diploma in Personal Advice. London: ODPM.

Daly, G. (1996) *Homelessness: Policies, Strategies and Lives on the Street.* London: Routledge.

Dane, K. (1998) *Making it Last: A Report on Research into Tenancy Outcomes for Rough Sleepers.* London: Housing Services Agency.

Dawson, A. (1994) Professional Codes of Practice and Ethical Conduct. *Journal of Applied Philosophy*, 11: 2,145–53.

Dean, H. (Ed.) (1999) *Begging Questions.* Bristol: The Policy Press.

Dermer, S.B., Hermesath, C.W. and Russell, C.S. (1998) A Feminist Critique of Solution Focused Therapy. *American Journal of Family Therapy*, 26: 239–50.

Derrida, J. (1995) *Specters of Marx: The State of the Debt, the Work of Mourning, and the New International.* London: Routledge.

DeShazer, S. (1985) *Keys to Solutions in Brief Therapy.* New York: Norton.

DeShazer, S. (1988) *Clues: Investigating Solutions in Brief Therapy*. New York: Norton.
DeShazer, S. (1991) *Putting Differences to Work*. New York: Norton.
DeShazer, S. (1994) *Words were Originally Magic*. New York: Norton.
Devore, W. and Schlesinger, E.G. (1991) *Ethnic Sensitive Social Work*. New York: Macmillan.
DfES (2003) *Homeless Places: The Uneven Geographies of Emergency Provision for Single Homeless People*. London.
Dingwall, R. and Lewis, P. (Eds.) (1983) *The Sociology of Professions*. London: Macmillan.
Doel, M. and Marsh, P. (1992), *Task Centred Social Work*. Aldershot: Ashgate.
DoH (1999) *Consent to Treatment*. Health Service Circular HSC1999/031 London: Department of Health.
Donald, J. (1992) *Sentimental Education*. London: Verso.
Donnison, D. and Ugerson, C. (1982) *Housing Policy*, London: Penquin.
Dordick, G.A. (1997) *Something Left to Lose: Personal Relations and Survival Among New York's Homeless*. Philadelphia: Temple University Press.
Douglas, M. (1986) *How Institutions Think*. Syracuse University Press, Syracuse, N.Y.
Douglas, T. (1995) *Survival in Groups: The Basics of Group Membership*. Buckingham: Open University Press.
DTLR (2002) *Homeless Persons Act*, Stationery Office.
Duck, S. (1999) *Relating to Others*. (Mapping Social Psychology Series) Milton Keynes: Open University Press.
Edwards, A. (2001) *Supporting Personal Advisors in Connexions: Perspectives on Supervision and Mentoring from Allied Professions*. Occasional paper, Canterbury: Centre for Career and Personal Development.
Edwards, A. and Seal, M. (2004) *Multi-agency Perspectives on Assessment and Assessment Frameworks*. Occasional paper. Canterbury: Centre for Career and Personal Development.
Egan, G. (1998) *The Skilled Helper. Model, Skills and Methods for Effective Helping*. 6th edn., Monterey, CA: Brooks/Cole.
El Ansari, W., Phillips, C.J. and Hammith, M. (2001) Collaboration and Partnerships: Developing the Evidence Base. *Health, Social Care and Community* V11. No.3: 23–45.
Ellis, A. (1962) *Reason and Emotion in Psychotherapy*. New York: Lyle Stuart.
ELSC (2004) *Managing Practice*, www.elsc.org
Engestrom, Y. and Mietten, J. (1996) *Cognition and Communication at Work*. Cambridge: Cambridge University Press.
Epson, D. and White, M. (1995) *Termination as a Rite of Passage in Constructivism in Psychotherapy*. Washington: American Psychological Association.
Epston, D. (1998) *Catching up with David Epston: A Collection on Narrative-based Papers, 1991–1996*. Adelaide: Dulwich Centre Publications.
Eraut, M. (1994) *Developing Professional Knowledge*. London: The Falmer Press.
Erikson, E.H. (1948) *Children and Society*. Harmondsworth: Penguin.
Erikson, E.H. (1977) *Childhood and Society*. London: Granada.
Eungjun, M. (1999) *Reading the Homeless: The Media's Image of Homeless Culture*. London, Connecticut: Praeger.
Everitt, E. (1995) *Evaluation in the Voluntary Sector: A Culture of Lying*. Department of Public Policy, Occasional Paper. Bristol University.
Field, K. and Philpott, C. (2001) Mentoring in Schools: From Support to Development. In Edwards, A. (2001) *Supporting Personal Advisors in Connexions. Perspectives on*

Supervision and Mentoring from Allied Professions. Canterbury: Centre for Career and Personal Development Occasional Paper, Michaelmas Term.

Fisher, J. (1973) Is Casework Effective? A Review. *Social Work,* 18.1.99: 5–20.

Fitzgerald, R.C. (1970) Reactions to Blindness: An Exploratory Study of Adults with Recent Loss of Sight. *Archives of General Psychiatry,* 22.

Fleman, K. (1999) *Room for Drugs: Guidelines for Direct Access Services after the Winter Comfort Trial.* London: Release.

Foord, M., Palmer, J. and Simson, D. (1998) *Bricks without Mortar.* London: Crisis.

Franklin, B. (1999) More Than Community Care: Supporting the Transition from Homelessness to Home. In Hutson, S. and Clapham, D. (Eds.) *Homelessness: Public Policies and Private Lives.* London: Cassell.

Freddolino, P.P. and Moxley, D.P. (1992). Clinical Care Update: Refining and Advocacy Model for Homeless People Coping with Psychiatric Disabilities. *Community Mental Health Journal,* 28: 4. 337–52.

Freire, P. (1972) *Pedagogy of the Oppressed.* London: Penguin Books.

Garland, R.J. and Dougher, M.J. (1991) Motivational Interviewing in the Treatment of Sex Offenders. In Miller, W.R. and Rollnick, S. (1991) *Motivational Interviewing: Preparing People to Change Addictive Behaviour,* 2nd Ed. New York: Guilford Press.

Geertz, C. (1998) *The Interpretation of Cultures: Selected Essays.* New York: Basic Books.

Giamo, B and Grunberg, J. (1992) *Beyond Homelessness: Frames of Reference.* Iowa: University of Iowa Press.

Giddens, A. (1991) *Modernity and Self-Identity: Self and Society in the Late Modern Age.* Stanford: Stanford University Press.

Giddens, A. (1987) Structuralism, Post-structuralism and the Production of Culture. In Giddens, A. and Turner, H. (Eds.) *Social Theory Today.* Cambridge, Polity Press.

Gilchrist, A. (2000) The Well-connected Community: Networking to the Edge of Chaos. *Community Development Journal,* 35: 264–75.

Gillet, C. (1996) Personal Communication. Unpublished data at the National Institute of Research in Agronomy, Thonon-les-Bains, France.

Glasser, I. and Bridgeman, R. (1999) *Braving the Street: The Anthropology of Homelessness.* New York: Bergham Books.

Glassman, U. and Kates, L. (1990) *Group Work. A Humanistic Approach.* London: Sage.

Goffman, E. (1971) *The Presentation of Self in Everyday Life.* Harmondsworth: Penguin.

Goodall, R. (1999) *Homeless for a Thousand Years.* Unpublished.

Griffiths, S. (1997) *Benefit Shortfalls: The Impact of Housing Benefit Cuts on Young Single People.* London: Shelter.

Grinder, J. (1996) *Turtles all the way Down: Prerequisites for Personal Growth.* California: Metamorphous Press.

Groundswell (2000) *Participation Handbook.* Groundswell: London.

Gullo, S.V., Cherico, D.J. and Shadick, R. (1974) Suggested Stages and Response Styles in Life-Threatening Illness: A Focus on the Cancer Patient. In Schoenberg, B., Carr, A.C., Kutscher, A.H., Peretz, D. and Goldberg, I.K. (Eds.) *Anticipatory Grief.* New York: Columbia University Press.

Gutheil, I.A. (1993) Rituals and Termination Procedures. *Studies in Social Work,* 63: 163–76.

Habbermas, J. (1984) *Theory of Communicative Action.* San Francisco: University of California Press.

Hagan, J. and McCarthy, B. (1997) *Mean Streets: Youth Crime and Homelessness.* Cambridge: Cambridge University Press.

Hamm, J. (1996) *Steps from the Street: A Report on Direct Access Hostel Provision*. London: CHAR.

Harper, K. and Hardy, L. (1998) *An Evaluation of Motivational Interviewing*. Middlesex Probation Service.

Harris, T.A. (1970) *I'm OK – You're OK*. London: Pan.

Harrison, M. (1996) *Emergency Hostels: Direct Accommodation in London*. London: Single Homelessness in London and the London Borough Grants Committee.

Hawes, D. (1997) *Older People and Homelessness: A Story of Greed, Violence, Conflict and Ruin*. Bristol: The Policy Press.

Hayes, N. (2000) *Foundations in Psychology*. 3rd edn., London: Thompson Learning.

Health and Safety Commission (1974) Health and Safety Act, London, HMSO.

Heap, M. (1988) *Hypnosis: Current Clinical Experimental and Forensic Practices*. London: Croom Helm.

Hearn, J. (1995) *Child and Family Support and Protection, A Practical Approach*. London: National Childrens Bureau.

Hewitt, M. (1992) *Welfare, Ideology and Need: Developing Perspectives on the Welfare State*. Hemel Hampstead: Harvester Wheatsheaf.

Hilsenroth, M.F., Ackerman, S.F. and Blagys, M.D. (2001) Evaluating the Phase Model of Change during Short Term Psychodynamic Psychotherapy. *Psychotherapy Research*, 11: 29–41.

Himsworth, P. (1995) *No Home, No Vote, No Voice: Challenging the Disenfranchisement of Homeless People*. National Homeless Alliance: London.

HMSO (1974) *Health and Safety Act*. London.

HMSO (1998) *Data Protection Act*. London.

Hollin, C.R. (1989) *Cognitive Behavioural Interventions with Young Offenders*. London: Butterworth-Heinmann.

Hollis, F. (1964) *Social Casework: A Psychosocial Therapy*. New York: Random House.

Holmes, T.H. and Rahe, R.H. (1967) The Social Readjustment Rating Scale. *Journal of Psychomatic Research*, 11: 213–7.

Hopton, J. (1997) Towards a Critical Theory of Mental Health Nursing. *Journal of Advanced Nursing*, 25:3, 492.

Hornstein, H. A. and Heilman, M. (1986) *Managing Human Forces in Organizations*. McGraw Hill.

Horowitz M.J. (1985) Disasters and Psychological Responses to Stress. *Psychiatric Annals*, 15: 161–7.

Horowitz, M.J. (1976) *Stress Response Syndromes*. New York: Aronson.

Howarth, Judge, (2000) *The Winter Comfort Case. The Guardian*, July 2000.

Hoy, D. (1997) *Protecting the Individual: Confidentiality, Security and the Growth of Information Systems*. Health Systems Division, NHS Scotland.

Hudson, B. and MacDonald, G. (1986) *Behavioural Social Work: An Introduction*. London: Macmillan.

Hugman, R. (1991) *Power in Caring Professions*. Basingstoke: Macmillan.

Humphreys, R. (1999) *No Fixed Abode: A History of Responses to the Roofless and the Rootless in Britain*. Basingstoke: Macmillan.

Hutson, S. and Clapham, D. (Eds.) (1999) *Homelessness: Public Policies and Private Troubles*, London: Cassell.

Hutson, S. and Liddiard, M. (1996) *Youth Homelessness: The Construction of a Social Issue*. London: Cassell.

194   *Resettling Homeless People*

Illich, I. (1977) *Disabling Professions*. London: Marion Boyars.

Inglehart, M. (1991) Reactions to Critical Life Events: A Social Psychological Analysis. New York: Praeger Publishing.

Inskipp, F. and Proctor, B. (1993) *Making the Most of Supervision*. Twickenham: Cascade.

Ivey, A.E. (1990) *Development Strategies for Helpers: Individual, Family and Network Interventions*. London and New York: Brooks Cole.

Jacobs, K., Kemeny, J. and Manzi, T. (2003) *Power, Discursive Space and Institutional Practices in the Construction of Housing Problems*. Housing Studies.

Jacobs, M. (1999) *Psychodynamic Counselling in Action*. London: Sage.

James, M. (1977) *Transactional Analysis: For Psychotherapists and Counsellors*. New York: Longman Higher Education Paperback.

Jeffs, T. and Smith, M. (2002) *Social Exclusion, Joined-up Thinking and Individualization: New Labour's Connexions Strategy*. www.infed.org/achieves/connexions

JNC (2004) *Salary Scales and Assimilation Details*. London: Joint Education Services Circular, No 13.

Johnson, B., Murie, A., Naumann, L. and Yanatta, A. (1991) *A Typology of Homelessness. Final Report for Scottish Homes*. Edinburgh: Scottish Homes.

Jones, A. (1999) *Out of Sight, Out of Mind? The Experiences of Homeless Women*. London: Crisis.

Jones, A., Pleace, N. and Quilgars, D. (2002) *Firm Foundations: An Evaluation of the Shelter Homeless to Home Service*. Shelter.

Kahn, E. (1999) A Critique of Non-directivity in the Person-centred Approach. *Journal of Humanistic Psychology*, 39: 4, 94–110.

Kanfer, F.H. (1987) Self Regulation and Behaviour. In Heckhausen, H., Gollwitzer, P.M. and Weinert, F.E. (Eds.) *Jenseits des Rubikon*. Elmsford, NY: Pergamon Press.

Karpman, S. (1968) Fairy Tales and Script Drama Analysis. New York: Transactional Analysis Bulletin.

Kates, N., Grieff, B.S. and Hagen, D.Q. (1993) Job Loss and Employment Uncertainty. In Kahn, J. (Ed.) *Mental Health in the Workplace*, (156–76) New York: Van Nostrand Reinhold.

Kemeny, J. (1992) *Housing and Social Theory*. London: Routledge.

Kemp, P. and Rugg, J. (1998) *The Single Room Rent: Its Impact on Young People*. Centre for Housing Policy, University of York.

Kennet, P. and Marsh, A. (Eds.) *Homelessness: Exploring the New Terrain* (37–60). Bristol: Policy Press.

Kent, R. (1991) Motivational Interviewing and the Maintenance of Change. In Miller, W. and Rollnick, S. *Motivational Interviewing: Preparing People to Change Addictive Behaviour*. New York: Guilford Press.

Klee, H. and Reid, P. (1998) Drug Use amongst the Young Homeless: Coping Through Self-medication. *Health*, 2: 2, 115–34.

Kline, J., Harris, M., Bebout, R. and Drake, R.E. (1991) Contrasting Integrated and Linkage Models of Treatment for Homeless, Dually Diagnosed Adults. In Minkoff, K. and Drake, R.E. (Eds.) *Dual Diagnosis of Major Mental Illness and Substance Disorders*. San Francisco, CA: Jossey-Bass.

Kline, J.D. (1993) Challenges to the Clinical Case Management of the Chronic Mentally Ill: Emerging Special Populations. In Harris, M. and Bergman, H.C. *Case Management for Mentally Ill Patients, Theory and Practice*. US: Harwood.

Klinger, E. (1975) Consequences of Commitment to and Disengagement from Incentives. *Psychological Review*, 82: 1–25.

Klinger, E. (1977) *Meaning and Void: Inner Experience and the Incentives in People's Lives.* Minneapolis: University of Minnesota Press.

Koehn, D. (1994) *The Ground of Professional Ethics.* London: Routledge.

Kuebler-Ross, E. (1969) *On Death and Dying.* New York: Macmillan.

Lash, S. and Urry, J. (1987) *The End of Organised Capitalism.* Cambridge: Polity Press.

Lawton, B. and Feltham, C. (2000) *Taking Supervision Forward: Enquiries and Trends in Counselling and Psychotherapy.* London: Sage.

Leadbeater, C. (2000) *Living on Thin Air. The New Economy.* London: Penguin.

Lehman, A.F., Dixon, L.B., Kernan, E., DeForge, B.R. and Postrado, L.T. (1997) A Randomized Trial of Assertive Community Treatment for Homeless Persons with Severe Mental Illness. *Archives of General Psychiatry,* 54: 1038–43.

Leigh, C. (1993) *Right to Care: Good Practice in Community Care Planning for Single People.* London: CHAR.

London, J. (1913) *People of the Abyss.* New York: Arrow Books.

Macguire, J. (2002) Cognitive Behavioural Interventions. In Bradley, T., Cooper, A. and Sycamore, R. (2004) *Day Centres Handbook: A Good Practice Guide.* London: Homeless Link.

Main, T. (2003) How to Think About Homelessness: Balancing Structural and Individual Causes. *Journal of Social Distress and the Homeless,* 7: 1, 41–54.

Maslow, A.H. (1954) *Motivation and Personality.* New York: Harper.

Mayer, J. and Timms, N. (1970) *The Client Speaks.* London: Routledge and Kegan Paul.

McCluskey, J. (1993) *Reassessing Priorities. The Children Act 1989 – A New Agenda for Young Homeless People?* London: CHAR.

McCluskey, J. (1994) *Acting in Isolation: An Evaluation of the Effectiveness of the Children Act 1989 for Young Homeless People.* London: CHAR.

McCluskey, J. (1994) *Breaking the Spiral: Ten Myths on the Children Act and Youth Homelessness.* London: CHAR.

McCluskey, J. (1997) *Where There's a Will: A Guide to Developing Single Homelessness Strategies.* London: CHAR.

McKenna, T. (1999) *Food for the Gods.* London: Macmillan.

McKnight, J. (1996) *The Careless Society: Community and Its Counterfeits.* London: Basic Books.

Means, R. and Smith, R. (1996) *Community Care, Housing and Homelessness Issues, Obstacles and Innovative Practice.* Bristol: The Policy Press.

Meekosha, H. (1993) *Body Battles: Disability, Representation and Participation.* London: Sage.

Meyersohn, K. and Walsh, J. (2001) Ending Clinical Relationships with People with Schizophrenia. *Health and Social Work,* 26: 3, 188–200.

Middleton, L. (1997) *The Art of Assessment.* Birmingham: Venture Press.

Middleton, L. (1999) Could do Better. *Professional Social Work,* Nov.

Miller, W.R. and Brown, J.M. (1991) Self-regulation as a Conceptual Basis for the Prevention and Treatment of Addictive Behaviours. In Heather, N., Miller, W.R. and Greeley, J. (Eds.) *Self-control and the Addictive Behaviours.* Sydney: Pergamon Press.

Miller, W.R. and Rollnick, S. (1991) *Motivational Interviewing: Preparing People to Change Addictive Behaviour.* 2nd edn. New York: Guilford Press.

Milner, J. and O'Byrne, P. (2002) *Assessment in Social Work.* London: Macmillan.

Minority Rights Group International (2004) *Minority Rights in Development Aid Policies – 2. The Heritage of Past Decades,* London: MRGI.

Morgan, D. (1988) A Scientific Assessment of Neuro-linguistic Programming. In Heap, M. (1988) *Hypnosis: Current Clinical Experimental and Forensic Practices.* London: Croom Helm.

Morse, G.A. (2003) Review of Case Management for People who are Homeless: Implications for Practice, Policy and Research. *Psychiatric Services*, 53: 3, 242–56.

Morse, G.A., Calsyn, R.J., Klinkenberg, W.D., Trusty, M.L., Gerber, F., Smith, R., Tempelhoff, B., Ahmad, L. (1997) An Experimental Comparison of Three Types of Case Management for Homeless Mentally Ill Persons. *Psychiatric Services*, 48: 4, 497–503.

Munro, M. and Madigan, R. (1993) Privacy in the Private Sphere. *Housing Studies.* 8: 1, 29–45.

Murray, J.A. (2001) Loss as a Universal Concept: A Review of the Literature to Identify Common Aspects of Loss in Diverse Situations. In *Journal of Loss and Trauma* Vol. 6: 3.

NASW (1992) *Standards for Social Work Case Management.* NASW: London.

National Health Service, (2002) *Joining up Local Approaches to Promote Health and Well Being in the Community.* Health Development Agency.

Neale, J. (1997) Hostels: A Useful Policy and Practice Response? In Burrows, B., Please, N. and Quilgars, D. (Eds.) *Homelessness and Social Policy.* London: Routledge.

Neale, J. (1997) Theorising Homelessness: Contemporary, Sociological and Feminist Perspectives. In Burrows, B. Please, N. and Quilgars, D. *Homelessness and Social Policy.* London: Routledge.

North, C., Moore, H. and Owens, C. (1996) *Go Home and Rest? The Use of an Accident and Emergency Department by Homeless People.* London: Shelter.

Office of National Statistics (1998) *Drug Use of Young People.* London: ONS.

Oldman, J. (1995) *Reflections on the 1995 Resettlement Conference.* Connect Issue 3. National Homeless Alliance.

Oldman, J. (1996) *Reflections on the 1996 Resettlement Conference.* Connect Issue 6. National Homeless Alliance.

Orford, J. (1985) *Excessive Appetites: A Psychological View of Addictions.* New York: Wiley.

O'Riordan, B., Carr, A. and Turner, R. (2003) Irish Child Sexual Abuse Victims. *Child Abuse Review.* 12: 3, 190–204.

Orwell, G. (1943) *Down and Out in Paris and London.* London: Penguin.

Park, G. (2002) *Someone and Anyone: Assessment Practice in Voluntary Sector Services for the Homeless in London.* London: Kings Fund.

Parkes, C. M. (1972) *Bereavement.* New York: International Universities Press.

Parson, T. (1955) *Family Socialization and Interaction Process.* Simon and Schuster.

Parton, N. and O'Byrne, P. (2000) *Constructive Social Work.* Basingstoke: Palgrave Macmillan.

Passaro, J. (1966) *The Unequal Homeless: Men on the Streets, Women in their Place.* London: Routledge.

Pavlov, I. (1960) *Conditional Reflexes: An Investigation of the Psychological Activity of the Cerebral Cortex*, New York: Dover Publications.

Perlmann, H.H. (1979) *Relationship, the Heart of Helping People.* Chicago: University of Chicago Press.

Perls, F. (1982) *Gestalt Approach and Eyewitness to Therapy.* London: Bantam Books.

Phillips, J. (2001) *Group Work in Social Care.* London: Jessica Kingsley.

Pleace, N. (1998) Single Homelessness as Social Exclusion: The Unique and the Extreme. *Social Policy and Administration*, 32: 1, 46–59.

Please, N. (2000) The New Consensus, the Old Consensus and the Provision of Services for People Sleeping Rough. *Housing Studies*, 15: 4, 581–94.

Please, N and Quilgars, D. (1996) *Health and Homelessness in London: A Review*. London: Kings Fund.

Pratt, M. (1992) *Imperial Eyes, Travel Writing and Transculturation*. London: Routledge.

Prochaska, D. and DiClemente, C. (1982) Transtheoretical Therapy: Towards a More Integrative Model of Change. *Psychotherapy: Theory, Research, and Practice*, 19: 276–88.

Ram Dass, B. (1985) *How Can I Help: Stories and Reflections on Service*. London: Alfred A Kompf.

Randall, G. and Brown, S. (1993) *The Rough Sleepers Initiative: An Evaluation*. London: HMSO.

Randall, G. and Brown, S. (1994) *The Move In Experience: Research into Good Practice in Resettlement of Homeless People*. London: Crisis.

Randall, G. and Brown, S. (1995) *Outreach and Resettlement with People Sleeping Rough*. London: DoE.

Randall, G. and Brown, S. (1996) *From Street to Home: An Evaluation of Phase 2 of the Rough Sleepers Initiative*. London: HMSO.

Randall G. and Brown, S. (1999) *Ending Exclusion: Employment and Training Schemes for Homeless Young People*, York: Joseph Rowntree Foundation.

Randall, G. and Brown, S. (2002) *The Support Needs of Homeless Households*. London: ODPM.

Reeve, K. and Coward, S. (2004) *Life on the Margins: The Experiences of Homeless People Living in Squats*. London: Crisis.

Reid, W.J. and Shyne, W.W. (1969) *Brief and Extended Casework*. New York. Columbia University Press.

Renzetti, C.M. (1992) *Violent Betrayal. Partner Abuse in Lesbian Relationships*. London: Sage.

Reynolds, H. (2001) Supervision in Counselling and Psychotherapy. In Edwards, A. (2001) *Supporting Personal Advisors in Connexions: Perspectives on Supervision and Mentoring from Allied Professions*. Occasional paper, Canterbury: Centre for Career and Personal Development.

Rice (1975) YMCA.

Ridgeway, P.A., Simpson, F., Wittman, F. D. and Wheeler, E. (1994) Home-making and Community Building: Notes on Empowerment in Place. *Journal of Mental Health Administration*, 21: 4, 417–8.

Rob, M. and Cameron, P.M. (1998) Supervision of Termination in Psychotherapy. *Canadian Journal of Psychiatry*, 43: 397–402.

Rog, D.J., Holupka, C.S., McCombs-Thirnton, K.L., Brito, M.C. and Hambrick, R. (1996) Case Management in Practice: Lessons from the Evaluation of the RWJ/HUD Homeless Families Program. *Journal of Prevention and Intervention in the Community*, 15: 2, 67–82.

Rogers, C. and Freiberg, H.J. (1994) *Freedom to Learn*. 3rd edn. New York: Merrill.

Rowe, M. (1999) *Crossing the Border: Encounters between Homeless People and Outreach Workers*. Berkeley, Los Angeles, University of California Press.

Rowlands, J. (1991) *How do we Know it is Working? The Evaluation of Social Development Projects*, and discussed in Rubin (1995: 17–23).

Rowntree, J. (1995) Mixed Fortunes: The Funding of the Local Voluntary Sector. *Social Policy Research*: March.

Rubin, F. (1995) *A Basic Guide to Evaluation for Development Workers*. Oxford: Oxfam.

Ruddick, S.M. (1996) *Young and Homeless in Hollywood: Mapping Social Identities.* New York: Routledge.
Ryan, M. (2004) *Client Centred Therapy* http://world.std.com/~mbr2/index.html
Rybczynski, R. (1987) *Home; Explorations of a Concept.* New York: Routledge.
Satyamurti, C. (1981) *Professionals Relationships: Boundaries of Power.* London: Routledge.
Saunders, B., Wilkinson, C. and Allsop, S. (1991) Motivational Interviewing with Heroin Users Attending a Methadone Clinic. In Miller, W.R. and Rollnick, S. (1991) *Motivational Interviewing: Preparing People to Change Addictive Behaviour.* 2nd edn. New York: Guilford Press.
Scaife, J. (2001) *Supervision in the Mental Health Professions – A Practitioners Guide.* Hove: Brunner-Routledge.
Schapiro, H. (1996) *Waiting for the Man: Popular Music Culture and Drug Use.* London: Random House.
Schein, E. H. (1985) *Organizational Culture and Leadership.* London: Jossey Bass Wiley.
Schofield, P. (1998) *Resettlement Works.* London: National Homeless Alliance.
Schön, D.A. (1983) *The Reflective Practitioner. How Professionals Think in Action.* Aldershot: Avebury.
Seal, M. (1998) *Working With a Jaundiced Eye.* Voluntary Action Camden: London.
Seal, M. (2004) *Reflections on Ten Years of Training.* Unpublished.
Seal, M. and Stretch, A. (1992) What's in a Name: Towards a Definition of Resettlement Work. *Housing Today,* 6: 4, 45–9.
Secker, J. and Hill, K. (2001) Broadening the Partnerships: Experiences of Working across Community Agencies. *Journal of Inter-professional Care.*
Seligmann, M.E.P. (1992) *Helplessness: On Depression, Development and Death.* New York: Freeman.
Sheldon, B. (1982) *Behaviour Modification, Theory Practice and Philosophy.* London: Routledge.
Sheperd, R. (2002) Resistance to Changes in Diet. *Proceedings of the Nutrition Society,* 61: 2, 267–72.
Shipton, G. (1997) *Supervision of Psychotherapy and Counselling.* Milton Keynes: Open University Press.
Shontz, F.C. (1975) *The Psychological Aspects of Physical Illness and Disability.* New York: Macmillan.
Shulman, L.S. (1987) *Knowledge and Teaching: Foundations of the New Reform.* Harvard.
Shulman, L. (1991) *Interactional Social Work Practice: Towards an Empirical Theory.* Itasca, Il: Peacock.
Sinason, V. (1992) *Client Worker Relationships in Caring Professions.* London: Routledge.
Skinner, B. F. (1958) Reinforcement Theory. *American Psychologist,* 13, 94–9.
Skyrme, D.J. (1997) *From Information Management to Knowledge Management: Are You Prepared?* Paper delivered at the Online conference, Reading.
Smith, A. (2004) Youth Work and Assessment. In Edwards, A. and Seal, M. (2004) *Multi-agency Perspectives on Assessment and Assessment Frameworks.* Occasional paper, Canterbury: Centre for Career and Personal Development.
Smith, D. (2002) *Housing Homeless Families with Children and the Children (Scotland) Act, 1995.* Shelter.
Smith, N. and Wright, C. (1992) *Customer Perceptions of Resettlement Units.* London: HMSO.

Smith, P. (1995) *Single Homelessness and the London Boroughs: A Good Practice Guide to Policies and Initiatives Developed by Local Authorities in the Capital.* London: SHIL.

Snow, D.A. and Anderson, L. (1993) *Down on Their Luck: A Study of Homeless Street People.* Los Angeles: University of California Press.

Social Exclusion Unit (1996) *Rough Sleeping:* Report by the Social Exclusion Unit. London: The Stationery Office.

Social Exclusion Unit (2002) *More Than a Roof: A Final Evaluation of the Rough Sleepers Initiative.*

Solomon, J. (1999) Models of Continued Professional Development. *Journal of In-service Education,* 25: 2.

Sorianro, F. (1995) *Conducting Needs Assessments: A Multi-disciplinary Approach.* California: Sage.

Standing Conference on Drug Abuse (1999) *Policy Guidelines for Working with Young Drug Users.* London: Standing Conference on Drug Abuse.

Steward, I. and Joines, V. (1999) *TA Today: A New Introduction to TA.* Nottingham: Lifespace Publishers.

Stewart, M. and Taylor, M. (1995) *Empowerment and Estate Regeneration: A Critical Review.* London: Policy Press.

Susser, E., Valencia, E., Conover, S., Felix, A., Tsai, W. and Wyatt, R.J. (1997) Preventing Recurrent Homelessness among Mentally Ill Men: A Critical Time Intervention after Discharge from a Shelter. *American Journal of Public Health.* 87: 2, 256–62.

Sutherland, S. and Scherl, D. (1970) Patterns of Response among Victims of Rape. *American Journal of Orthopsychiatry,* 40: 503–11.

Tavecchio, L.W.C. (1999) Attachment, Social Network and Homelessness in Young People. *Social Behaviour and Personality.* 2: 3, 45–54.

Tew, J. (2002) Going Social: Championing a Holistic Model of Mental Distress within Professional Education. *Social Work Education,* 21: 2.

Thompson, N. (1995) *Theory and Practice in Health and Social Welfare.* Buckingham: Open University Press.

Timms, N. (1983) *Social Work Values: An Enquiry.* London: Routledge.

TLC Group (2004) *Beware the 5 Stages of Grief.* Counselling for Loss and Life Changes: Dallas: Texas.

Tomlinson, H. (1997) *Professional Values in Informal and Community Education.* London: YMCA.

Torstendahl, R. and Burrage, M. (Eds.) (1996) *The Formation of Professions, Knowledge, State and Strategy.* London: Sage.

Van Bilsen, H.P.J.G. (1991) Motivational Interviewing: Perspectives from the Netherlands, with particular Emphasis on Heroin Dependant Clients. In Miller, W.R. and Rollnick, S. (1991) *Motivational Interviewing: Preparing People to Change Addictive Behaviour.* 2nd edn. N.Y.: Guilford Press.

Van Doorn, A. and Cain, M. (2003) *To Boldly go where the Homeless Sector has Never Gone Before.* In HSA Occasional Papers, Spring. York: York University.

Waldron, J. (1993b) Homelessness and the Issue of Freedom. In *Liberal Rights: Collected Papers, 1981–1991.* Cambridge: Cambridge University Press.

Warnes, A. and Crane, M. (2000) *Meeting Homeless People's Needs: Service Development and Practice for the Older Excluded.* London: Kings Fund.

Wasylenki, D.A., Goering, P.N., Lemire, D., Lindsey, S. and Lancee, W. (1993) The Hostel Outreach Program: Assertive Case Management for Homeless Mentally Ill Persons. *Hospital and Community Psychiatry,* 44: 9, 848–53.

Watson, S. and Austerberry, H. (1986) *Housing and Homelessness: A Feminist Perspective.* London: Macmillan.

Watts, K. and Bennet, D. (1991) *Theory and Practice of Psychiatric Rehabilitation.* Chichester: John Wiley.

Weber, M. (1948) *Essays in Sociology.* Edited by Gerth, H.H. and Wright Mills, C. London: Routledge.

Wenger, E. (1999) *Communities of Practice. Learning, Meaning and Identity.* Cambridge: Cambridge University Press.

Whitaker, R. (1999) *The End of Privacy.* New York: The New Press.

White, M. (1993) Deconstruction and Therapy. In Gilligan, S. and Price, R. (Eds.) *Therapeutic Conversations.* New York: Norton.

White, M. (1995) *Re-authoring Lives: Interviews and Essays.* Adelaide: Dulwich Centre Publications.

White, M. (1996) *Conference on Narrative Approaches.* Doncaster.

White, M. with Epston (1990) *Narrative Means to Therapeutic Ends.* New York: Norton.

Whitechapel, (1998) Resettlement Recording Policy. In Bevan, P. (1998) *The Resettlement Handbook.* London: National Homeless Alliance.

Williamson, D. (2000) *Direct Access Centres Handbook of Good Practice.* London: National Homeless Alliance.

Wilson, A. and Charles, K. (1997) *Making Partnerships Work: A Practical Guide for Public, Private, Voluntary and Community Sectors.* York: York Publishing Services: Joseph Rowntree Foundation.

Wilson, H. (1970) Speech on launch of Shelter campaign about the recognition of the need for statutory housing for homeless people.

Woods, J. (2001) Supervision from an Informal Education/Youth Worker Perspective. In Edwards, A. *Supporting Personal Advisors in Connexions Perspectives on Supervision and Mentoring from Allied Professions.* Canterbury: Centre for Career and Personal Development. Occasional paper Michaelmas term.

Worden, J. (1988) *Grief Therapy.* London: Routledge.

Wright, T. (1997) *Out of Place: Homeless Mobilizations, Subcities, and Contested Landscapes.* New York: City of New York University Press.

Wyler, S. (1999) *New Deal, Big Deal? The Experience of Homeless Young People in the First Year of the Governments New Deal.* London: Crisis.

Yablonski, L. (1989) *The Therapeutic Community: A Successful Approach for Treating Drug Abusers.* New York: Gardiner Press.

Zahourek, R. and Jensen, J.S. (1973) Grieving and the Loss of the Newborn. *American Journal of Nursing,* 73: 836–9.

Zell, D. (2003) Organizational Change as a Process of Death, Dying and Rebirth. *Journal of Applied Behavioural Science,* 39: 73–96.

Index